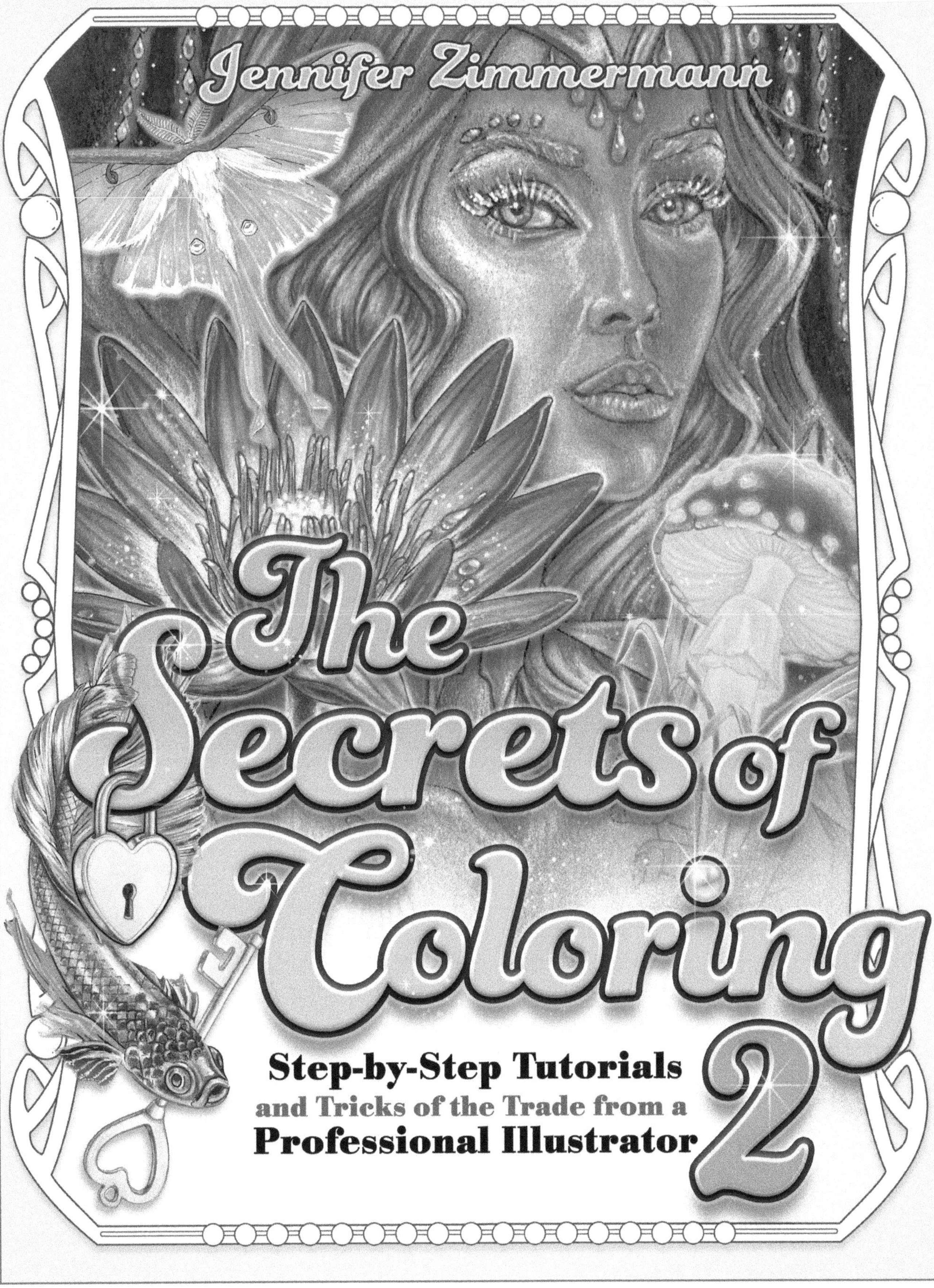

Jennifer Zimmermann

The Secrets of Coloring 2

Step-by-Step Tutorials and Tricks of the Trade from a **Professional Illustrator**

Thank You...

To my amazing family who continues to support me, through my artistic journey...
especially to my husband who always gives me the green light!

Special thanks to:

Lilicence and Selina (Coloured_by_me) for creating the techniques in their fantastic tutorial spotlights,
Irena Herman (Black_Aneri) for her inspirational coloring, staging, and photography...
and Christina Spicuzza, my amazing pencil research partner and swatch expert!

To my fantastic administrators and team:
Karen, Tina, Michelle, The Jills, Mary, Cindy, Maria, Belinda, Angelique and Pauly

To the fiercest females – my beautiful models:
Tamara, Mel, Lisa & Ayla

To Gerry Hampton for teaching me some of the invaluable skills that I apply to my own instruction today

To Kay for her endless knowledge, kindness, patience and priceless advice

and finally...to my many friends who constantly encourage me and proudly share my art!

The Secrets of Coloring 2

I'd like to take a moment to assure the purchaser of this book that the recommendations I've made are of my own honest opinion and research after teaching art and working as a professional artist for over twenty years. Although some of the products I've used here have been given to me to sample, I have not been paid by any manufacturer to post positive feedback or to endorse their products in this book. I have chosen the best supply for each tutorial in my opinion and based on my experience, and in many cases I have recommended possible alternatives for those who have difficulty obtaining certain materials due to location or budget. My recommendations for products can be purchased through affiliate links, at no additional cost to you. This in turn contributes a small percentage towards the purchase of new materials which enables me to create books such as this. I thank you for your trust and your ongoing support.

Foreword

THANK YOU, THANK YOU...

It is because of you that *The Secrets of Coloring* has been such a huge success! I am so blessed to have the support of this amazing coloring community – friends that believe in my art and my ability to teach what I know. I've received so much positive feedback from colorists around the globe and I am delighted that these lessons have helped so many improve their skills. I have read many private messages about how my book has helped you to have more confidence and how it has allowed you to create art at a more advanced level. I must admit that being tagged by you or your friends to take a look at your interpretations of my tutorials and coloring pages is so rewarding! I love seeing how these lessons are applied and how they may have supplied you with the finishing touches needed to take your art from good to fantastic! One of my greatest passions in life is helping people learn how to create art that they never thought they'd be able to! It IS possible with a little guidance. Just believe in yourself!

There are endless lessons that I could teach. The goal of this second volume is to expand upon the knowledge you've acquired in Volume 1. Although some of the concepts may seem a bit more advanced than in the first book, they are broken into small attainable steps, much like the first book… so that most are even for the beginner…it just takes patience and practice! In my research, I discovered that a big current trend is creating glowing drawings, and here you will find many ways to do this! I've also enlisted the help of some very prolific colorist friends, and here you will learn some *secrets* to achieve their trademark effects!

The Secrets of Coloring 2 is an interactive book with diagrams, visuals, demonstrations, explanations and step-by-step lessons in which you will learn about coloring and drawing supplies – as well as money and time-saving tips. Watch how I do it, then try it yourself!

It is my hope that you will take these lessons and run with them, taking your coloring pages to the next level of sophistication or even creating new dynamic work of your own. Although we will discuss the newest approaches, most of what is covered is "tried and true" from my experience as an illustrator and art teacher for over two decades combined. It is important to keep this book intact as a reference guide, so be sure to protect it from the elements so that it may benefit you for years to come.

I hope that you have tried many of the lessons in the last volume and that you are as excited as I am about the newest ones! It is my goal only to teach you what you wish to learn. I do try to take your requests in the form of messages through my Facebook artist page as time permits. I also read reviews of my books to help guide me in the decision-making process before starting the next venture! I am so appreciative of the people who take time out to leave a review – both formal reviewers and colorists whom wish to share their personal experiences. If there's a Volume 3, I will certainly cross-check my request list, as well as the reviews to see what I can be doing to better assist my followers. By the way, this book has taken me out of my own comfort zone as I try to develop content that will appeal to you – some may not necessarily be what I am accustomed to creating. I welcome this challenge as it has forced me to think outside of the box and make me a stronger and more versatile artist! I am very proud to have found the key to unlock the "secrets" to some of these tricky effects.

I appreciate your continued support which in turn allows me to do what I love most: to create and teach art and to inspire others! Let's continue the wild ride we started on this colorful journey and collaboration – I promise to keep the tutorials flowing! Please enjoy this book! As always, Happy Coloring :)

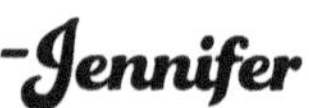
-Jennifer

Sign up for Jennifer's newsletter to receive occasional freebies
and stay up to date:

ModernColoring.com

To purchase Digital Downloads:
etsy.com/shop/ModernColoring

Other Books available on Amazon!
The Secrets of Coloring Vol. 1, Glamourista and Bella Futura!

Artist Page: **Modern Coloring: Jennifer Zimmermann**
facebook.com/moderncoloring/

Color Along Tutorials:
youtube.com/c/ModernColoringJenniferZimmermann

instagram.com/moderncoloring/

pinterest.com/moderncoloring/

twitter.com/moderncoloring

Amazon Author Page: **amazon.com/author/jenniferzimmermann**

Do you love this book?
**Thank you for leaving a review!
It is very much appreciated :)**

Table of Contents

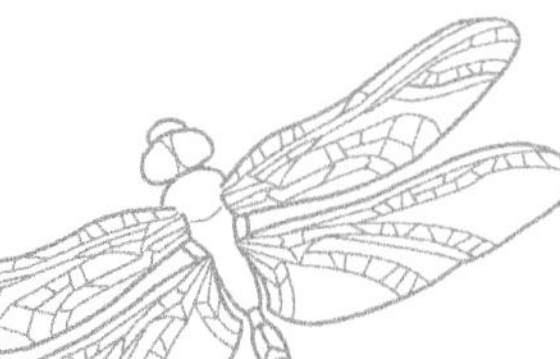

Getting Started

This book was created to guide you and allow you to test out possibilities before purchasing loads of additional art supplies. Some colorists prefer to purchase a second copy of a book in which to practice while keeping the original copy pristine! However, keep in mind that you can make copies of the practice and final coloring pages onto quality card stock or heavyweight paper as well as toned paper. These supplies are used to create the tutorials you will see, and I recommend this if you are determined to achieve my exact results.

I do want to remind you that it is often less expensive to print something at a copy center rather than at home, and you are allowed to make personal copies of the pages in this book, but copying onto paper for anyone other than yourself would be violating this privilege. I am again including a copy permission agreement at the end of this book to allow you to print up to ten pages at a time for personal use at a business copy center. Commercial copying services don't want to risk running into copyright issues, and some refuse to make copies entirely, so my permission will help to eliminate that possibility.

Chapter 1: Beyond the Basics

Ready for the Next Level... Advanced Blending , Investment Supplies, Markers & What's Hot

Smoothing with Advanced Supplies – As you may recall, we briefly discussed basic and traditional methods of blending colored pencils in Volume I of *The Secrets of Coloring*. In addition to the most commonly used methods of blending, many colorists set out to create the perfect smooth surface, with no evidence whatsoever of paper tooth. Although I usually prefer traditional approaches and a little colorless blender pencil, it is possible to achieve these "smoother" results by incorporating some additional blending tools. Be aware that some of these additions may contain minerals or chemicals that may bother your eyes or have an unpleasant odor. They may also produce unexpected results with different brands or even colors. It is always best to test your sensitivity first and use these mediums with proper ventilation, as it is wise to first try them on a test page. What are the benefits of using a blender? You can use less pencil (less expensive and less of a likelihood of "bloom"); it will increase vibrancy of your colors; get rid of some of the paper tooth and create a smoother surface. The drawbacks? It can be smelly or hazardous to breathe in; may stain your page; so not great for double-sided art; you must allow it to dry before reworking; sometimes it simply doesn't have much of an effect at all!

What are the different types of blenders?

If you are using watercolor pencils, choose a water-based colorless blender like Tombow or use a water brush that you fill yourself. If you're using wax or oil non-water-soluble pencils, opt for an alcohol-based or mineral spirits type of solvent or a colorless blender. Some examples of solvents are: Bio-Shield (environmentally friendly and readily available in the U.S.), Gamsol, Zest-it, or Alcohol – Applied with a blending stump, tortillion, cotton swab or brush. Blender marker examples are: Artist's Loft Colored Pencil Blender, Copic Blender and Prismacolor Blender.

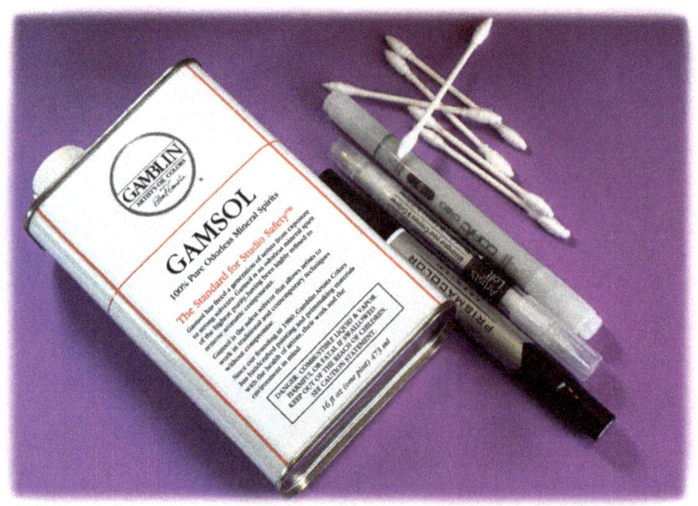

The Importance of Mixed Media…Making an Investment – As you may recall from my last book, I often use mixed media for multiple reasons, including preventing wax bloom! Although you may certainly use what you already have, many of the lessons here will use more than pencil alone. I suggest that you invest in a few tried and true supplies: at least one decent set of pencils and an inexpensive set of alcohol markers, a Mono Zero Eraser Pen, plus a few "finishing supplies" such as a Black Verithin, a white gel pen (Uniball Signo "Angelic" is my current go-to), white paint marker (such as Posca Extra Fine PC-1M) and some glitter and fluorescent or "fluo" neon gel pens like Pentel Milky Pop (Lolliz sets are inexpensive and contain both). If it's in your budget I'd also recommend that you keep a white Caran D'Ache Luminance pencil on hand – I will use it a lot here!

Marker Discoveries – In this book you will notice that in addition to numerous pencils, I am using various marker brands. The truth is that not every company makes every color! A prime example: Fluorescent Red. I sometimes look for the perfect color – a color that will make or break the effect I am trying to achieve. If I can't find it in my go-to brand's collection, I must go elsewhere. The upside: I have found some less expensive markers that do a nice job and come in a plethora of colors. I've also listed some as budget substitutes in these tutorials!! The downside: oftentimes they only come in sets. I've also heard many stories about obscure brands having an increased tendency to leak. I will say that Copic brand hasn't ever leaked on me. However, despite the brand, one way to prevent this is by ALWAYS storing your markers horizontally, especially if they are dual-ended (a drawer is a good thing to have). This disperses the ink evenly, making it less likely that you'll be agonizing over an ink blob on your paper! Also, never shake your markers without caps on. Speaking of caps…wouldn't it be great if ALL manufacturers would design marker caps to snap easily onto the opposite end of the marker while in use? This feature prevents our runaway caps from getting lost and our markers from drying out prematurely. Of all the major alcohol-based brush nib marker brands I own, only my Prismacolor Premier and Copic Ciao markers have this feature.

The Newest Trends in the coloring world include GLOWING EVERYTHING and lots of realistically colored portraits every way you turn! In addition to using tan or grey toned paper, a professional technique of drawing with bold and bright colors on dark colored paper is becoming quite popular among colorists! Staying with current trends, in this book, I have created my own offering of some "Theatrical Skin Tone" tips just for you! You can apply these techniques to any portrait you wish. However, if you are looking for more portraits to color, please check out my two portrait-heavy coloring books: *Glamourista* and *Bella Futura*.

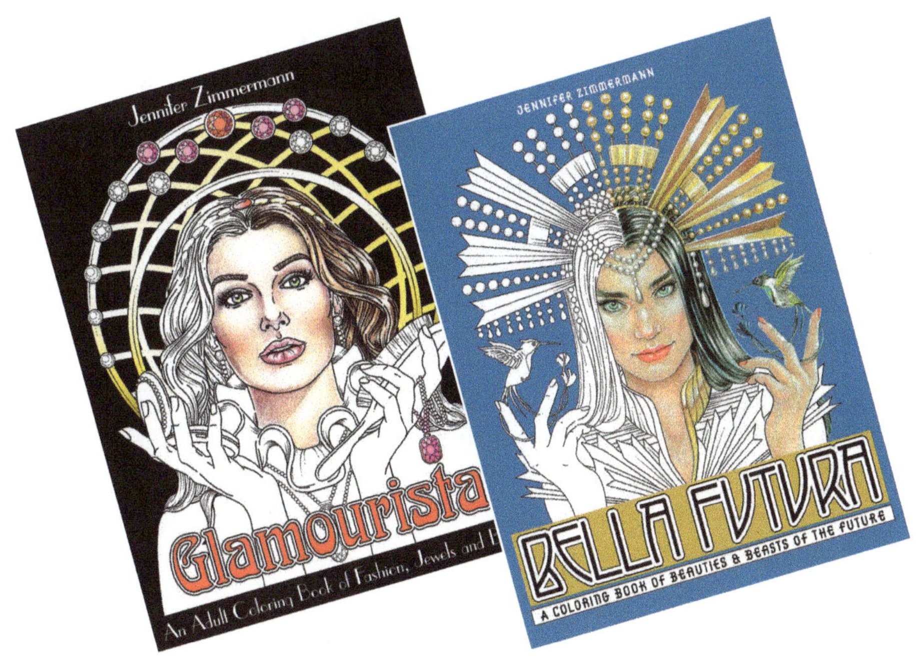

Chapter 2: Ingenious Time, Stress & Money Saving Hacks

I can't take credit for inventing these hacks, but they are great! I urge you to test them!

Mixed Media Saves More Than Just $$

As you know, I encourage mixed media for a variety of reasons. Combinations such as marker under pencil will save you time, potentially save you money (if you use top-of-the-line pencils), and save your wrists (not as much burnishing to fill in the paper tooth)…but most importantly leave you with a brighter, richer end result!

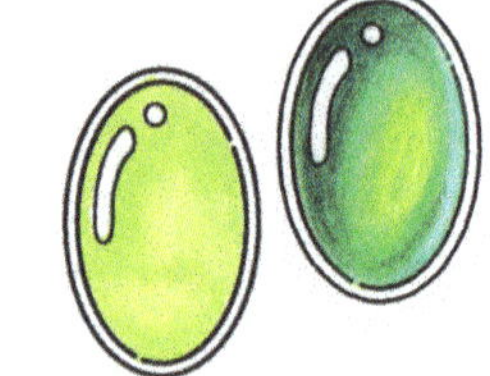

If It's Broke, Fix it!

Broken Pencils: If your pencil is seriously off center, it's defective and you should contact the manufacturer and request a replacement. However if your lead is loose you can try **one** of three things:

1. If it has an open end, Krazy/Super Glue it. Add a dot of glue and let it dry.
2. Clamp it down and hit it with some hot air – a hot blow dryer will help mend a broken core. Be sure to keep the dryer moving and rotate the pencil!
3. Place on a foil-covered sheet and allow it to "bake" in the sun or on a *very low* temp in the oven, rotating often. *Keep an eye on your pencils during any of these processes to avoid total melting or warping.

Extend Your Pencil Life: You can also use Krazy/Super Glue to prolong the life of a pencil stub by gluing it to an unsharpened graphite pencil to extend it, instead of buying pencil extenders (which don't allow you to sharpen pencils to the very end in many sharpeners). This works best with Prismas and flat-ended pencils because they will glue flush.

Compact & Convenient Mineral Spirits :) Much like nail polish in a jar, you can keep your Gamsol in an air-tight baby food or jam jar with a wound up strip of sponge – pull it out when you need to do some serious blending! You can also use it in a water brush on larger areas for watercolor-like effects.

Don't Erase, Scrape! Scraping overly thick colored pencil with an X–acto knife with a #11 blade held **flush** to the surface of the paper will prevent a hassle! Just be careful to hold it the right way to prevent tears.

Got Smears? A tablet or hair styling glove - one with only two fingers, made out of thin, slippery fabric can help! These are now even sold with some sets of markers (TouchNew 168-Marker Set). Or buy a glove separately! They are inexpensive (they range from 99¢ to $10 and will help to prevent smearing.

Choose Your Paper Wisely! Knowing your plan ahead of time is helpful. See Lilicence's finished version of the Glow Princess from Chapter 5. You might notice that she's got a warm halo around her glow. She didn't use any yellow though! The reason is that the white pencil is more neutral than the paper she used, which leans a little towards the cooler whites (Hammermill Premium Color Copy Card Stock, 100 Bright).

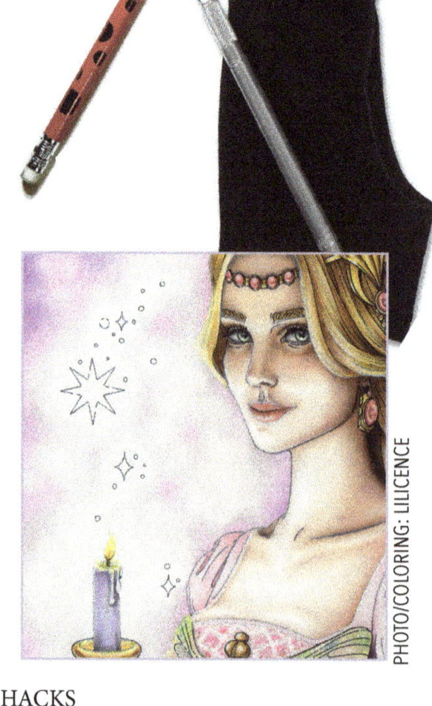

Chapter 3: Colored Pencils – Testing, Testing 1, 2, 3...4, 5!

Pencils are the most frequently used tool in the coloring world. Since writing my last volume of *Secrets*, many more pencils have become available on the market. How do you choose with so many options? A lot of it boils down to your goals: Are you a beginner or a long-time colorist? Are you on a tight budget? Do you care if your colorings are still vibrant a few years from now? Did you know that art supplies sold in a U.S. storefront must be compliant with ASTM D4236, and EN71 standards in Europe? These numbers refer to the pencils' materials and their potential toxicity – many of these newer pencils are produced in parts of the world where these safety standards are potentially not policed in the same manner. This may be something to consider especially if you have pets or small children that could ingest them.

I am constantly asked, "What less expensive pencils are best?" So, I set out to find out what makes a pencil brand popular. I did extensive research with the help of my friend Christina! Since I use Prismacolor Premier pencils for the majority of my tutorials, and they are the most widely used pencil, I felt it would be helpful to recommend some others that might work as substitutes...and match my colors as closely as possible. *Please note: There will be some gaps in my charts because I am comparing mostly 72-piece cost-friendly sets to 150-piece "Prismas". The following list includes nothing above $75. Most sets are less than that, some being just a fraction! I'm not including student grade pencils – it is simply impossible to achieve what I am teaching in these tutorials with inferior blendability and quality in general.

Before we get into affordable pencils, let's talk about the cream of the crop, Caran D'Ache Luminance. Why are they so expensive? The truth is, sometimes you do get what you pay for. "Lumis" as they are known in the coloring world, are lightfast-rated. This means that there is information published on how well they will withstand being left in daylight and before fading (if at all), and they are some of the least likely to fade on the market. Most pencils are not tested for this. These pencils also happen to be creamy and very blendable, they have unmatched opacity, and they break less than any pencil I've owned. Their skin tone colors are unparalleled, which is why I have chosen to use them for my skin tone tutorial. If your goal is to be sure that your art stays intact just as when you created it, it may be worth it to spend this extra money. However, not everyone can afford a full set of Luminance pencils. Regarding budget-sensitive pencil brands, I've polled colorists to see what works best for them. Although Prismacolor pencils aren't cheap, they are a lot less expensive than some European brands, especially in the U.S. If you can afford them, I recommend them over anything else to start. However, there seem to be newer "indie" brands cropping up all of the time that are affordable…and popular with colorists. What is important to the colorists I've polled?

-Cost　　　　　*-Superior sharpening*　　*-Available as sets vs. open stock*　*-Numbered colors *and* names*
-Blendability　*-Less breakage*　　　　*-Available in Europe, Australia*　*-Light-fastness*
-Color range　*-Wax bloom-free*　　　　 *and the U.S.*
-Vibrancy　　*-Wax vs. oil base*　　　*-Intensity on dark surfaces*

Prismas and Polys are the most popular pencils, but which less costly brands are faves among colorists I've polled? This is not a complete list, but 10 of the most popular (in no particular order):

- Black Widow　*- Schpirerr Farben*　*- Marco Raffine*　*- Guang Hui*　*- Koh-I-Noor Polycolor*
- Castle　　　*- Colleen*　　　　　*-Marco Renoir*　　*- Hero*　　　*- Lyra Rembrandt*

*To clarify, I am not suggesting that the more affordable brands will perform the <u>exact</u> same way as the Prismacolor Premier pencils used for tutorials in this book. Brands have entirely different characteristics: hardness, blendability and coverage. Some work much better than others for very specific uses. However, it is important to have options, plus pencils are very much a personal choice. With that said, see the *very close* color conversion charts for 150-count Prismacolor vs. five of the most popular 72-piece+ affordable pencils according to the people who color (in no particular order), in the back of the book.*

Chapter 4: The Elements and Principles of Art

How these concepts apply to coloring

One way to learn something seemingly complicated is to break it down to its basics…to deconstruct it. We touched on the basics of Color Theory in *The Secrets of Coloring Vol. 1*, and a few of the terms below are explained in more detail in the first book. Let's take time to learn the rest. It's important to understand these terms because they will help you see how the parts work together to create something visually dazzling – this knowledge will serve you better when you are watching tutorials or following color-alongs. Plus you'll be able to pinpoint your own strengths and weaknesses which will assist you in developing a more sophisticated approach to coloring! Since so many colorists are looking to take their projects to the next level, let's talk a little about the Elements & Principles of Art & Design and see how they apply to coloring.

Elements (the basic components of art):

Line - As you would find in most coloring books which are comprised of "line art", **Line** is described as a connection of two or more points. Lines can be curvy, straight, thick, thin, jagged, vertical, horizontal, etc. In coloring, you might use "hatched" lines.

Shape/Form - **Shape** is described as the area inside of a closed **Line**. Shapes are 2-D and can be organic or geometric. **Form**, on the other hand, is a shape with the appearance of volume and dimension. Form can refer to either implied 3-D objects, such as the sphere shown, or to actual dimensional objects themselves (such as decorative crafts, like glitter added to your colored images, or actual props in your staged photos of coloring pages). See **Black_Aneri**'s colored Betta page! Check out her Instagram for some serious staging inspo!

Value - **Value** is the perceived lightness or darkness of a color. Value is often measured on a scale in percentages of grey (0-100%). Greyscale images are based on the Value scale!

Color - **Color** is made of light and comprised of three properties: Hue (the color's name), **Value** (the color's relative lightness or darkness) and Intensity (Brightness, Chroma, Saturation, Purity). Color can be lightened, dulled, or darkened (tints, tones, shades). Color has visual temperature and is charted on a color wheel. Color can be organized in groups called color schemes which create "mood" in a piece of art (see *The Secrets of Coloring Vol. 1* for a customizable color wheel and more detailed information on color properties and some basic color schemes).

Texture - **Texture** refers to surface quality. Texture can be real (such as the "tooth" of paper) or implied (only the appearance of something tactile such as a drawing of a cookie). **Texture** can be rough, smooth, gritty, silky, slimy, etc.

Space - Layout/Perspective - **Space** has two meanings:
1. The arrangement (layout) in an image area. Space can be positive or negative (the object itself vs. blank area around it, or between it and other objects).
2. The appearance of flatness (2-D) vs. illusion of dimension (3-D perspective) and depth. Through Color we can create multiple levels of depth. Successful landscape images use **Color** and **Value** to create Space!

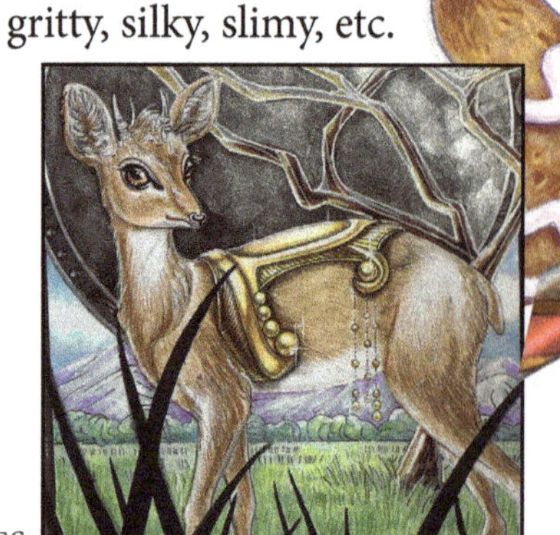

Principles (the connection between the Elements – making them work together):

Balance - Balance is the dispersal of visual weight within an image. There are three kinds of balance: symmetrical (the same objects on two sides), asymmetrical (a sense of similarity created by different objects) and radial (circular arrangement of objects or those stemming from a center point - a mandala, for example, is a balance of **Shape** and **Line**). Look at Michelle's gorgeous *Glamourista* gem!

Pattern - Pattern is comprised of regularly repeating elements (Examples: both checkerboard and camouflage are patterns of **Shape** and **Color,** whereas plaid would be a pattern of **Line** and **Color**).

Rhythm/Movement - Rhythm and Movement go hand-in-hand because they are tools the artist uses to direct the viewer's eye to an area of importance in an image. **Movement** is the creation of motion or action when objects align and point us in a direction. **Rhythm** is a repetition of similar elements, like **Shapes**, that may be used to help direct us there.

Proportion/Scale - **Proportion** is the size relationship among parts vs. the whole. **Scale** is a relationship between objects to one another in an image. (Examples - Proportion: The human head is said to be five eyes wide. Scale: A picture of a person compared to a large object makes that person seem small) - using **Shapes** to measure.

Emphasis - a focal point in an image, created by use of different elements. Example: a portrait doesn't necessarily have to be centered to make it the focus. Saturated, contrasting **Colors** or contrasting **Values** in the foreground will separate it from a dull, low contrast or mono-chromatic background. The viewer's eye will to go to the brighter area.

Unity/Variety/Contrast - Similarities vs differences. **Unity** is the parts working together to form a harmonious and cohesive image. **Variety** is creating visual interest by accentuating many differences in the elements in an image. **Contrast** is extreme differences between elements. (Example: **Color** might be cool vs. warm to create interest.)

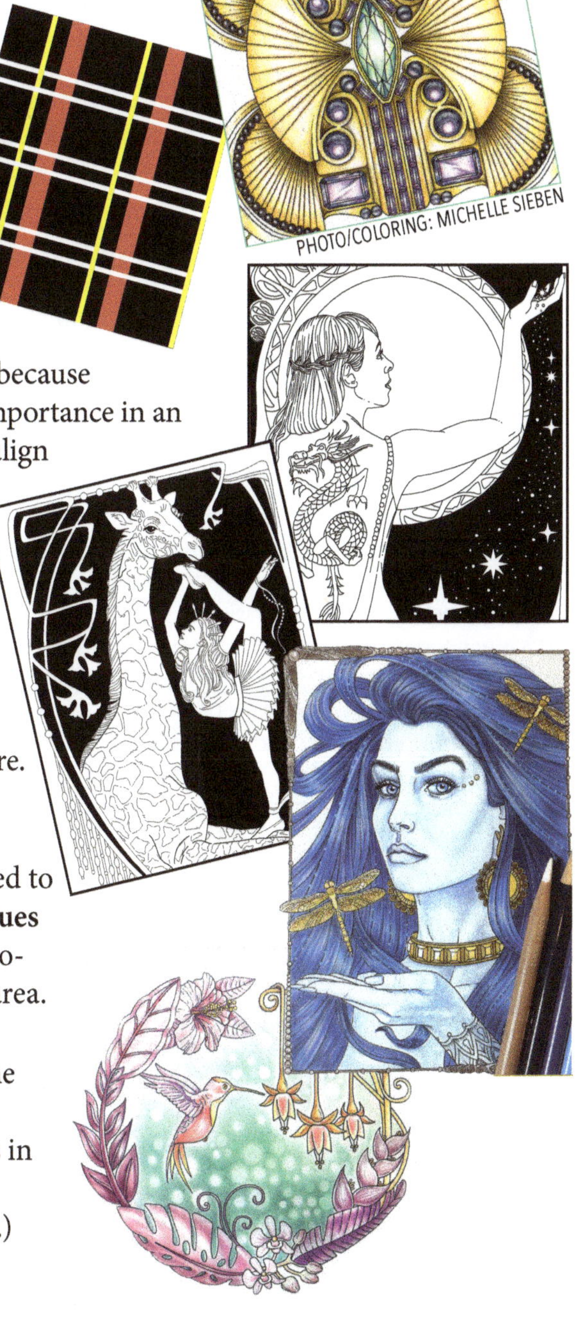

Chapter 5: Simple Background Solutions & Color Swaps

I always do my best to address the concerns of my followers. I've repeatedly been asked to offer suggestions for filling large empty spaces on coloring pages, and to make suggestions for various backgrounds. There is more to coloring than a plain blue sky! I will say that for colorists at any level I recommend that you purchase some of the "investment supplies" from Chapter 1, so that your options aren't limited and your end results look professional. You can find *most* of these materials on a budget. Although I adore the wonderfully unique PanPastels (Chapter 10) for quick and easy backgrounds too, the following ideas only involve the use of supplies that are common-place, inexpensive and easy to get ahold of – or have easily obtainable substitutes. Nothing fancy required...

Rich Black Background/Starry Sky

You will need: - A black marker, preferably brush-tip, paint or alcohol-based (Posca or Sharpie)
- Any waxy white colored pencil (Prismacolor, Luminance)
- A white gel pen (such as Uniball Signo)

Adding solid black backgrounds with marker, or simply purchasing coloring books that offer them (like the Luna Moth coloring page!), looks great with an otherwise bright drawing because it creates drama! You can of course use something as inexpensive as a Sharpie, but for a richer black I'd recommend a paint-based marker.

Black Background – Here I've used a Black Posca Brush Marker – a fantastic tool! Notice that I use the very tip to get into small spots. I utilize the full brush to fill in the larger areas. I recommend that you keep rotating your page as you cover the outer edge of each shape you are filling. Drag the marker tip TOWARDS YOU (**fig. A & B**), to the right of the inside outline of whatever shape you are trying to color. This will keep your edge clean and it will give you the most control. Brush markers are so versatile, which is why I generally prefer them over chisel, bullet, or fine point tips. More bang for your buck. Did you know that Sharpie brand is now producing brush markers? They are relatively inexpensive and work well! Their only limitations are the few colors offered and lack of an affixed color name/number label.

Starry Sky – Take it a step further and turn it into a starry sky! In the next photo (**C**) I have added a few white colored pencil "pings" by creating "+" shapes lightly in several areas of the black background. *Note: paint marker doesn't take a layer of pencil as evenly as alcohol marker does. These will become my brightest stars. I've also added a few dots by picking a point to make a mark and swirling outwards slightly in a circular motion (not shown). Next I add a layer of white gel pen, dotting it heaviest in the center of the stars I want to illuminate (**D**). With swift motions, I also add little bright stars all over the background and on top of some of the swirled pencil marks (**E**). Cluster them together to form constellations. Afterwards I touch up the "pings" (**F**) with a sharp white pencil to smooth out some of the dotted centers. I may choose to add another set of pencil "+" shapes to each ping, only lighter and rotated 45 degrees.

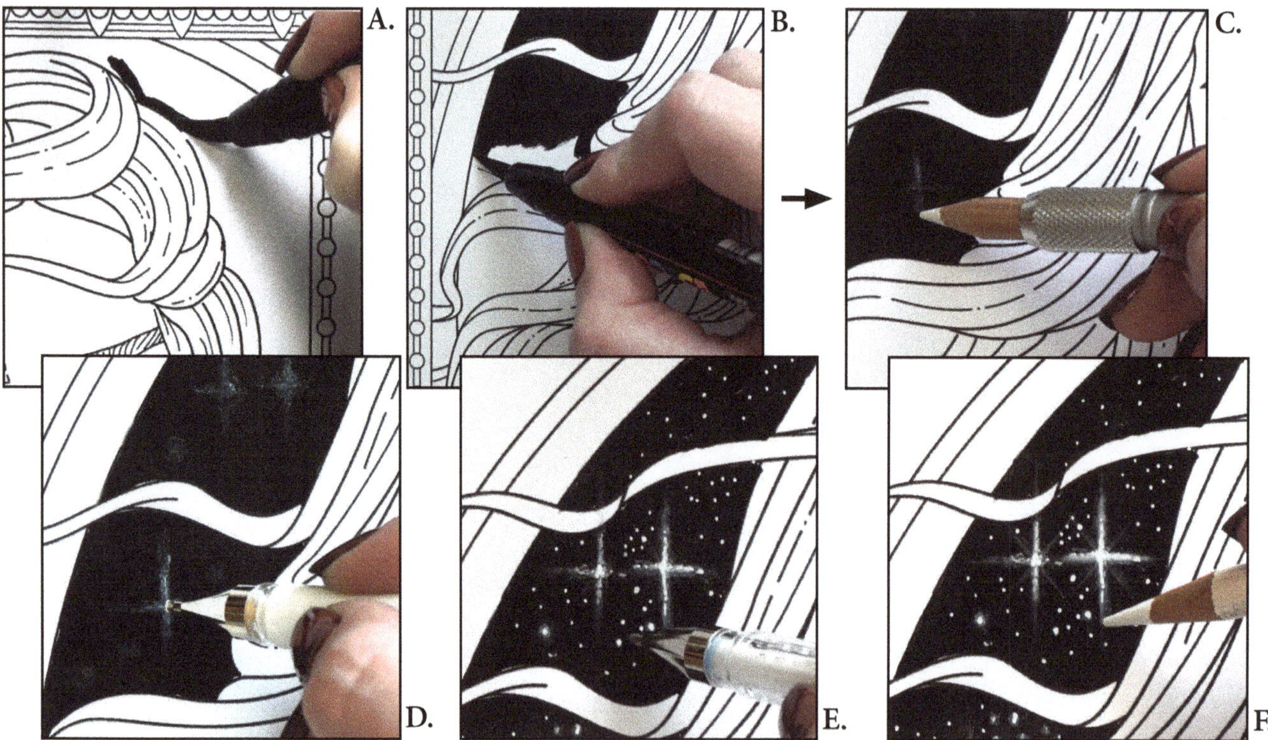

A.

B.

C.

D.

E.

F.

Did you know? *You may want to choose a black background when your main focus (**Emphasis**) is a neon or glowing object, or one that you want to look translucent – it will really set it off! Or try adding white PanPastel for a smokey or nebula effect! (See the Luna Moth tutorial in Chapter 10.)*

Radiant Circle Backdrop

You will need:

- The Jungle Circle line art page (or any circular coloring page)
- Polychromo pencils: 137, 134, 119, 128, 107, 247, 199, 101
- Optional: Copic Colorless Blender marker

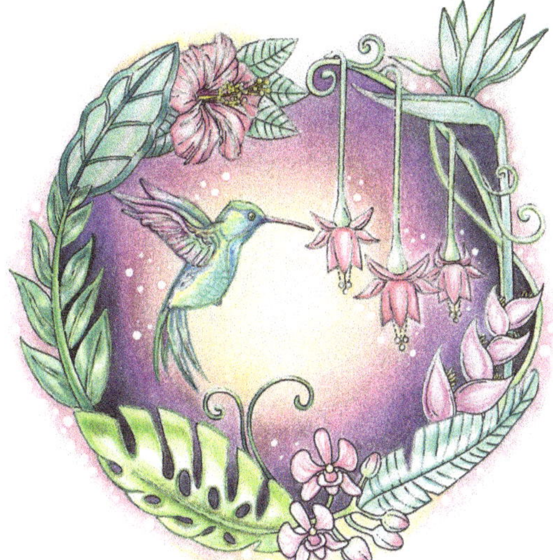

1 I start by using 137 Blue Violet. I turn my paper 360º using curved hatching strokes – lighter as I move inwards, leaving the center alone.

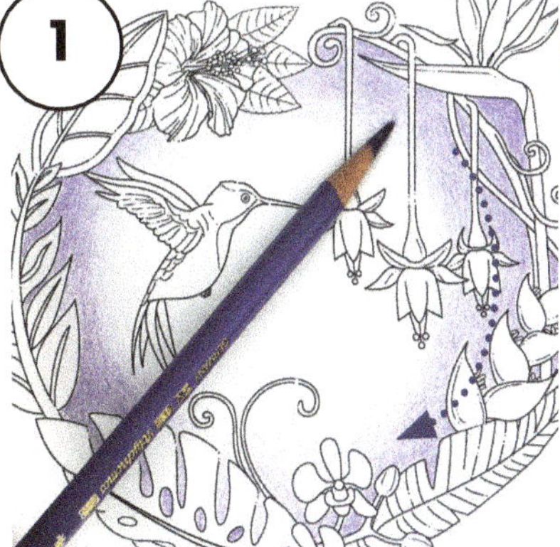

2 Next I use 134 Crimson to blend the edges of the 137 as I work inward, an inch or so, over the white with light hatching strokes.

3 Then I blend 119 Light Magenta with the edges of the 134, as the white center gets smaller! I'm careful not to extend it too far.

4 I use 128 Light Purple Pink circling inward until about where the bird's feet and innermost flower begin. I add a layer in small circles all over!

5 Now I brighten the middle, still leaving a little white showing. Using 107 Cadmium Yellow, I blend into the 128 but it looks a little too muddy.

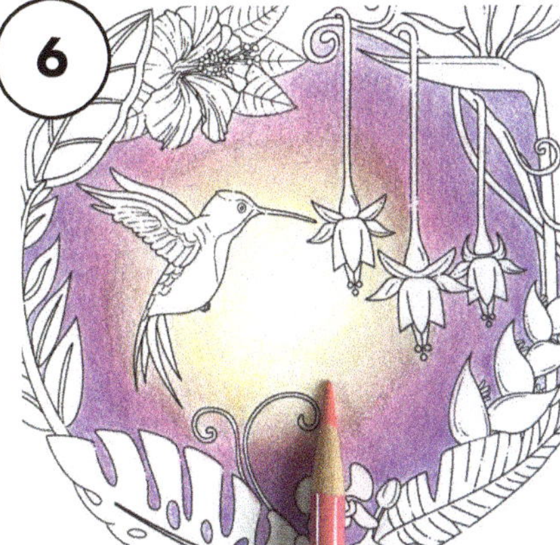

6 To counteract the dull orange resulting from the mix, I add layer of 128 over the edges and back into the previously colored areas, intensifying the color.

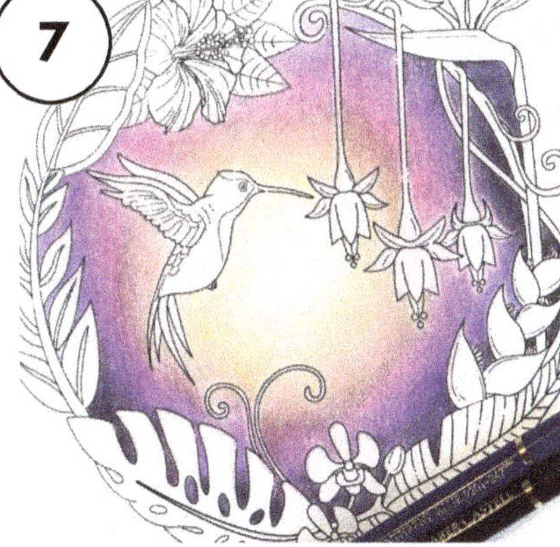

7 Next, I use 247 Indianthrene Blue towards the outer part of the picture, over the edges of the 137. I also add a very light coat of 199 Black up to the plants, blending it in small circles.

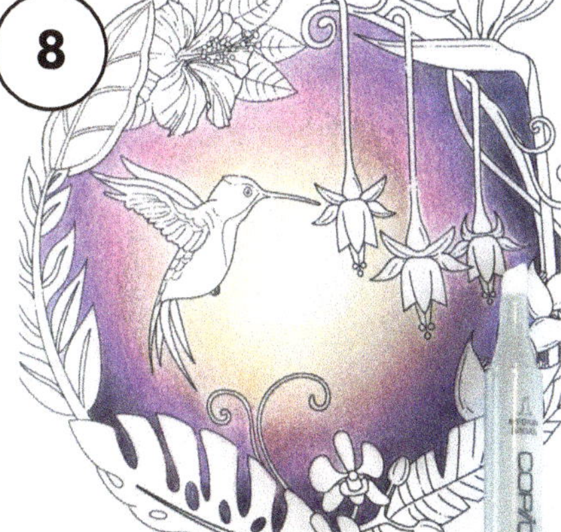

8 Finally, I smooth everything with the lighter colors I've already used and a 101 White Polychromo. I use a Copic Colorless Blender marker over the very corners to deepen/smooth the darks.

Green Haze Background

You will need:
- The Holiday Gift line art page
- Prismacolor Premier pencils: 989, 920, 912, 907, 908, 935, 913
- White gel pen or Posca marker

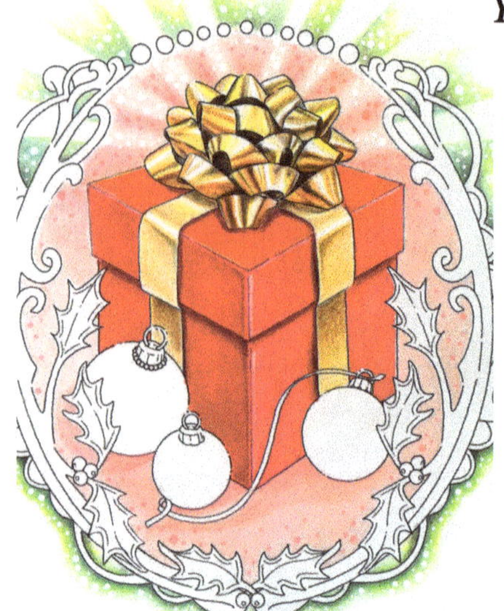

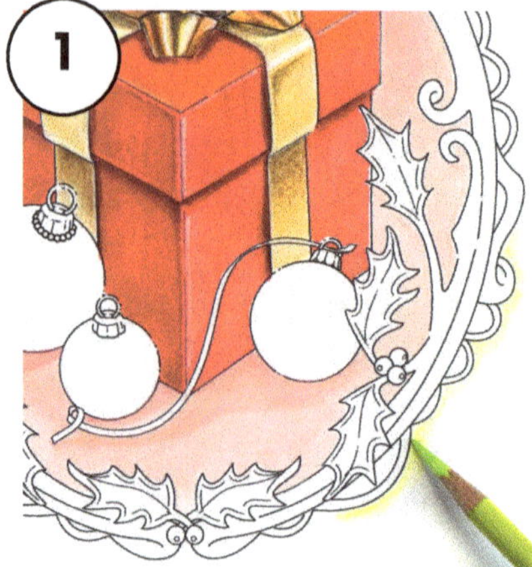

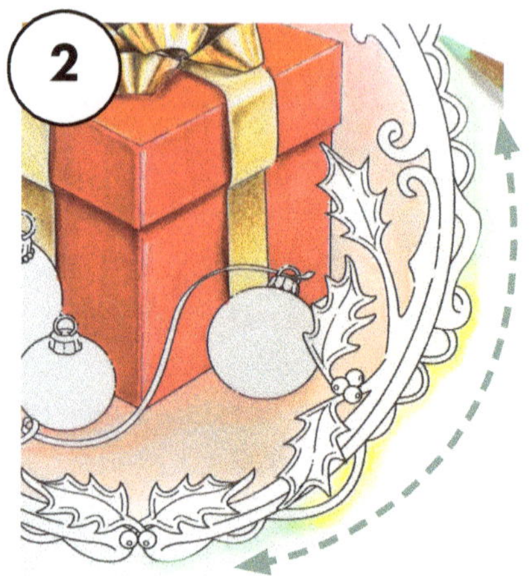

1-2: I begin by using a 989 Chartreuse pencil outside of the border from "three o'clock to five o'clock." I add some 920 Light Green above and below the 989, extending it up to about the corner of the gift and downward to about the "six o'clock mark."

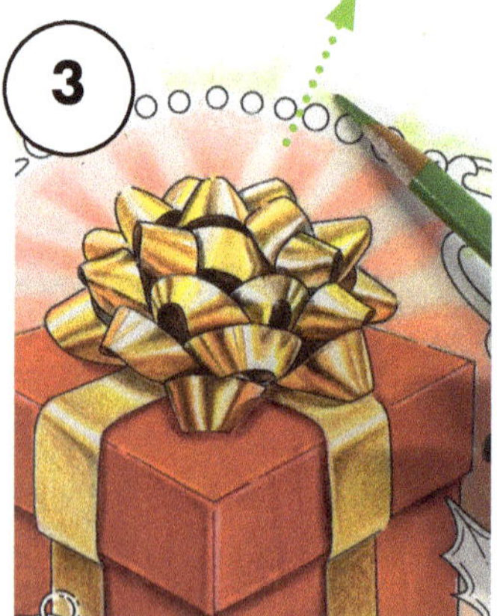

Since I used the "Polka Dot Rays" tutorial (next page), I'm extending the pink rays from inside by drawing directionally, using 912 Apple Green.

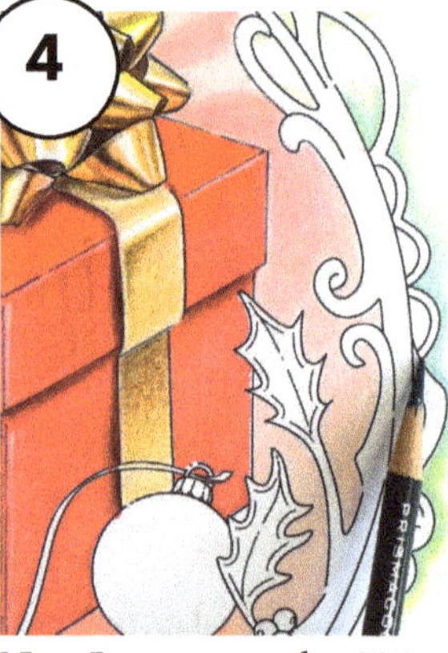

Now I use my cooler 907 Peacock Green against the frame to deepen over both previous colors, leaving 989 and 920 showing.

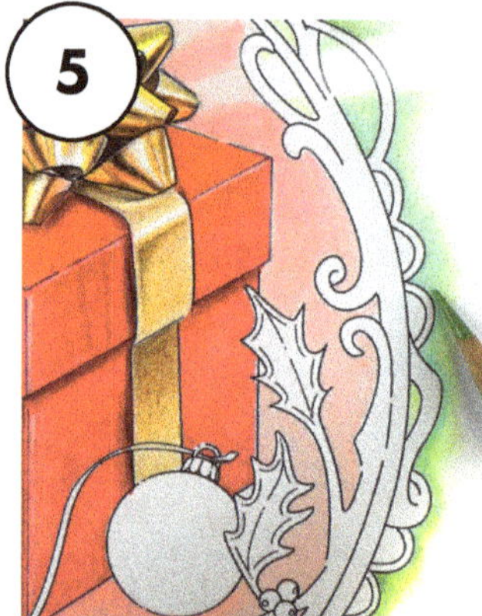

Over the 907 I blend the outside edges with warmer 912 and extend the "haze" outward.

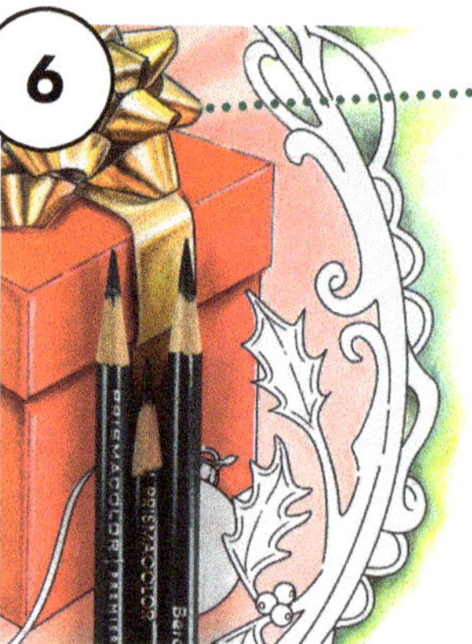

I use a little more 907 plus 935 Black and 908 Dark Green up to where the rays begin. If you are using a different coloring page, stop the haze wherever you'd like!

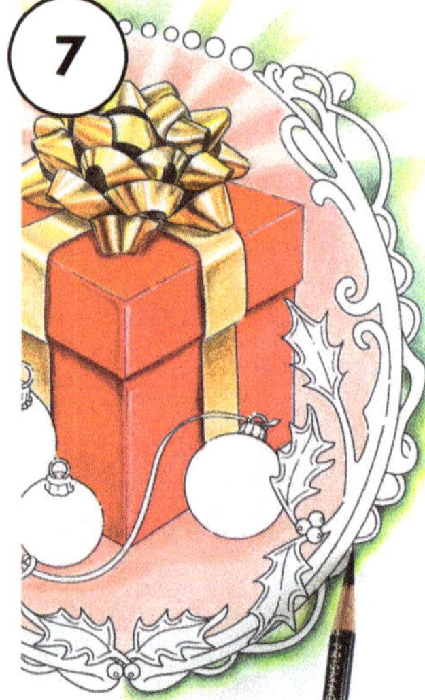

I do this all the way around the frame – repeating on the other side. Then with a very sharp 935 pencil I perfect the edges touching the frame and smooth out the paper texture.

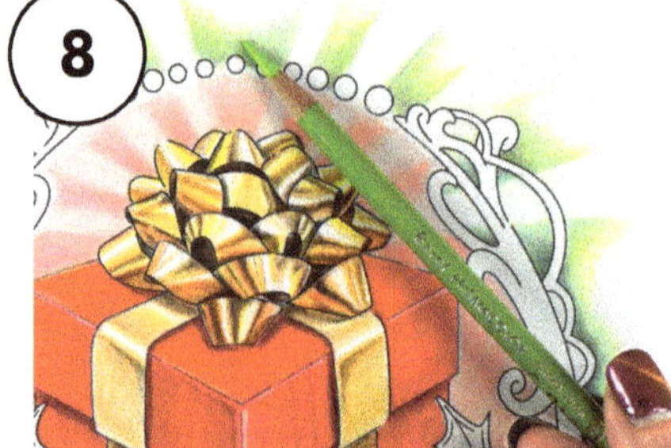

Near the top, I extend the haze outward and warm it up a bit more with 913 Spring Green, intensifying the color and the glow all around.

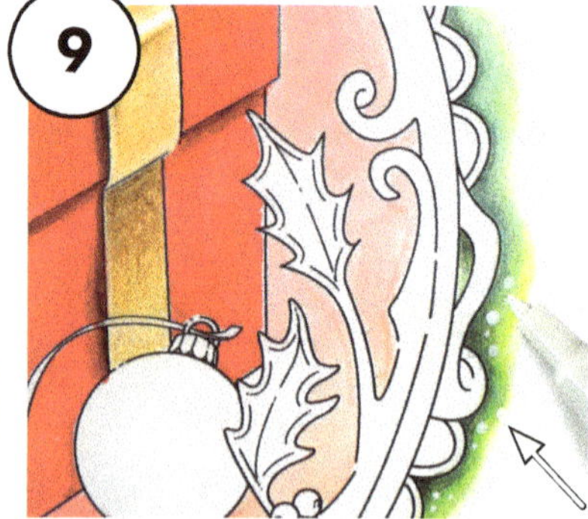

For the final touch I add Posca dots in slightly different sizes in the green haze, especially towards the outside edges. They magically appear to blend into the white paper!

2 Easy Peachy-Pink BackDrops – Which is your Favorite?

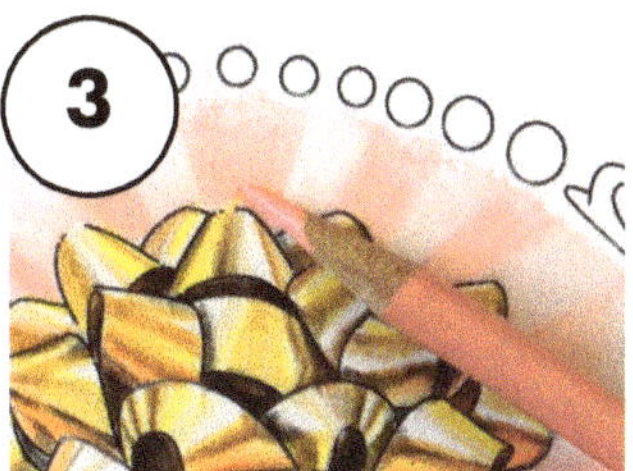
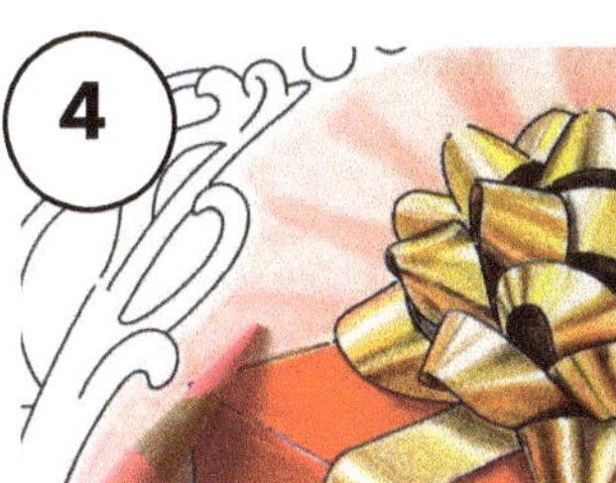

You will need:

- The Holiday Gift line art page
- White Posca marker or gel pen (Uniball Signo)
- White Luminance pencil 001
- Primsacolor Premier pencils: 928 Blush Pink, 929 Pink, 926 Carmine Red
- TouchNew dual-ended markers in 28 Fruit Pink and 9 Pale Pink (**OR** Copic Sketch in R20 Blush and R22S Light Prawn **OR** Prismacolor Premier marker in 133 Deco Pink and 010 Blush Pink, **OR** Arrtx dual tip alcohol markers in 135 Pale Cherry Pink and 9 Pale Pink)

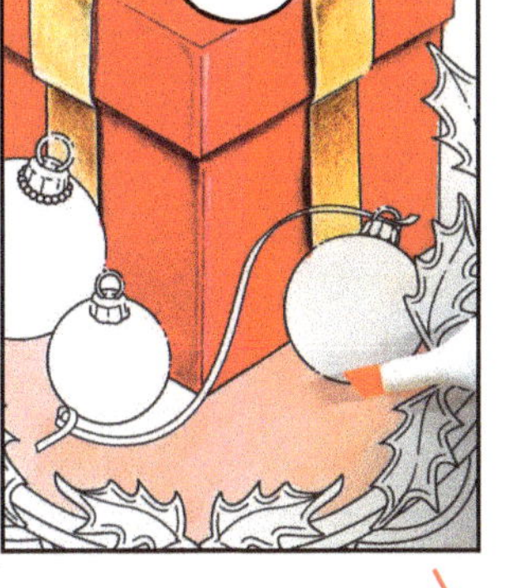

Polka Dot Rays

Start Here!

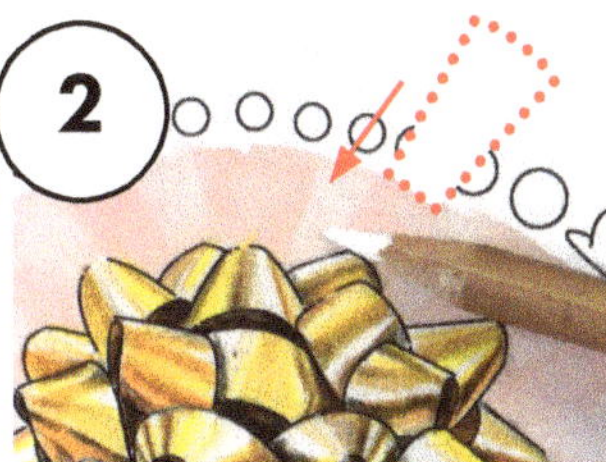

1

For either version, I start off by using both ends of my TouchNew Fruit Pink marker (or a similar sub) to block in the color. I use swift strokes, without overlapping or leaving space. This keeps it looking flawless!

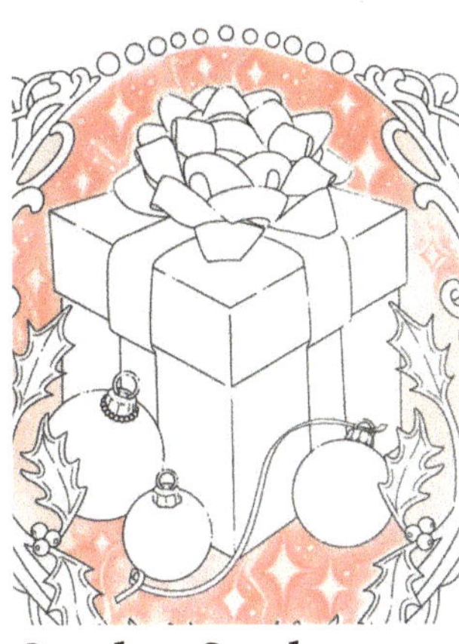

Smokey Starbursts

2 To create the white rays stemming from the gift, I use a 001 Lumi pencil.

3 928 is next, darkening the bottom half of each new pink ray and blurring the top edge.

4 929 Pink is used to gradually darken each ray as I move down toward the center (gift).

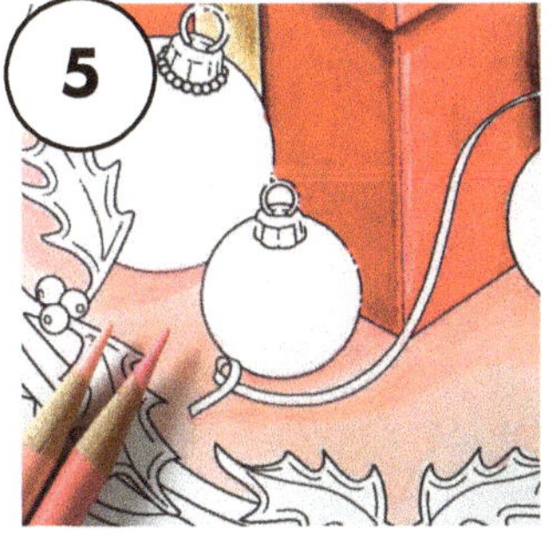

5

Now I begin to fill in solid "cast shadows" under the gift and ornaments with 929 and I soften the edges with my 928.

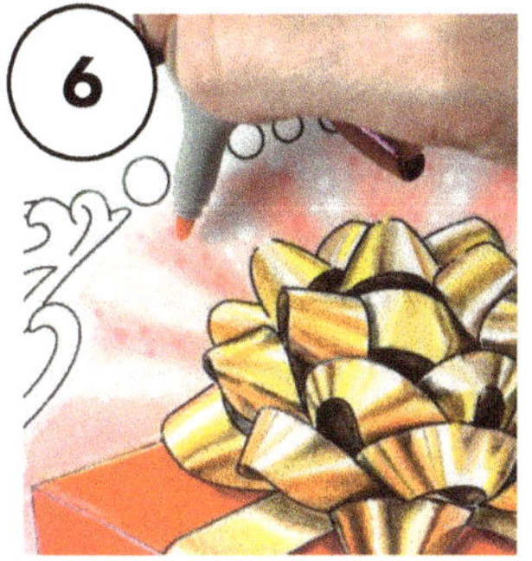

6

Finally, I use a White Posca to dot each white ray and a Pale Pink marker to dot my pink rays! I change my pressure to vary the size.

— *or* —

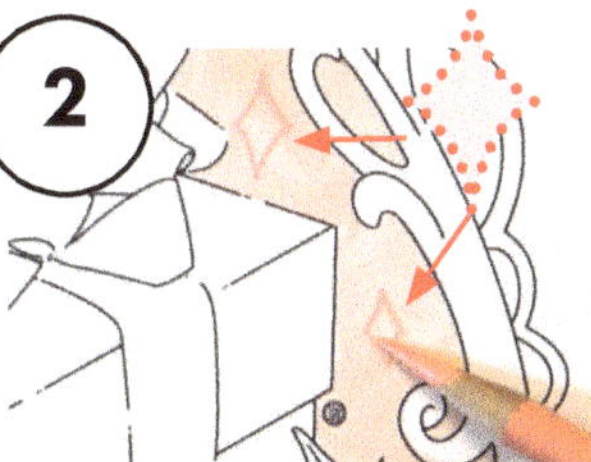

2 I use a Blush Pink pencil to draw in starbursts all over the pink marker background in different sizes.

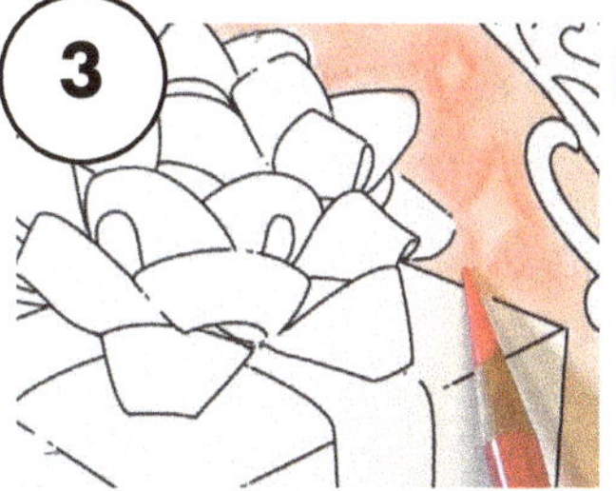

3 Next I add Pink around the outsides and fuzz some color between the starbursts.

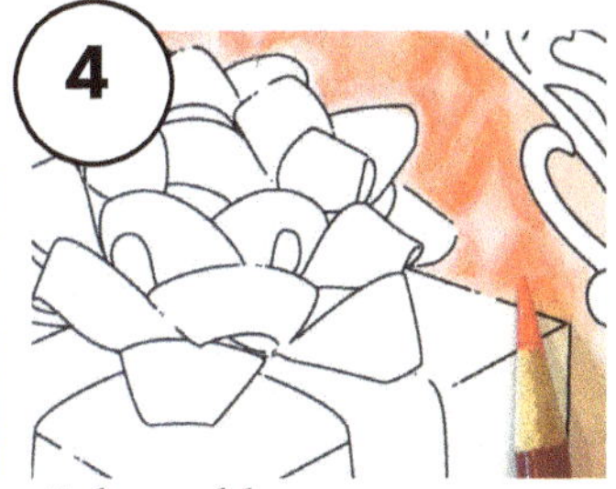

4 I then add more contrast with a bit of Carmine Red around the outsides.

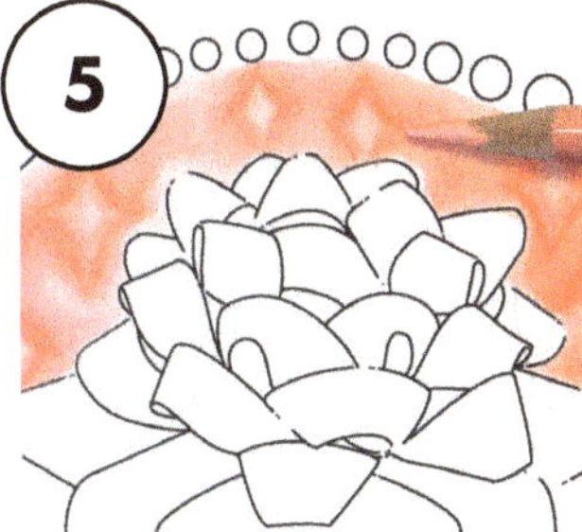

5 I use the Blush Pink again to smooth, soften and burnish the darker colors so it looks more refined.

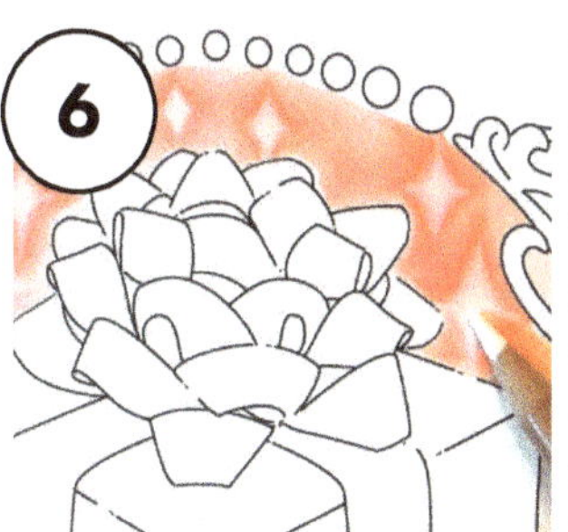

6 To finish, I lighten the inside of each shape with White Luminance. You can add a few dots of white gel pen in the center if needed!

"Smokey Bokeh" Colored Pencil Background – Special Guest Tutorial by Lilicence

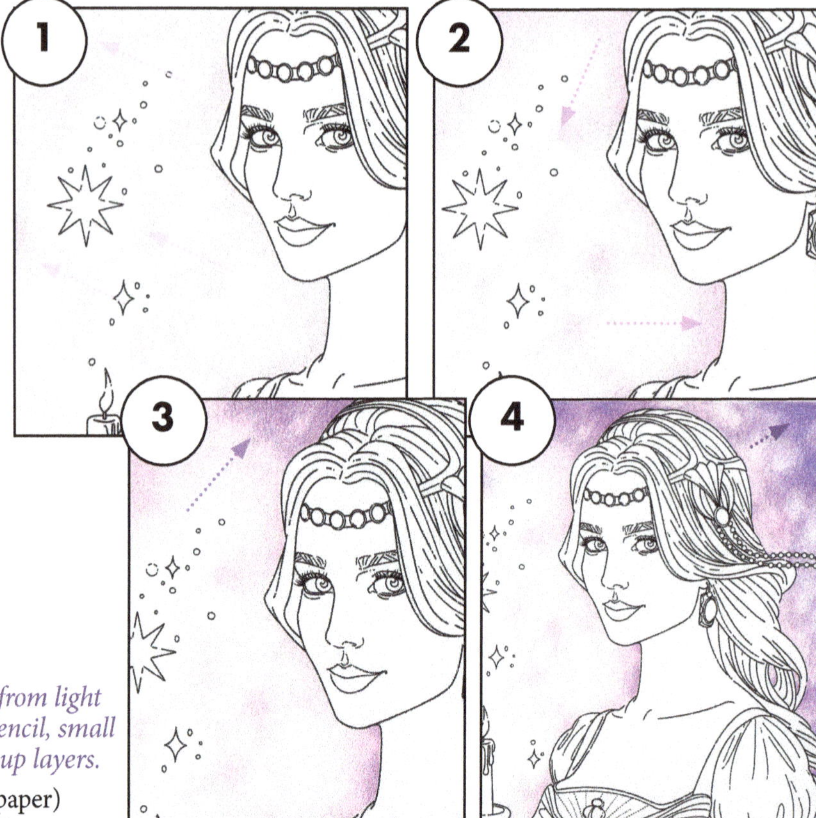

You will need: - 4-6 colors of pencils in a family
Used: Prismacolor Premier pencils: 1026, 956, 1008, 1007, 132, Luminance 001 (or Prisma 138)
- Glow Princess line art page

LILICENCE *is an absolutely amazing colorist, whose works convey mesmerizing luminance and seemingly complex backgrounds. Here she has created a dreamy, sophisticated yet surprisingly simple glow for us!*
Follow her on Instagram: **LILICENCE**

To create this effect Lilicence blends patches from light to dark, then back again! She uses a sharp pencil, small circles and minimal pressure to slowly build up layers.

1. Lilicence starts out leaving areas of white (paper) where the brightest glow will be, then she begins to shade patches around them in the lightest color, 1026 Grayed Lavender – slowly working her way outwards, all around, towards edges of the page. **2.** Next, she blends into the 1026 with a slightly darker color, 956 Lilac.
3. Leaving the previous colors showing - the lightest color remains in the center - she continues towards the outside edges with a darker hue, 1008 Parma Violet.
4. She then uses 1007 Imperial Violet, moving outward.
5. Once the darkest color, Dioxazine Purple 132, is used around the edges, the effect is half completed. Now the reversing begins... **6.** From outwards in, she goes back through every color, starting with the most recent, 1007, slightly burnishing the paper tooth, blending the gradation's transition edge. **7.** The 1008 is blended at the edges of the 1007. **8.** The 956 is blended at the edges of the 1008. **9.** The 1026 is blended at the edges of the 956. Finally, as seen in the completed image above, She uses a heavier hand + white pencil to smooth the edges where the lightest color meets the white paper, allowing the paper areas to continue to show through.

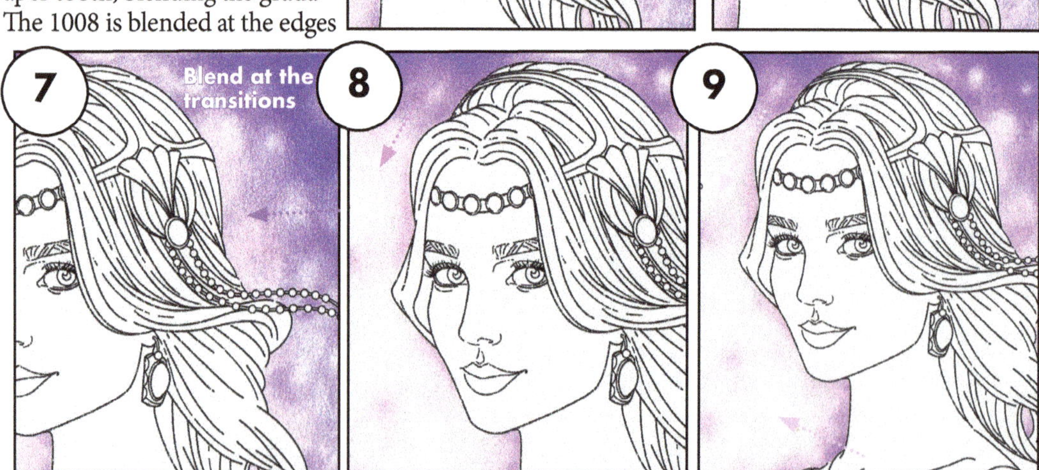

Use any of the previous suggestions for backgrounds, just swap colors! I am frequently asked to give examples of scheme swatches. These aren't *actual* color scheme types, but just the best descriptions to explain my ideas here. The mood, focal point and overall effect is up to us depending on how we apply color. Here I set out to create the same image four different ways, using only **Faber-Castell Polychromos**, a White Luminance pencil, white gel pen or Posca marker, and a black fineliner. Each *emphasizes* different elements within the design – making them look like entirely different images.

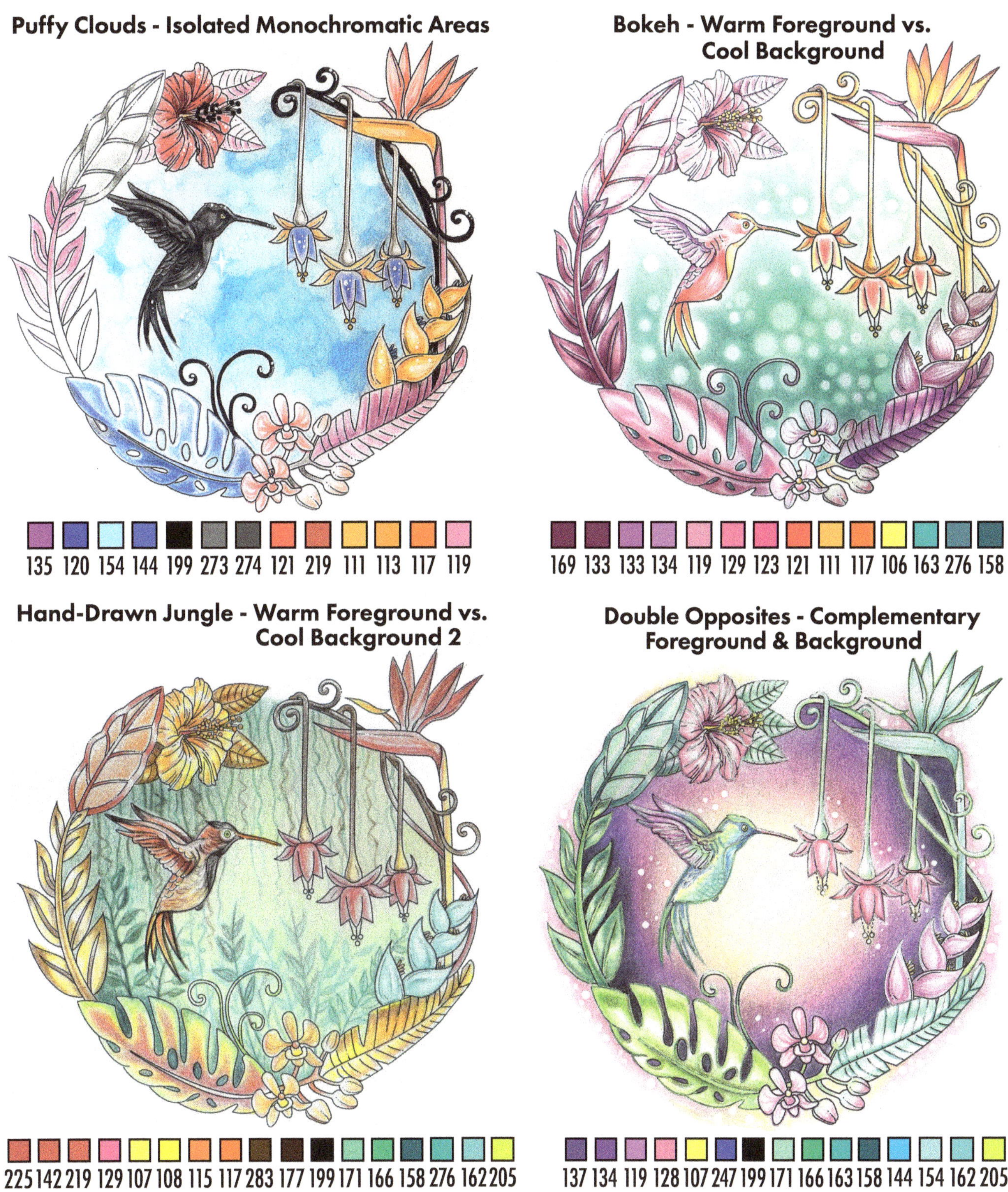

Puffy Clouds - Isolated Monochromatic Areas

135 120 154 144 199 273 274 121 219 111 113 117 119

Bokeh - Warm Foreground vs. Cool Background

169 133 133 134 119 129 123 121 111 117 106 163 276 158

Hand-Drawn Jungle - Warm Foreground vs. Cool Background 2

225 142 219 129 107 108 115 117 283 177 199 171 166 158 276 162 205

Double Opposites - Complementary Foreground & Background

137 134 119 128 107 247 199 171 166 163 158 144 154 162 205

Not all of these colors have Prismacolor substitutes. See ModernColoring.com, using your code in the back of the book for more information.

Chapter 6: Dynamic Varieties of Light and Shadow: The Parts of Light In Effect

Before we jump into tutorials, let's take a look at lighting a little more in depth. If you can figure out where to place your light and shadows, you can easily create more believeable dimension in your coloring or drawing!

SIMILAR LIGHT – DIFFERENT OBJECT

Where does the light go? Where do the shadows go? How do you know? If you have *The Secrets of Coloring Volume 1* you know that I emphasize what is referred to as **The Parts of Light**. In explaining the theory, I use a simple sphere as a model, which is how the concept is traditionally taught. Now we are ready to take it to a more intermediate level when we apply The Parts of Light to objects with completely different *forms* (Chapter 1, Elements &Principles).

These objects look strikingly different but the light source is almost the same. They are examples of "side lighting". Take note of the shadows created by each object. Do you notice there is some of the object's color mixed into the shadow? Shadows aren't just black! Light bounces off an object and onto the surface it sits upon!

The shape of the shadow is most often a stretched version of the object. The length of the shadow is determined by the distance from the object and strength of the light source. In addition, cast shadows get lighter and the edges get fuzzier the further they are from the objects casting them. Shadows are most crisp and dark right directly underneath the objects casting them. Look at the difference in the shadows between the organic forms vs. the geometric one.

The Parts of Light

1. Light Source
2. Highlight
3. Core Shadow
4. Cast Shadow
5. Reflected Light

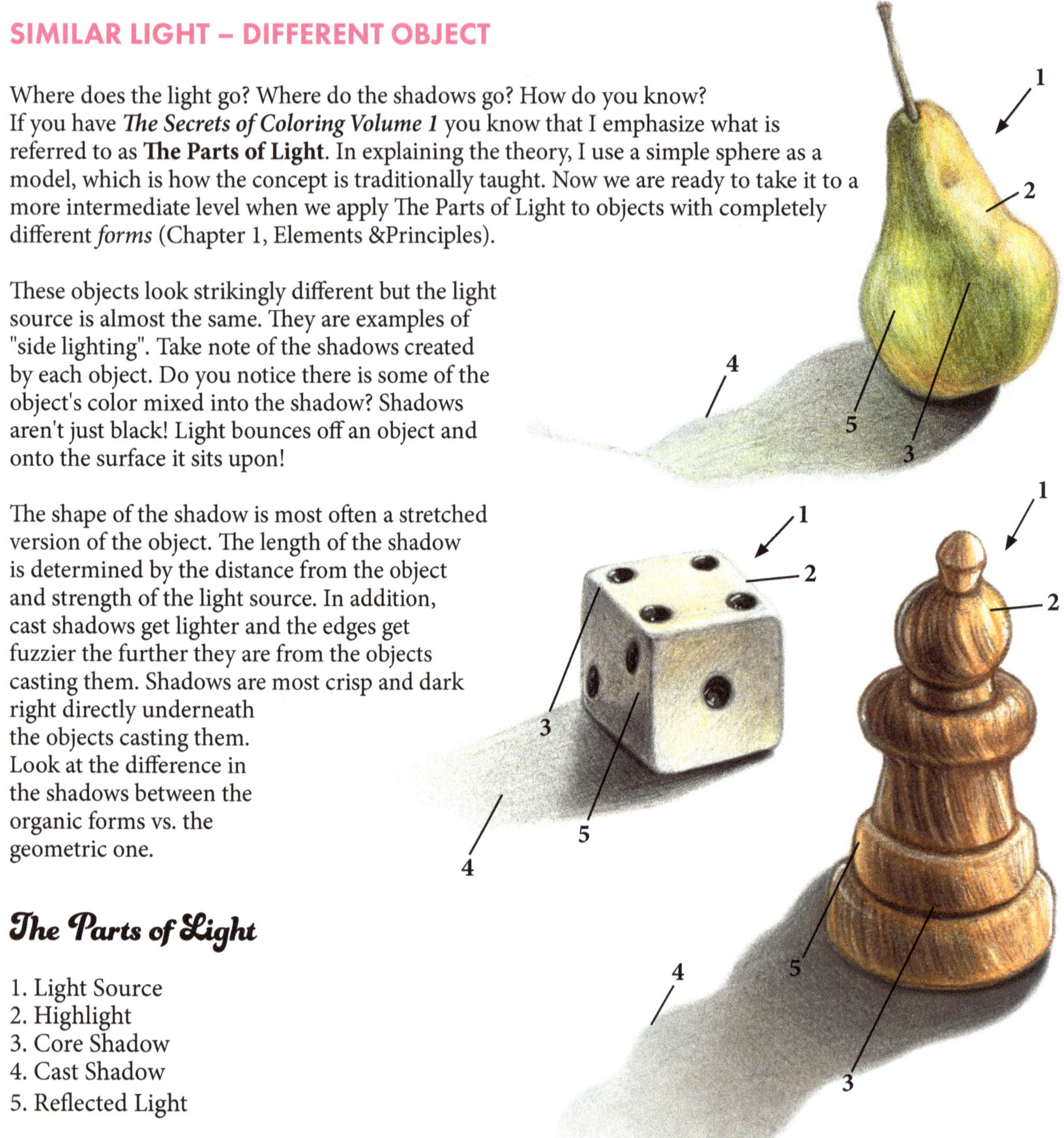

SIMILAR OBJECT– DIFFERENT LIGHT

The next few images are based on woodland scenes from a worm's eye point of view. What makes them so different? This is what you should be thinking about before tackling a scene! Imagine yourself a fairy trekking through the woodsy terrain. You'd likely find lots of mushies, moss and lichen. The greens would be vibrant from all of the rain, and the tiny world created here would be vast compared to the undersized inhabitants.

Depending on the time of day and the weather, the scene could look drastically different. Colors and contrast are greatly affected when sunlight isn't abundant...or when it's night time! Or when something is self-illuminating! Here are some examples using different light sources under different conditions. When you color are you cosidering the time of day is in your settings? Think about the location of the setting you are trying to create? Is it overall eery or warm and inviting? Consider your light source direction (direct, diffused, side, back or self-illuminating) and the materials your objects are made of! Take note of the relationship between the light placement and shadow direction here. Where is the core shadow? The highlights? The cast shadow?

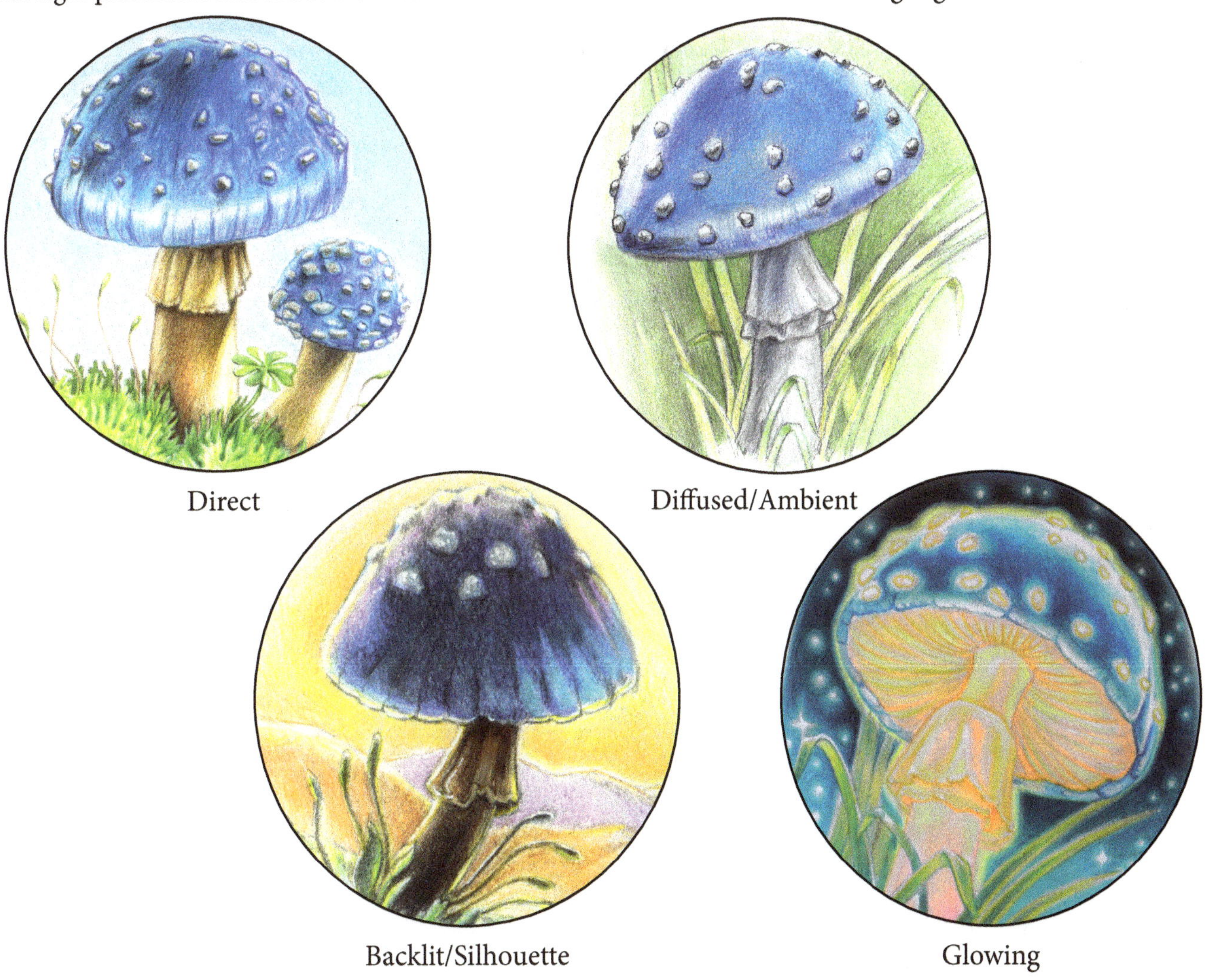

Direct

Diffused/Ambient

Backlit/Silhouette

Glowing

Chapter 7: Investigating Light – Transparent, Translucent, Opaque + Surface Textures

Although this may seem like a science project, the goal of the following step-by-step lessons is to provide you with examples of rendered objects with different degrees of reflection, transmission and absorption of light. We will also take a look at surface types – the defining characteristics of various materials. You might not find yourself coloring these exact objects, so instead perhaps think about utilizing the "big idea" information taught here to apply to your chosen subjects. As a side note, the "Candy Shoppe" and practice pages have been printed on "Faux Toned" backgrounds. For a limited time you can access a bonus PDF of this image on a white background to copy onto real toned paper for the best results. See the coloring page section in the back of the book for more information.

You might not care to learn how to draw a lollipop or an Easter bunny, but you might be wondering how to color something pearlescent! Candy is a great subject to study to practice drawing with light. When you are trying to realistically color something made of a similar finish, ask yourself each time, "Do I want it to look transparent or opaque? Should it be shiny or matte?" Use the "formulas" in these tutorials to help achieve the next level of realism on your own.

There's always an excuse for candy! Who doesn't love it? Well these treats are calorie-free, fat-free and sugar-free to draw, so enjoy these holiday delicacies without the guilt!

Milk Chocolate Easter Bunny

Opaque
Shiny

You will need:

- The Candy Shoppe "Faux Toned Paper" line art page
- Copic Sketch Milk Chocolate or other brand brush or chisel marker (budget substitute Arrtx 94 Brick Brown)
- Prismacolor Premier pencils: 1001, 942, 943, 1082, 945, 947, 938
- A colorless blender pencil
- White Posca marker or Uniball Signo gel pen

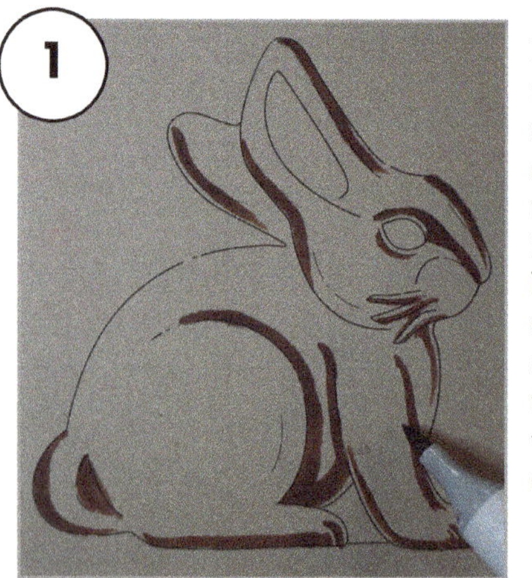

My first step is to use my Copic or another brand of marker, on the toned paper, in a light warm brown to create small areas of shadow – where the "form" would turn away or crease.

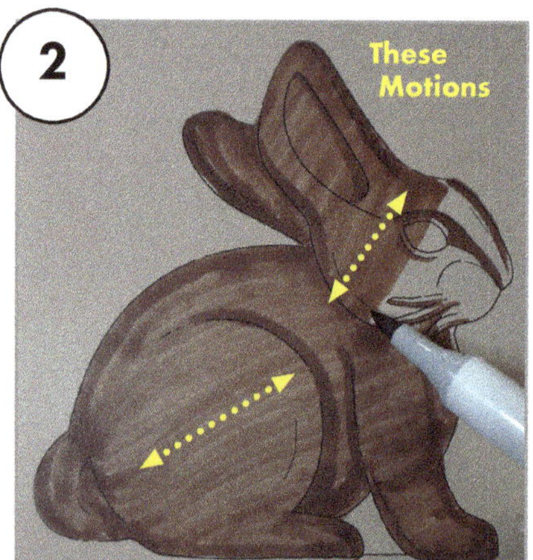

Using swift motions, I add one complete coat without gaps across the entire form, going right over the shadow marks I made in Step 1. It's easiest for me to cover the bunny's body and head in two sets of diagonal motions.

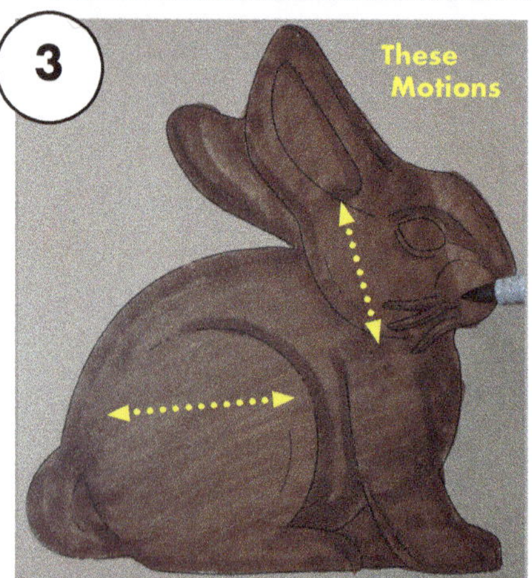

Now I add a second complete coat at a slightly different angle so that I cover any sign of marker strokes from the first coat for a seamless brown bunny.

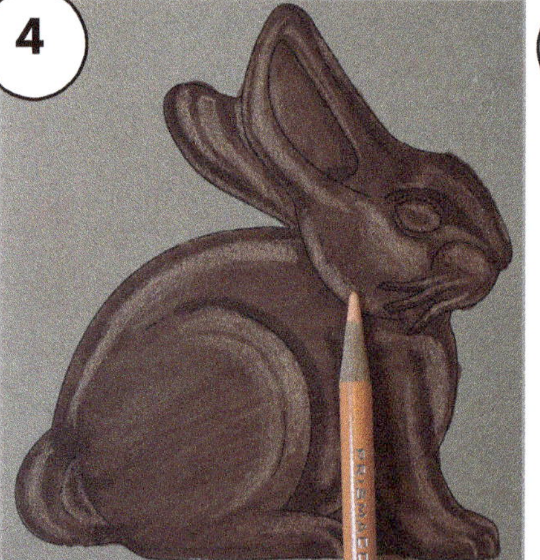

Using my first pencil, 1001 Salmon Pink, I add areas of reflection with a light hand, all over the bunny, where I think the light would go: along the back, front of the legs and feet, plus facial features.

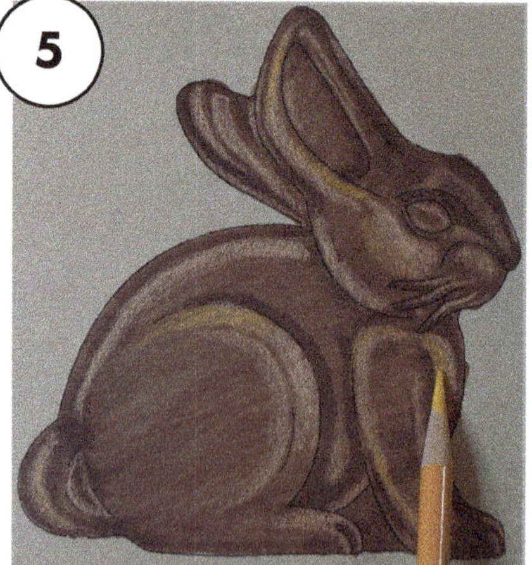

Next, I use my 942 Yellow Ochre, to warm up the reflections and add a little color variation in a few areas. This should be very subtle, to end up with a realistic effect.

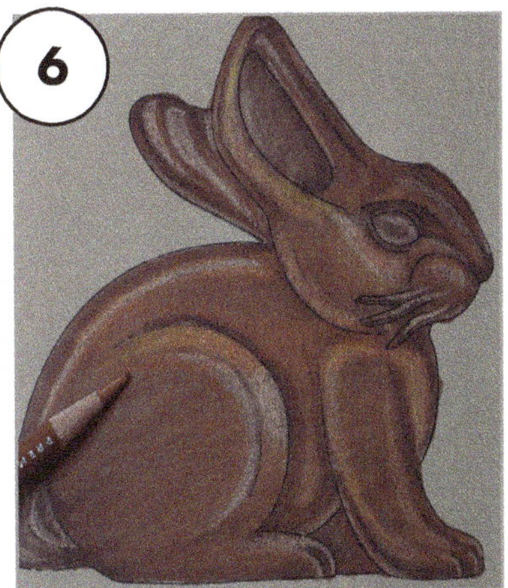

Then I add some warmth all over by applying a thin, even coat of 943 Burnt Ochre all over. I blend it carefully into the edges of the reflection sections, and add a light coat but I don't cover them completely.

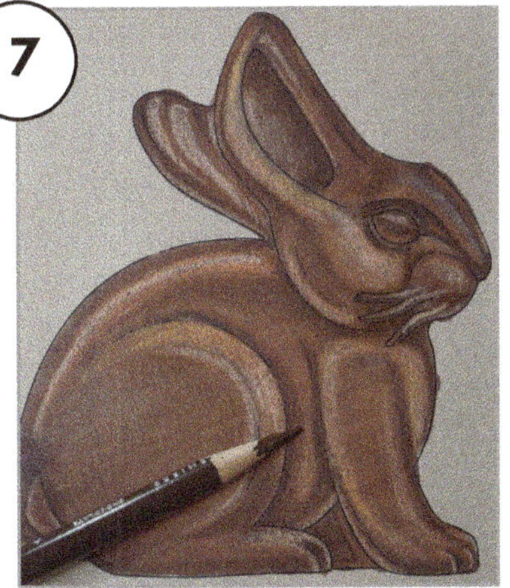

Now it's time for a little contrast. I use my 1082 Chocolate to deepen shadows under the neck, in the ear, in the crease and in the center of the eye, and the bottom of the hind leg and feet. Again, I use a light hand.

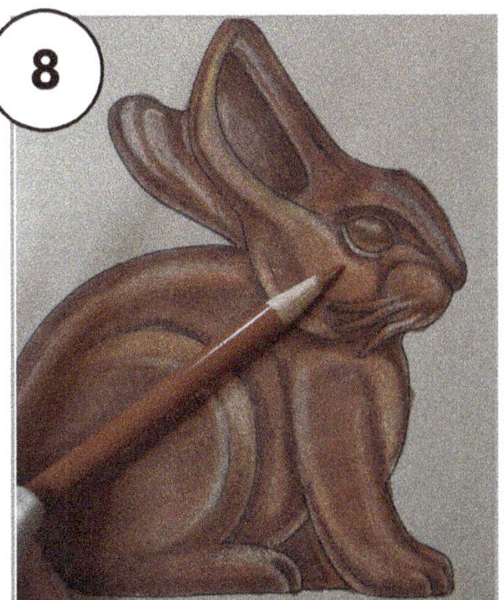

I warm up the bunny's cheek a bit while creating a darker value with 945 Sienna Brown.

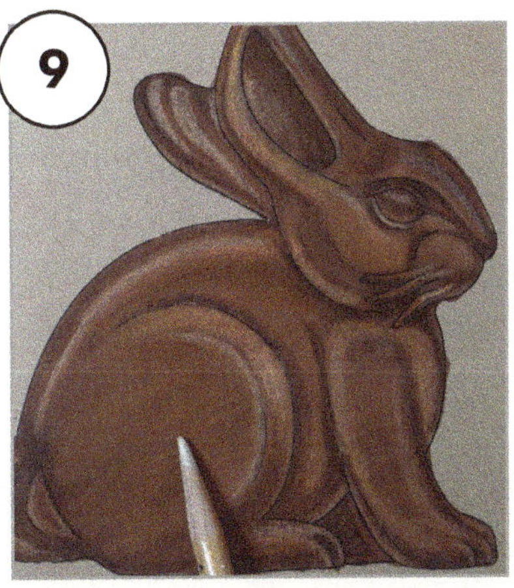

Now I use my colorless blender to blend all of the large areas of color and each reflection to make them all look smooth. Magic!

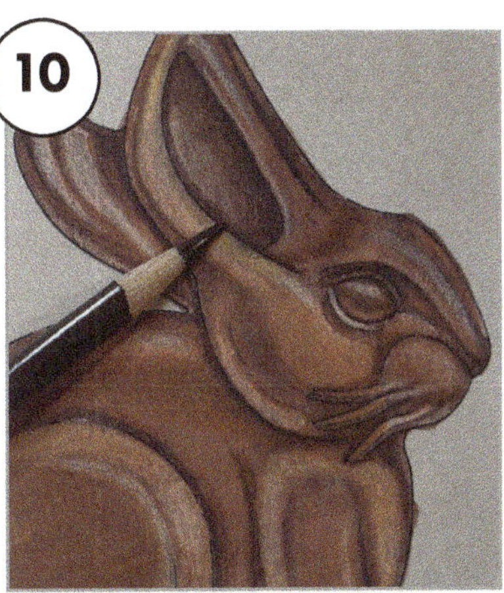

I add a small amount of 947 Burnt Umber to fuzz the line art that still shows and amp up the shadows only slightly. I don't go overboard here.

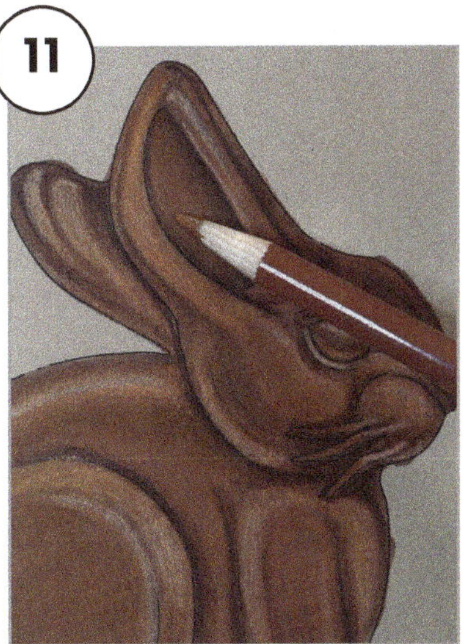

I warm up and darken the inside of the ear using 945 again.

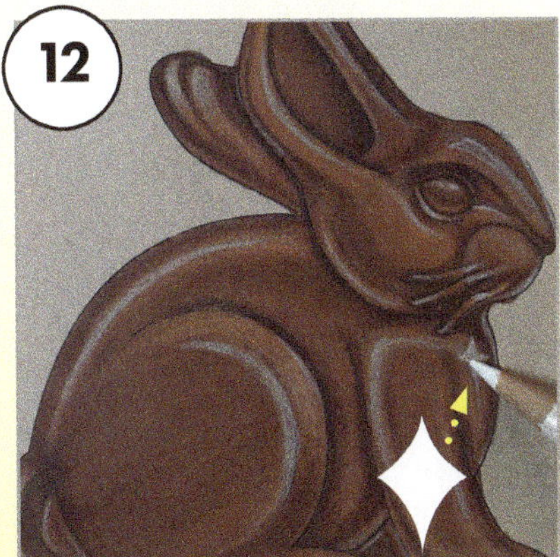

Here it is really starting to come to life with the addition of White 938 highlights. I blend the White into each reflection, keeping it "whitest" in the middle. I add a reflective "starburst" or "ping" shape to the chest.

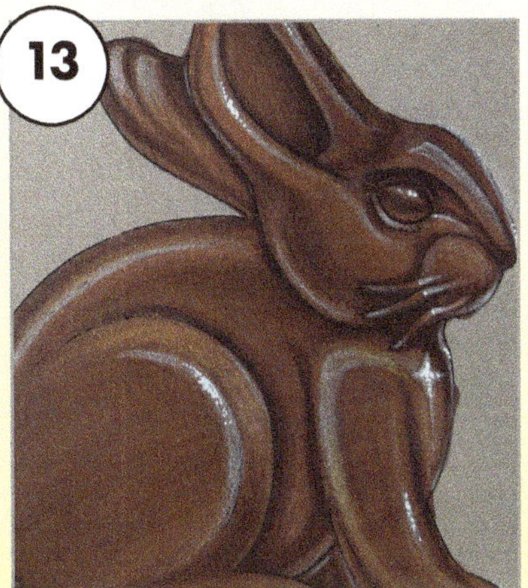

The finishing touch – tidy up and re-blend each color, add whatever nuances I need to, and brighten my "ping" and dotted white areas in the center of each highlight with a Posca.

Did you know?

It's very difficult to achieve a really deep, dark color with colored pencils alone. *Using mixed media, such as applying markers under pencil will add to the richness of your color. Additional examples can be seen in The Secrets of Coloring, Vol. 1*

Pink Foil Easter Egg

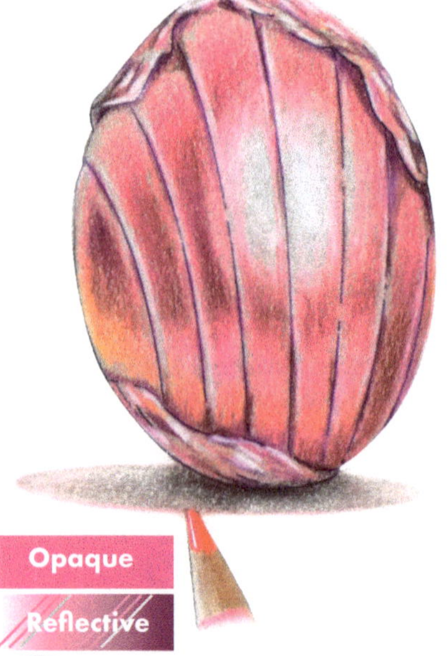

You will need:
- The Candy Shoppe "Faux Toned Paper" line art page
- White CD Luminance
- Prismacolor Premier pencils: 1038, 938, 994, 995, 1036, 931, 1099, 1077 Colorless Blender

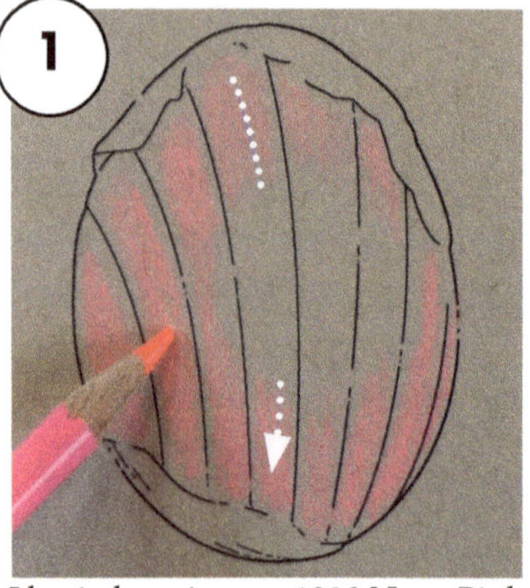

1 I begin by using my 1038 Neon Pink to fill all of the vertical sections, but leave an uncolored circular area, just right of center.

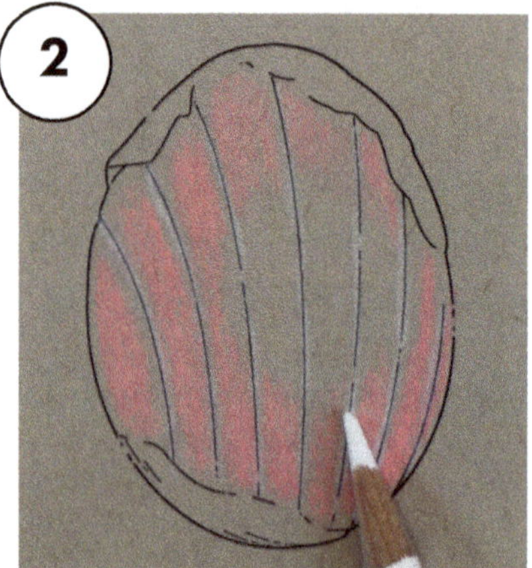

2 I use my 938 White to lightly cover over the vertical line art to tone down the *contrast*.

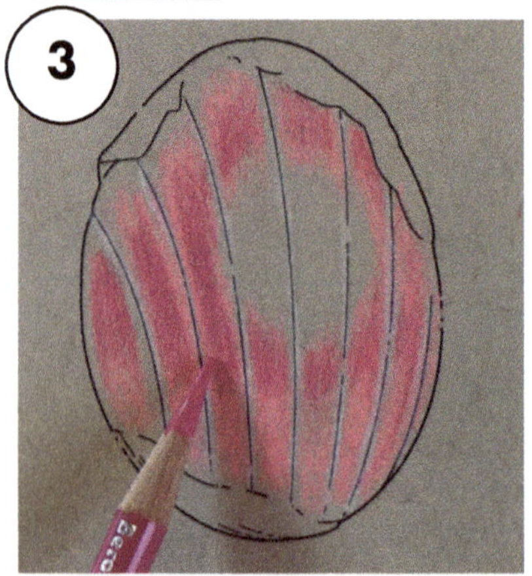

3 I then use 994 Process Red to color in the top half of the egg, avoiding the uncolored area and the edges of each vertical section.

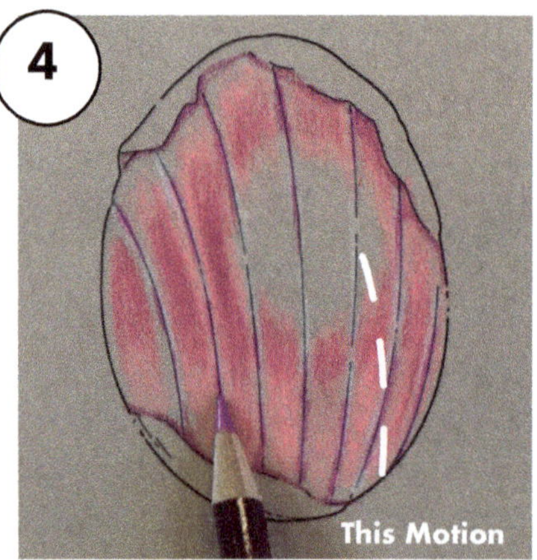

4 Next, I use Mulberry 995 to *emphasize* the vertical lines by drawing dashed lines on top.

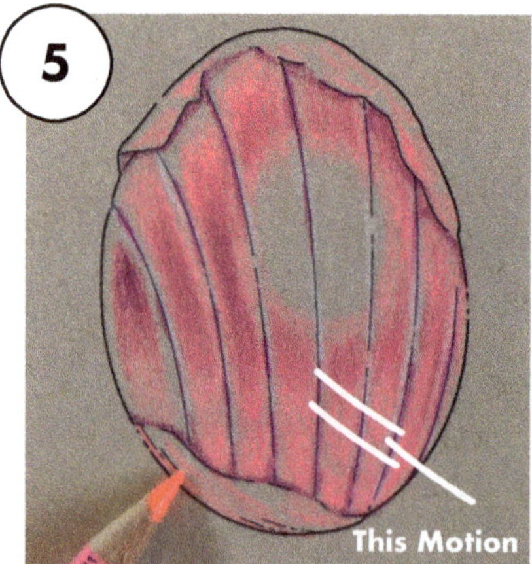

5 After that I focus on the top and bottom wrinkled foil areas, adding diagonal strokes with 1038 again.

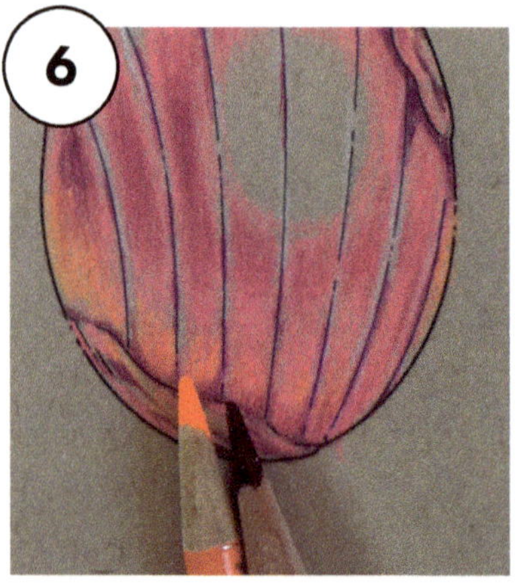

6 I create *variety* with 1036 Neon Orange adding it along the top of the wrinkled bottom, mainly on the left. I deepen above/below the wrinkled sections with 931 Dark Purple.

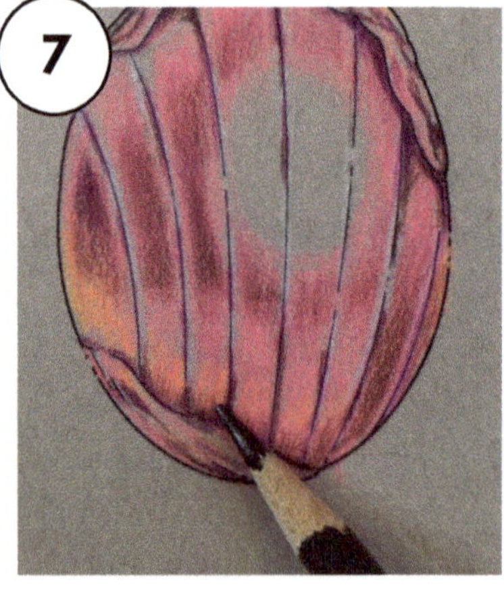

7 I add definition to and around the wrinkles and lightly on top of the 994 areas with 1099 Espresso.

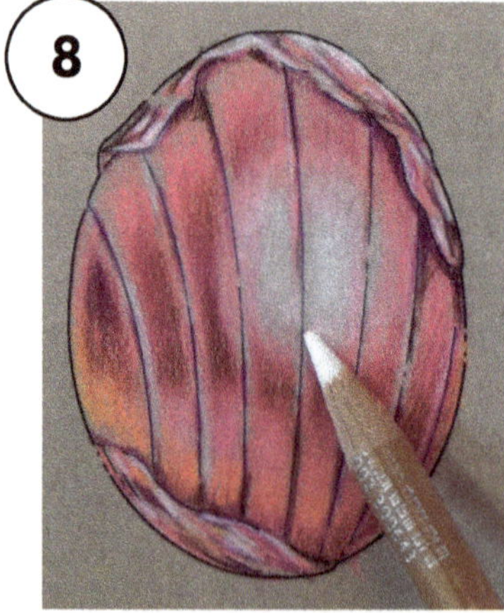

8 To finish, Luminance White highlights fill the center of the uncolored area, plus a few of the vertical lines, and the top and bottom wrinkles. I blend the imperfections with 1077 blender. I add a 1099 cast shadow underneath (darkest directly under the egg, with a little 1038 on the edges, as seen in the final image).

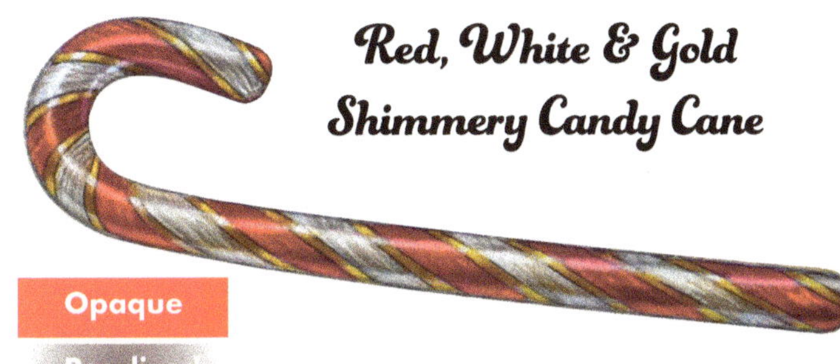

Red, White & Gold Shimmery Candy Cane

You will need:

- The Candy Shoppe "Faux Toned" line art page
- Prismacolor Premier pencils: 925, 938, 922, 924, 1008, 1072, 914, 1011, 1036 + optional sharp Black Verithin
- White CD Luminance + thin white gel pen
- Markers: Any medium red & light golden brown. I've used Copic R27 and TouchNew 41

Opaque

Pearlized

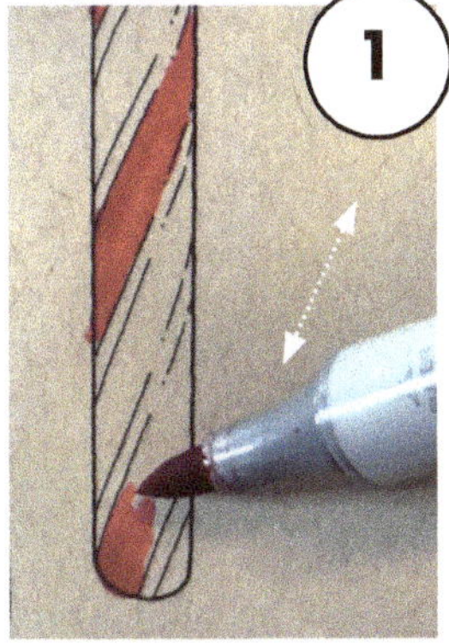

1

I begin by using a Copic R27 Cadmium Red brush marker, filling in every other wide area.

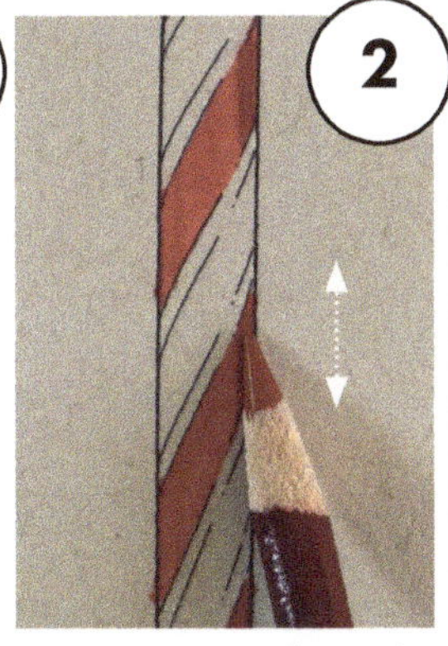

2

Next I use a single stroke of dark red down the right edge of the red areas using Scarlet Lake 925.

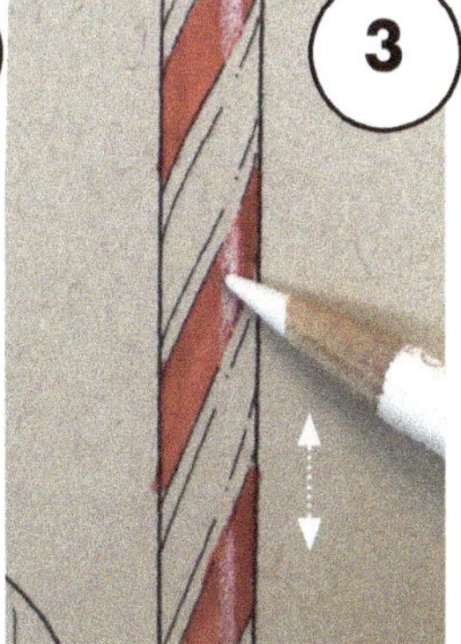

3

Just to the left of that stripe I create a bold white reflective highlight using 938 White.

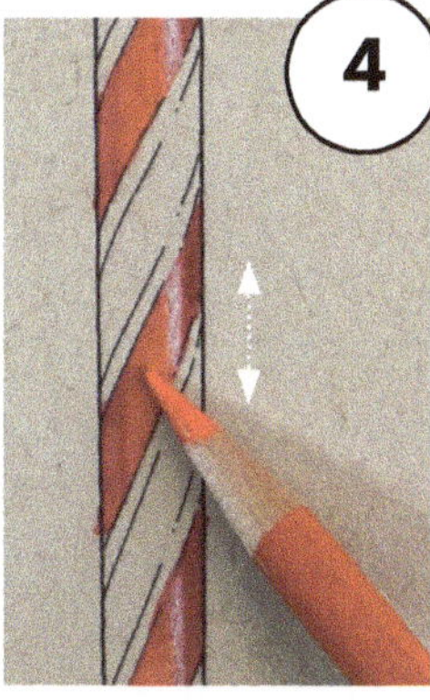

4

Now I fill the center of each "red stripe" with bright 922 Poppy Red.

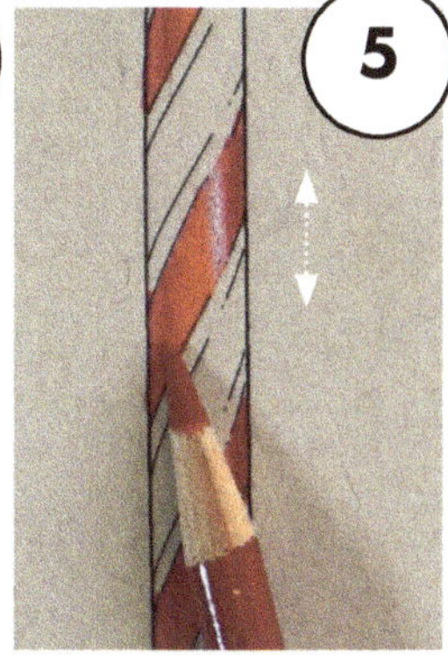

5

Then I use a thinner dark stroke down the left side of the 922 using 924 Crimson Red.

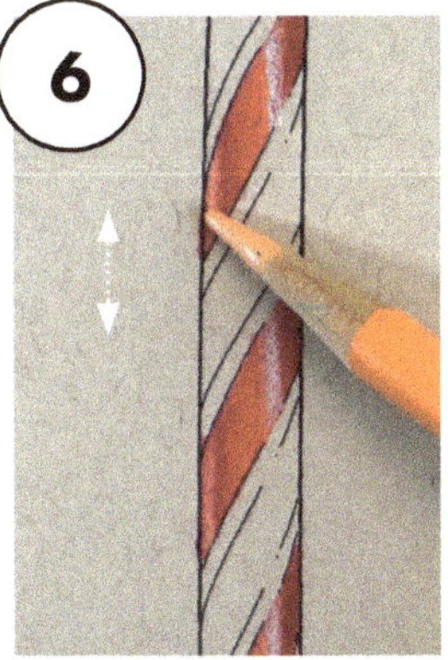

6

Next I use a 1008 Salmon Pink stroke on the left edge of each "red stripe" – *reflected light*.

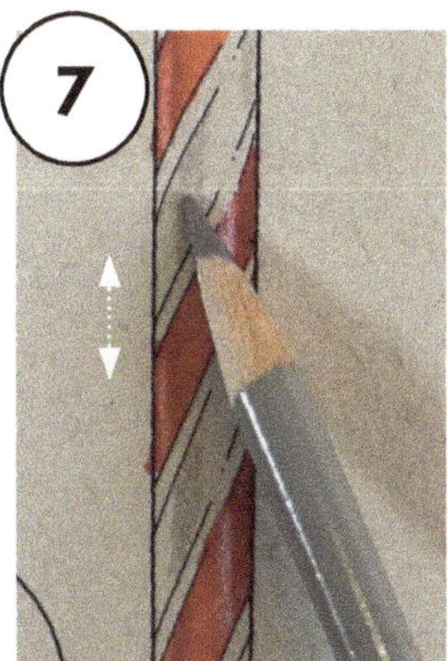

7

In the blank areas I vertically align strokes of 1072 Light French Grey, with the red strokes above.

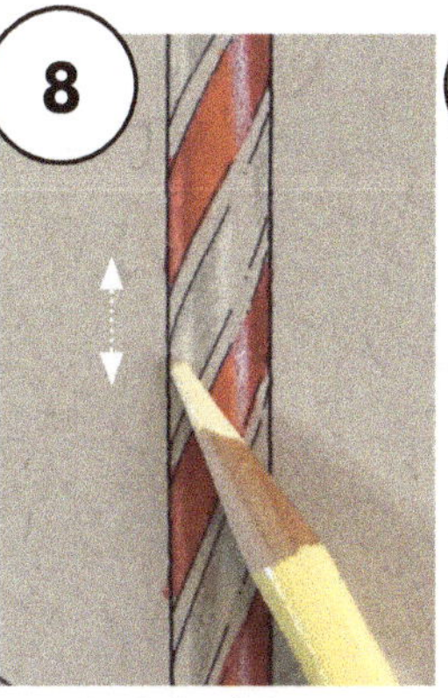

8

To the left of the 1072 I add a single stroke up the side, of reflected light with 914 Cream.

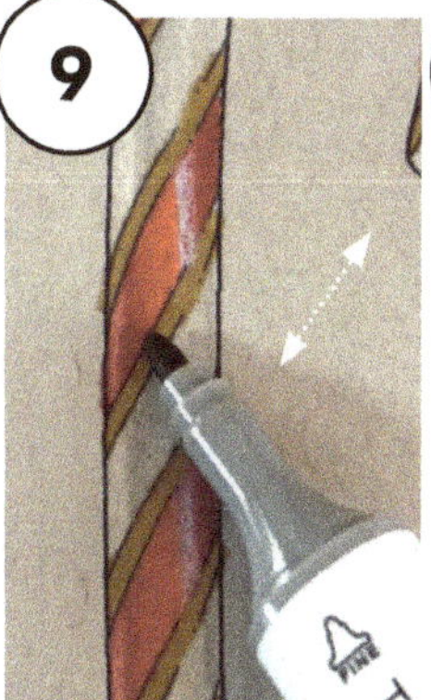

9

Now I fill in each narrow space with a marker. TouchNew 41 Olive Green.

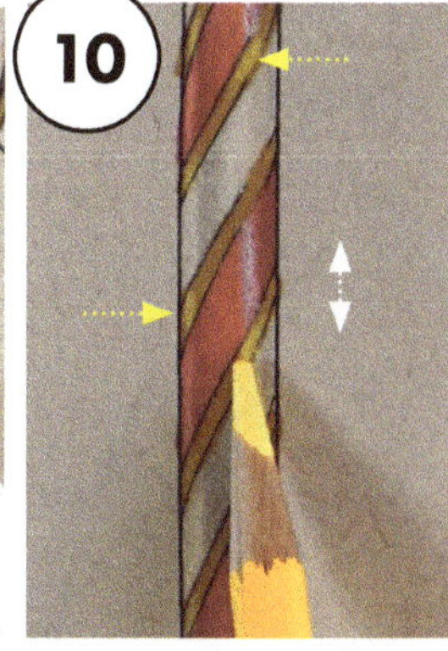

10

Tiny 1011 Deco Yellow highlights go on top of the marker aligning with the 938/914 strokes above.

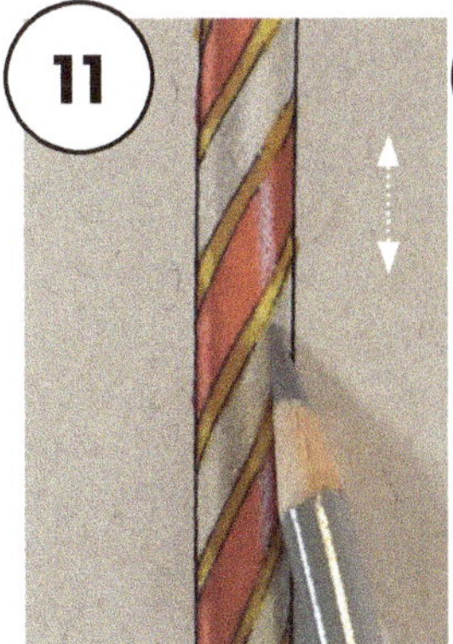

11

Again, I use 1072 for a little more contrast on the side of the "white stripes" of the candy.

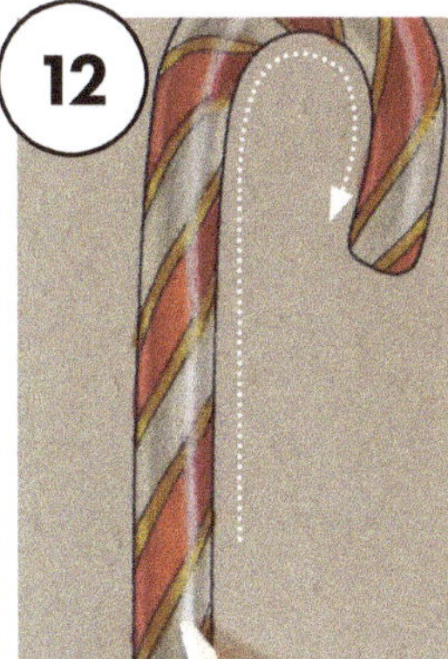

12

I am using a Luminance White to pump up the highlight. 1038 may be used alternatively.

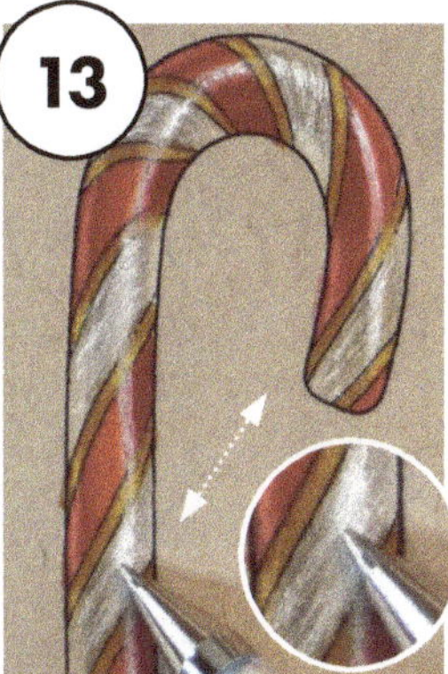

13

I add texture with a few skinny gel pen diagonal strokes in white areas.

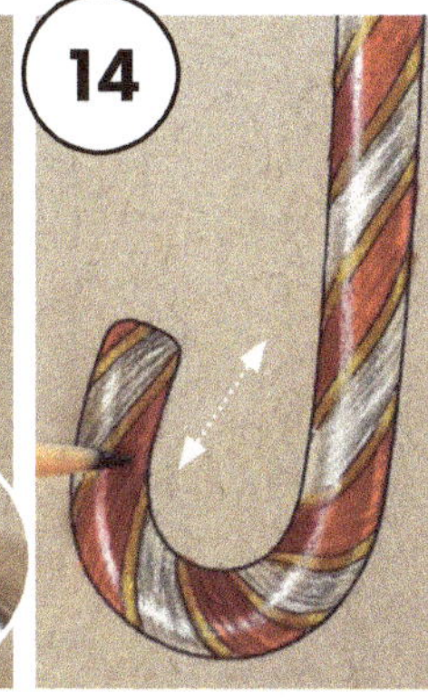

14

Optional: I add more texture using a Black Verithin in some areas.

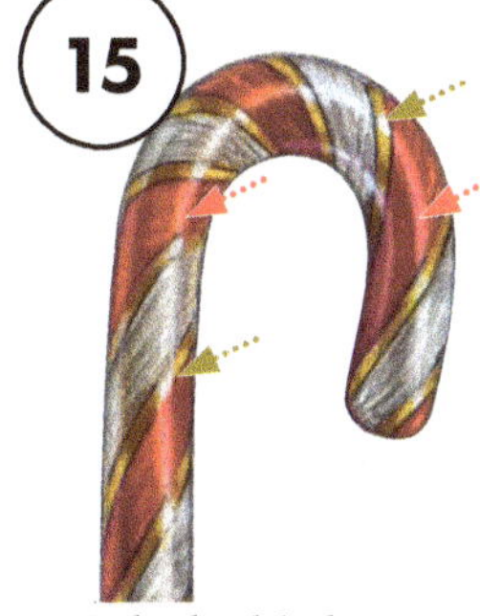

15

POP the highlights!! See arrows: add a hint of Neon Orange over the red area highlights and white gel on the gold ones!

Pearlized White and Blue Spiral Lollipop

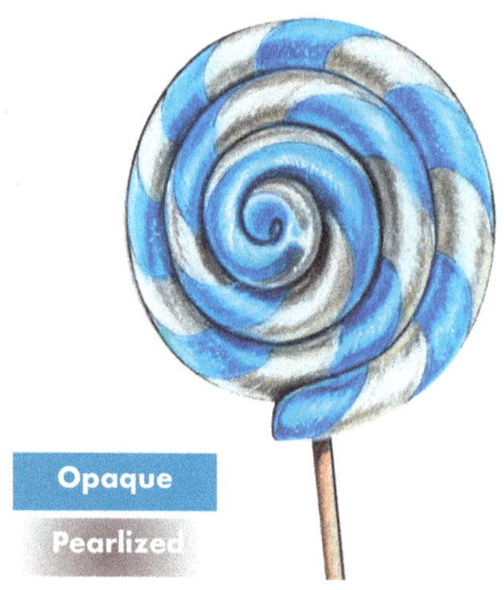

You will need:

- The Candy Shoppe line art page
- Primsacolor Premier pencils:103, 1072, 903, 940, 904, 1023, 140, 901, 914, 992, 946, 1008
- White gel pen (Uniball Signo)
- White Luminance pencil 001 or PC 938
- Optional: Verithin Black and Indigo Blue pencils or other hard brand

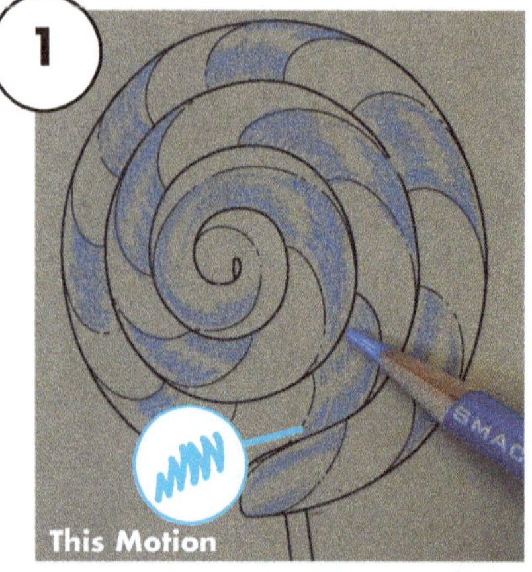

Spiral your page, just like your lollipop as you draw! Starting with 103 Cerulean Blue. Alternating sections, I create the *core shadow* in blue for every other area. I leave out the centers of most of them. I use a zig-zag scribbling motion.

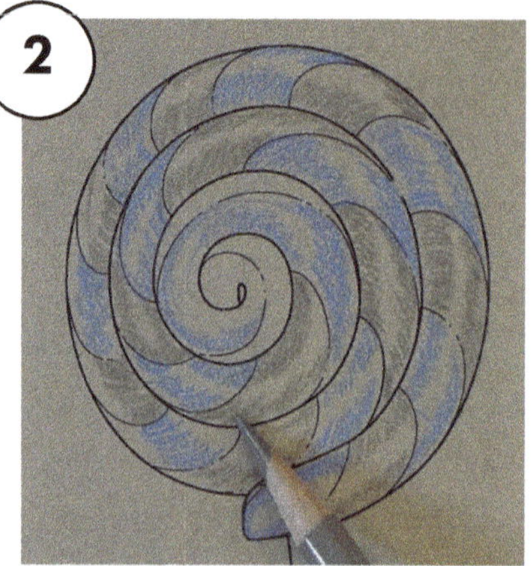

I do the same in the alternating sections using 1072 French Grey 50%, zig-zagging to match the curve of the spiral. I must use razor sharp pencils to create the pearlized effect in the end.

Tip: *Don't Forget to Rotate the Page!*

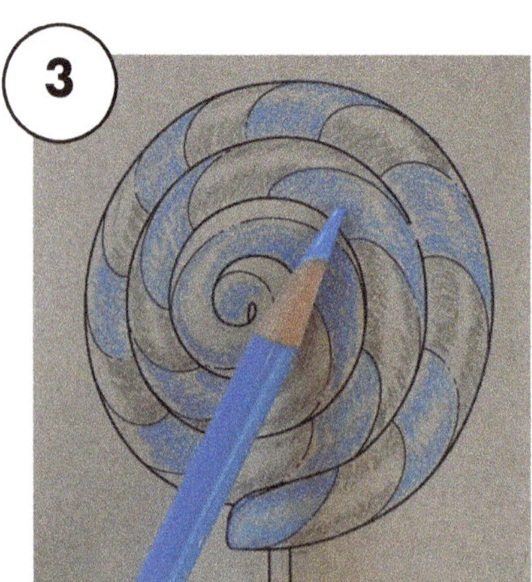

Now I add another layer of blue, but lighter and brighter – 903 True Blue over the darker blue, extending the color a little closer to the centers of the areas.

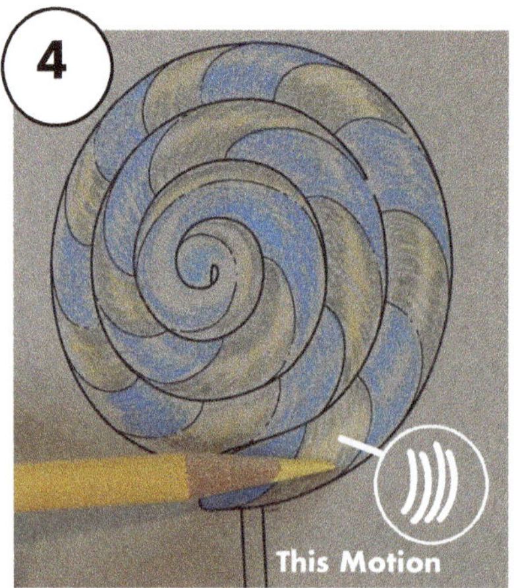

Next, I begin highlights with 940 Sand to each grey section, extending right over the centers but I use individual curved strokes that match the curve direction of each section!

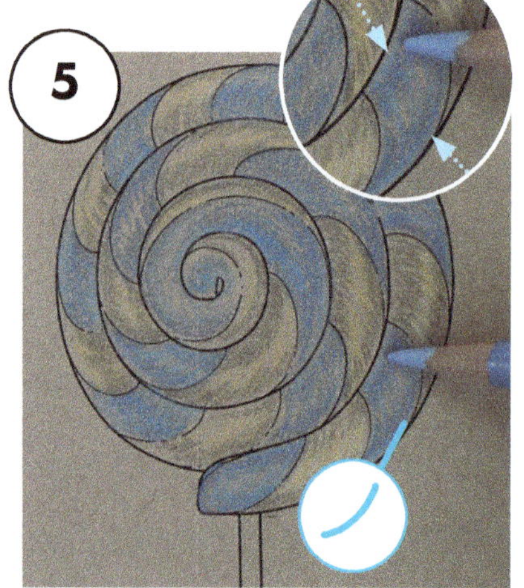

Then I use just a small single stroke of 904 Light Cerulean on the inner and outermost edge of each blue section to create *reflected light* next to the darker *core shadow*.

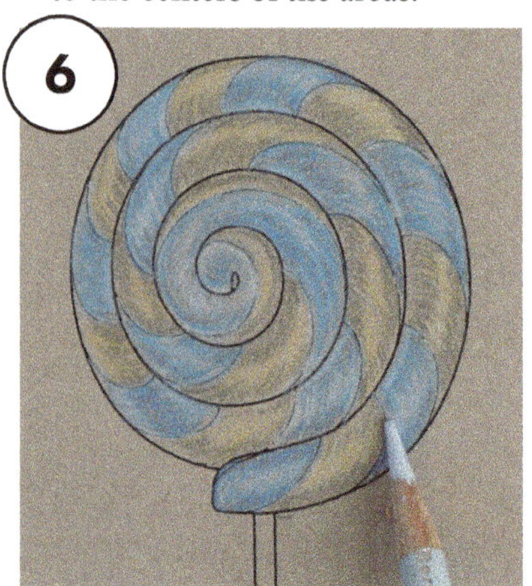

Now I begin the highlight of every blue section, just like in Step 4, in the same direction along the center of each section. I use 1023 Cloud Blue to do the trick.

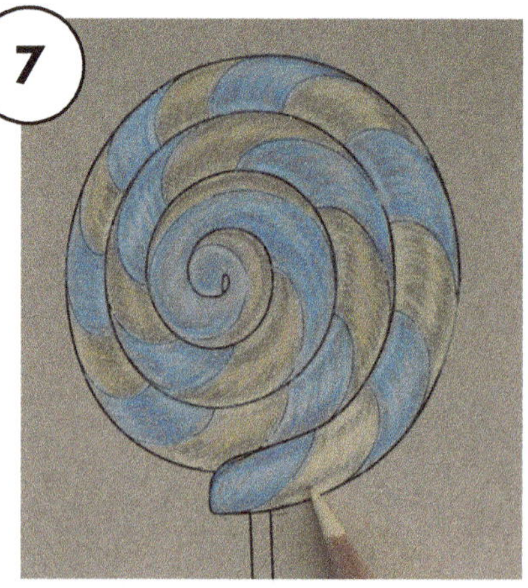

I add *reflected light* to each of the opposite sections to begin to take on the "pearlized white" look – a straight stroke of color on both inner and outer edges, just as I did in Step 5. This time I use my 140 Eggshell pencil.

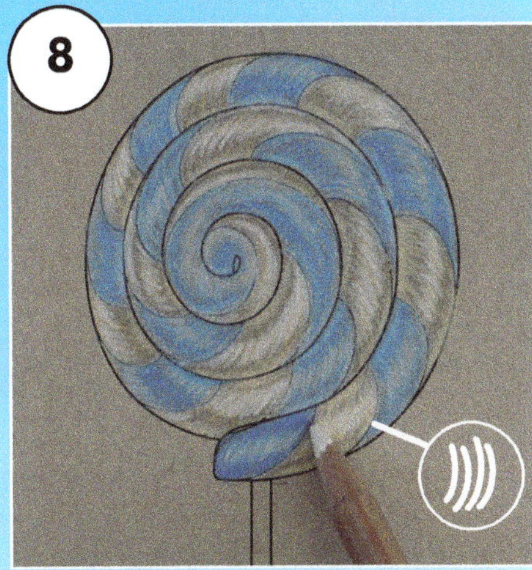

I use a White Luminance pencil (if you don't have one, a Prismacolor) to make the highlights pop. I use curved strokes on the centers of all the blue sections, sharpen my pencil and then all of the white sections to avoid contamination.

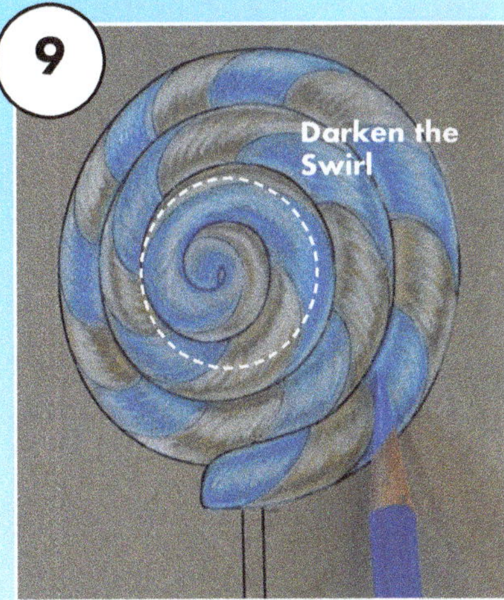

Then, going back through all of the colors I've used so far, I deepen a little or lighten a little as needed. I begin to "carve in" details such as the swirl in the middle, darkening around it.

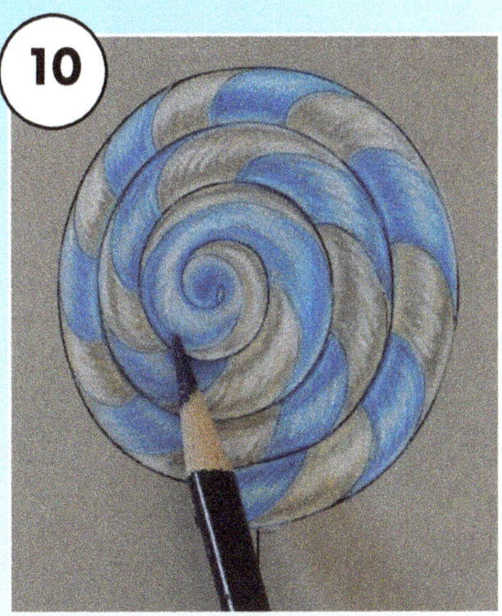

For some added punch I use one of my "magic colors" (instead of plain Black), 901 Indigo Blue. I add depth and richness to the shadow areas (cores and creases) by increasing the *contrast*.

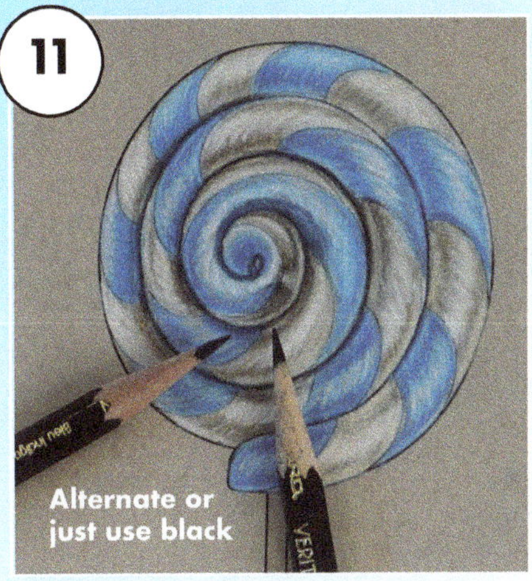

I alternate with optional Verithin Indigo Blue and Black pencils here to darken the creases of the lollipop spiral. You can use any hard pencil. The Indigo looks better in the blue creases!

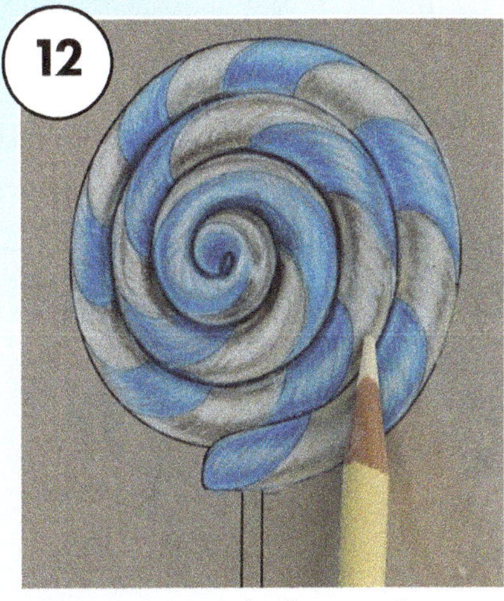

One more round of warmth on the edges of each "pearlized white" section. This time 914 Cream.

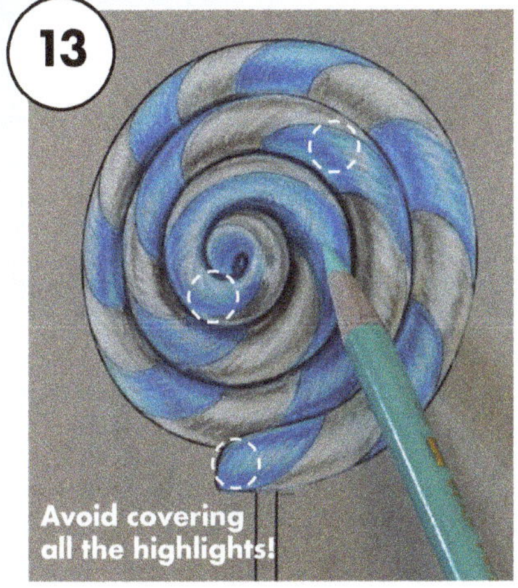

The blue could use a little warmth too, so I add a zig-zag layer on a few of the "protruding" blue sections, but leave some of the white highlights! 992 Light Aqua.

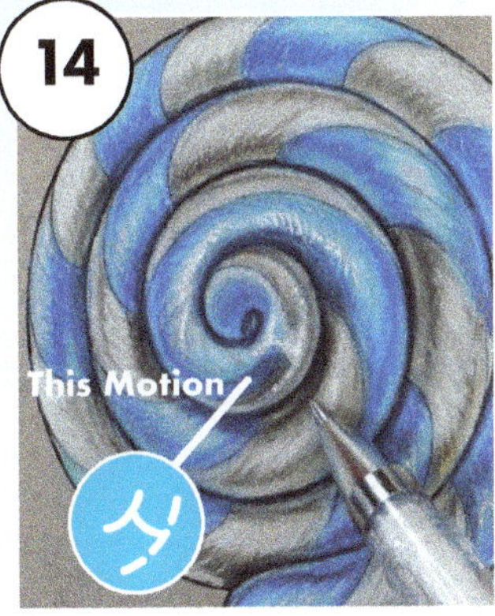

Now I add some sparkle! A little white gel pen dotted around the center swirl. I've added some subtle zig-zags on the white areas too.

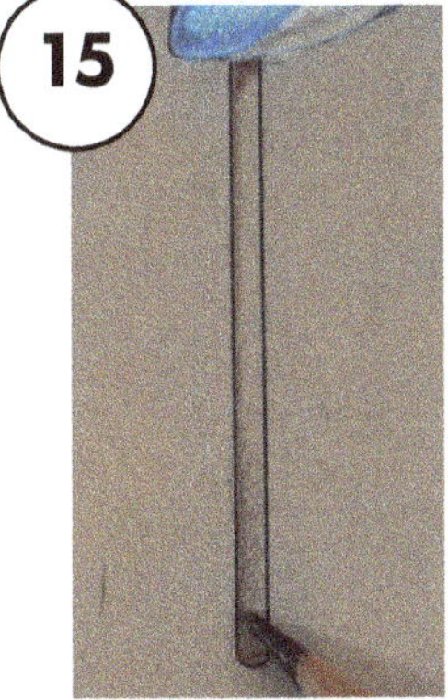

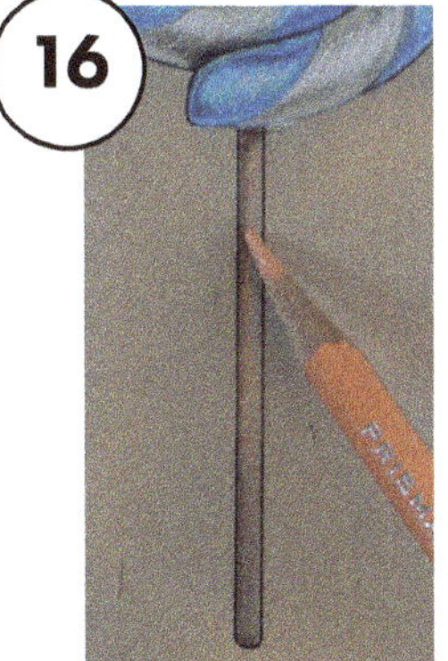

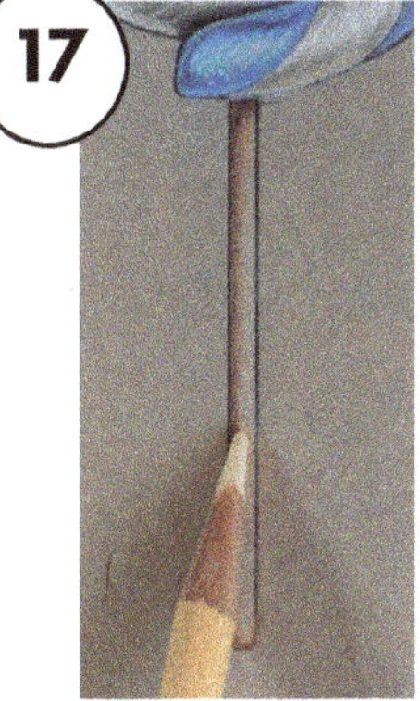

For the Wooden Stick: First I add a light application of 946 Dark Brown, directly under the lollipop and down the left side as a shadow, then I gradate darker again towards the bottom. I blend all of this except the very bottom with 1008 Salmon Pink, and finally I create an area of light using 914 Cream up and down the right side.

Purple Heart Lollipop

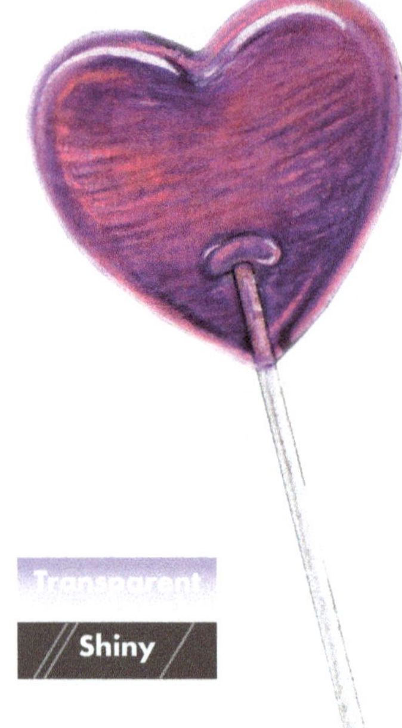

You will need: - The Candy Shoppe "Faux Toned Paper" line art page
- Prismacolor Premier: 1007, 934, 1008, 132, 1038, 994, 932, (938)
- Caran D'ache Luminance 001 and colorless blender
- White gel pen and neon pink fine gel pen (Lolliz seen here)
- White Posca marker

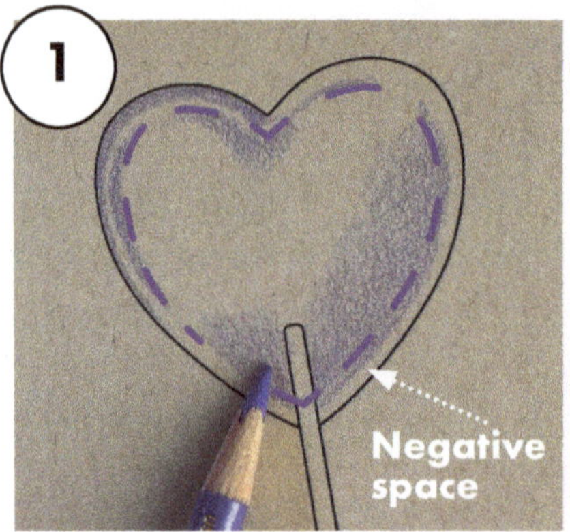

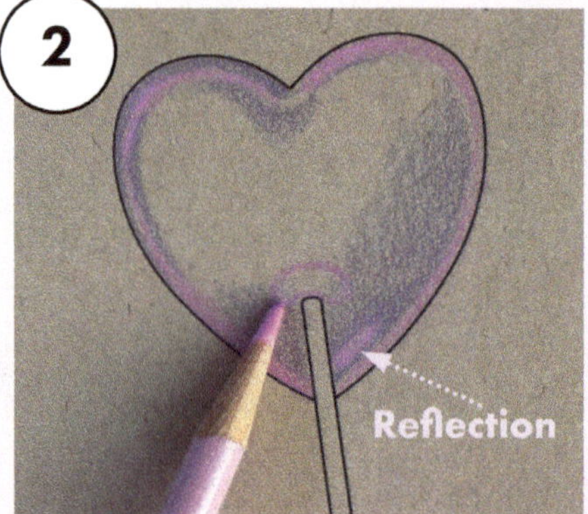

1. I begin with 1007 Imperial Violet – creating the illusion of dimension. It may help to draw a light "outline" just inside the heart. Very lightly with tiny circles I carve in the upper left and lower right edges and *negative space.*

2. Next I use a stroke of 934 Lavender all around the perimeter (and outline from the last step) of the heart, plus a secondary reflection, and I begin to draw in a bean-shaped air bubble at the top of the stick! (You can skip the bubble if you'd like.)

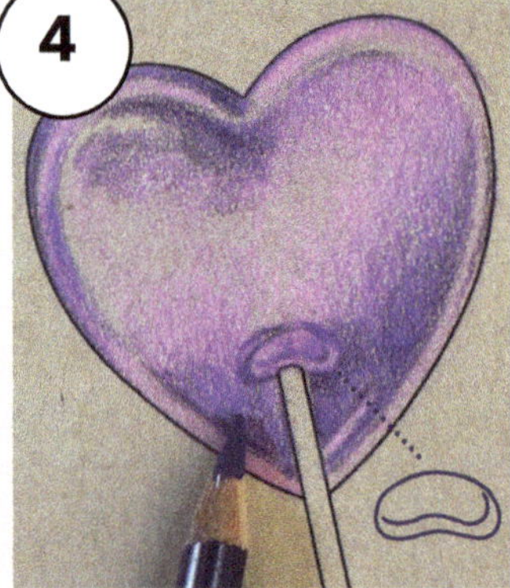

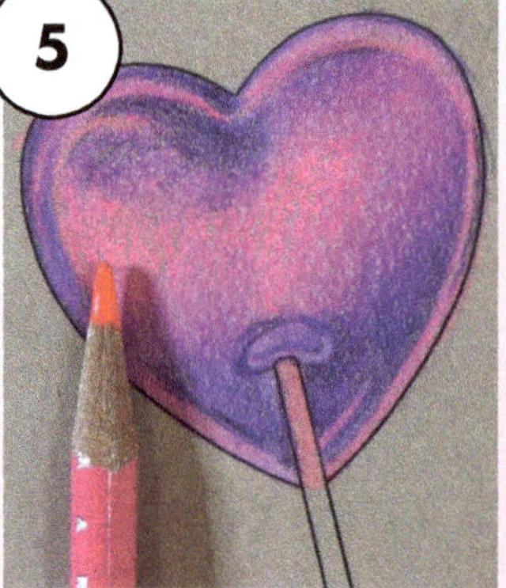

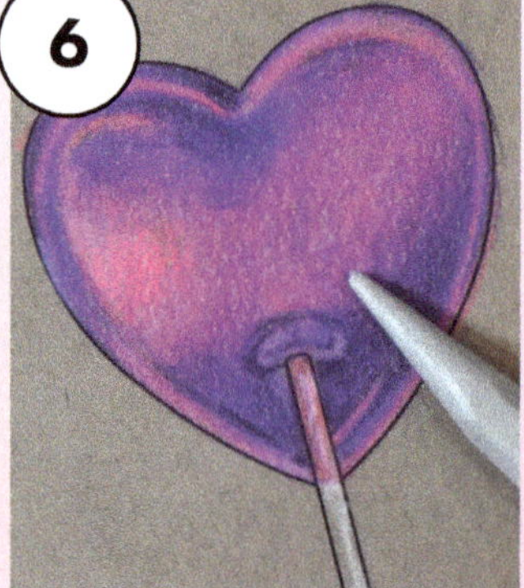

3. I use 934 to fill in some patches in the center (the bubble too) and top right (inside the "outline"). I blend it towards the bottom with 1008 Parma Violet.

4. Now I use 132 Dioxazine Purple to emphasize the top and lower right parts of the outline and the bubble. I darken the bottom of the heart lightly.

5. I use 1038 Neon Pink to fill in all of the blank areas and blend on top of the other colors, and top of the stick. See how saturated the colors are?

6. Now I use a wax-based colorless blender (Caran D'ache or PC 1077) to carefully smooth each area, using small circles.

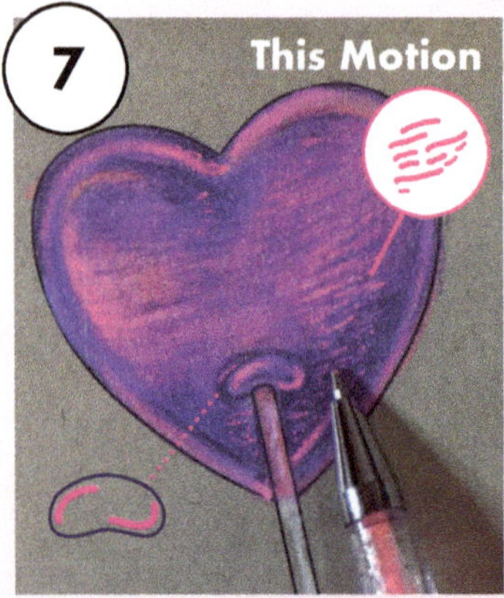

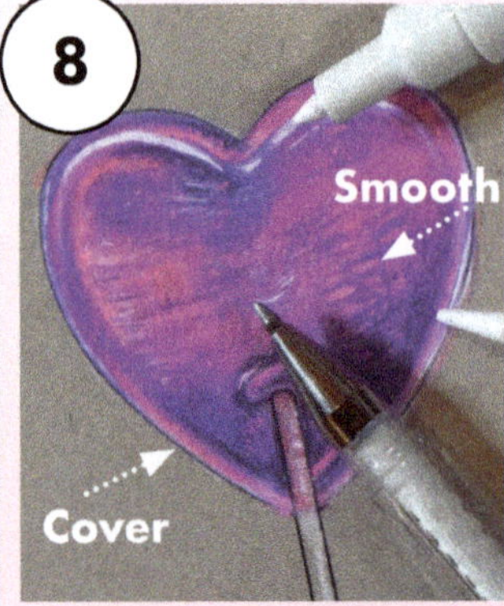

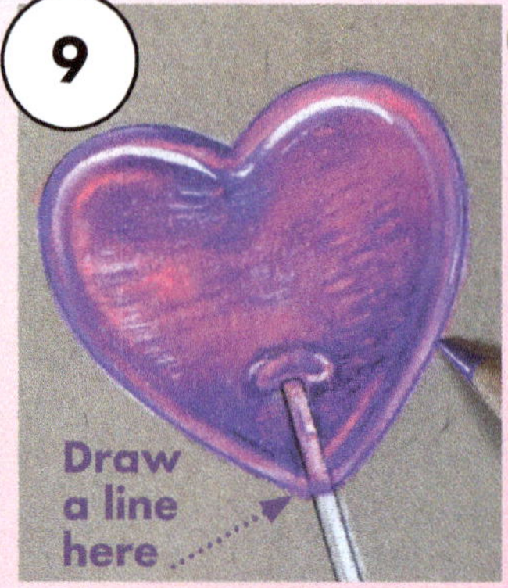

7. For texture, I add a few horizontal flicks of Neon Pink gel pen to the heart's right side, plus the reflection and bubble.

8. Lumi White pencil fills the right side of stick and smoothes out some of the flicks – and covers the line art. I add white gel pen and Posca highlights!

9. (If you added too much gel pen, scrape some off with 994 in the next step). I add a few dark flicks and a stroke over the line art using 932 Violet.

10. Finally, I use a sharp 994 Process Red in horizontal motions to add color and get in between some of the flicks and lessen the contrast. (You may use gel pen to cover the outline if you wish.)

Tiny Holiday Candy

You will need: - The Candy Shoppe "Faux Toned Paper" line art page
- Prismacolor Premier: 140, 1021, 122, 918, 922, 1034, 916, 944, 907, 910, 920, 929, 937
- Caran D'ache Luminance 001 (or Prismacolor 938)
- White gel pen

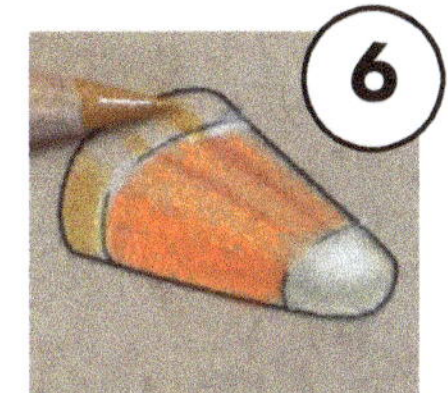 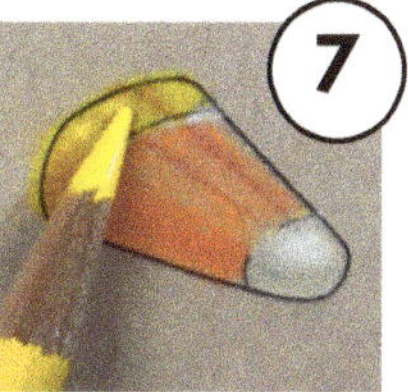 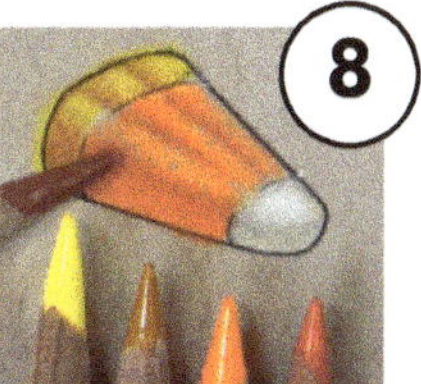 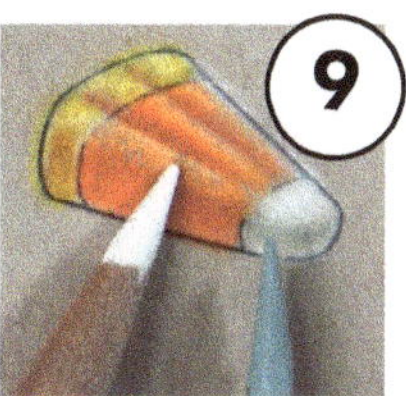

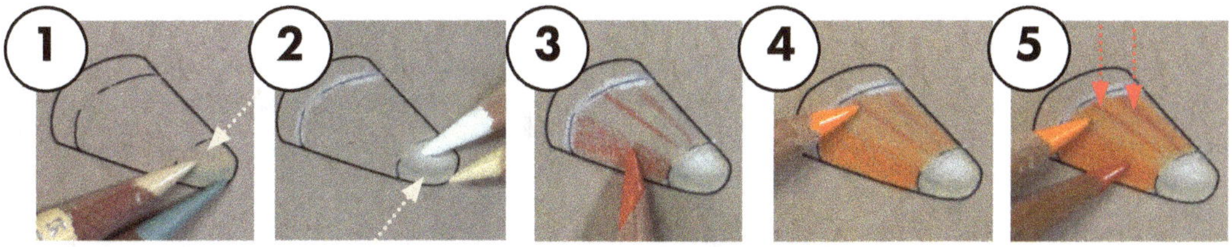

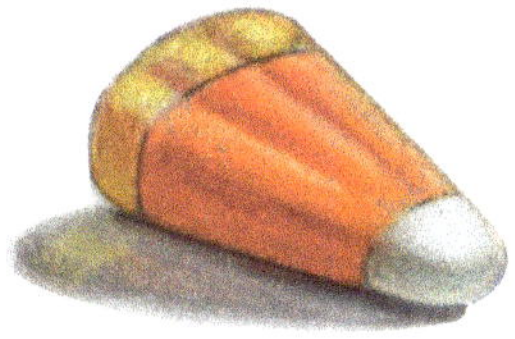

Candy Corn

Opaque
Matte

1. I create the "white" tip with Eggshell 140 on the top half and a fuzzy 1021 Jade Green stroke below.
2. Next I add a layer of Luminance White on top of the 140 and a stroke of 140 below the 1021.
3. Lightly, I fill the shadow side of the candy corn, and indentations (tapered lines) on top with a sharp 122 Permanent Red pencil.
4. Then I add a thin layer of 918 Orange to the top plane around the indentations, and directly over the shadow side.
5. I go back and re-define the indentations again and smooth the side with both 918 and 922.

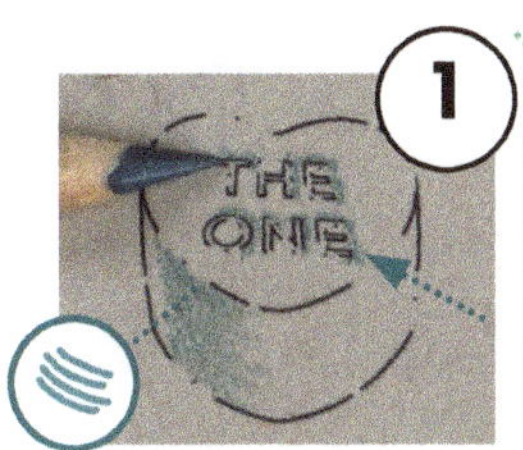 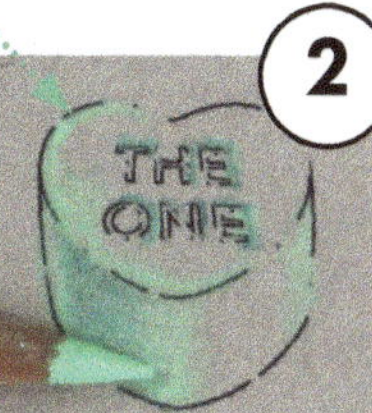  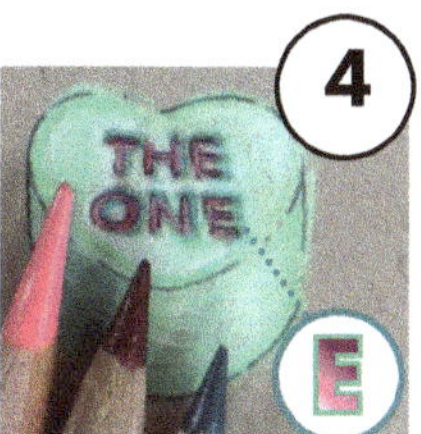

6. I then fill the last empty section. I start with 1034 Goldenrod on the side facing us, plus I extend the indentations from the orange to the "yellow" end of the candy corn.
7. I add 916 Canary Yellow to fill in the top plane of the yellow end and blend the 1034.
8. I go back and add another layer of each color, then add a core shadow with 944 Terra Cotta across the orange and yellow side. I also carefully deepen the indentations.
9. I use 001 to add a subtle highlight to the top edge of each ridge (next to indentations) and 1021 to define the tip again and line it up with the rest of the 944 core shadow. I've also used a white gel pen to whiten the very tip (not seen).

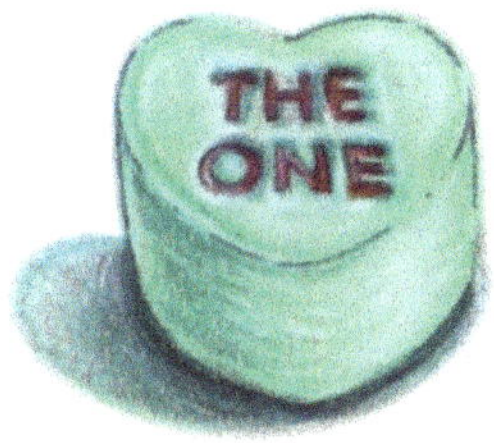

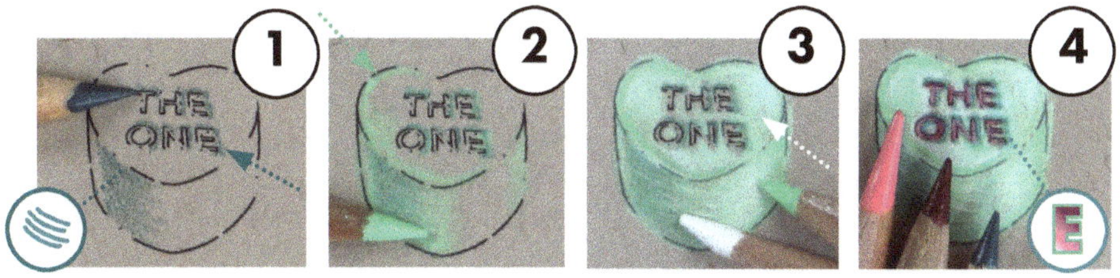

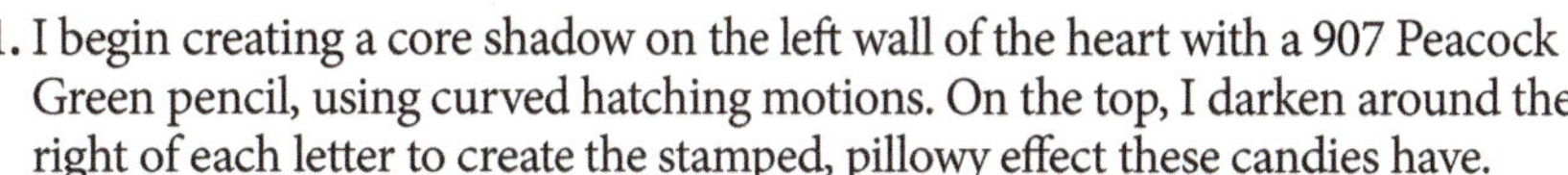

Candy Heart

Opaque
Matte

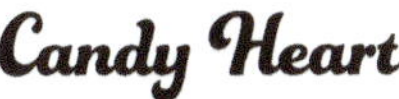

1. I begin creating a core shadow on the left wall of the heart with a 907 Peacock Green pencil, using curved hatching motions. On the top, I darken around the right of each letter to create the stamped, pillowy effect these candies have.
2. I add 910 True Green to the whole left side of the wall, covering over the 907, and the very edge of the right side, only leaving a small amount of paper showing in between. I also add a layer on the top plane: over the 907, on the left edge of the heart and around the letters.
3. Now I fill in the rest of the heart with 920 Light Green. I use my 001 Luminance White pencil to create a subtle highlight in the middle of the right side of the wall and the right side of the top plane, and under the word "ONE". I use horizontal flicking motions on the wall with both the 920 and 001 to create texture.
4. I create the letters by filling them carefully with a sharp 929 Pink pencil. Concentrating mostly on the top and right side of each letter, I add some random patches all over with a sharp 937 Tuscan Red, to create shadow from the pillowy green surrounding. 907 is used as needed to sharpen the shadows around the letters.

** See Chapter 6 to learn tips on creating cast shadows*

Fluorescent Gummy Bear

Although this tutorial may seem complicated, it's easy if great care is taken! To achieve these effects you'll need to follow carefully, using a few specific materials. There aren't many options for quality alcohol-based markers in fluorescent colors, especially reds. If you can find them in your part of the world, buy them! To create this little gem of a bear, one must use fluorescent or very bright colors to get a rich glow. In the meantime, these fairly inexpensive Stabilo water-based ones do the trick. I have used the elusive red fluorescent marker here, although this one is a lighter pinkish red. For a gummy that is more of a true red, look for a darker fluorescent red marker! Gummy bears are unique because they have mainly a satin finish, sometimes with a few shiny reflections.

Translucent
Satin

You will need:
- The Candy Shoppe "Faux Toned Paper" line art page
- Stabilo fluorescent marker in Red
- White CD Luminance 001 or Prismacolor pencil
- Prismacolor Premier pencils (or Other Wax-Based Brand) in 923, 1036, 1038, (938), 931
- White Posca paint marker or Uniball Signo gel pen
- Optional: colorless blender pencil (Caran D'ache or Prismacolor 1077)

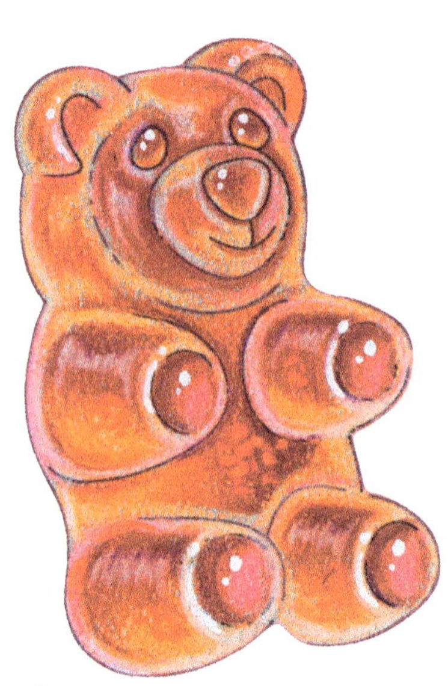

I begin by using 923 Scarlet Lake in tiny circular motions to fill areas of the face, the middle of the chest and belly, the upper right side of each leg, and crescents on the feet!

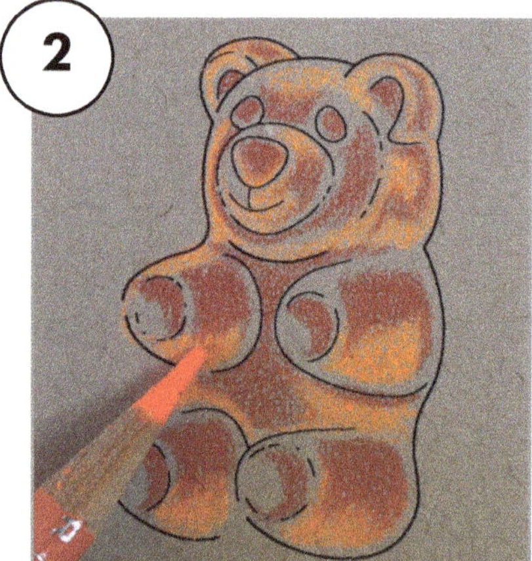

On the edges of each part I use 1036 Neon Orange to create a glow all around. I leave the edges of the legs and a few spots on feet and face empty for the next step.

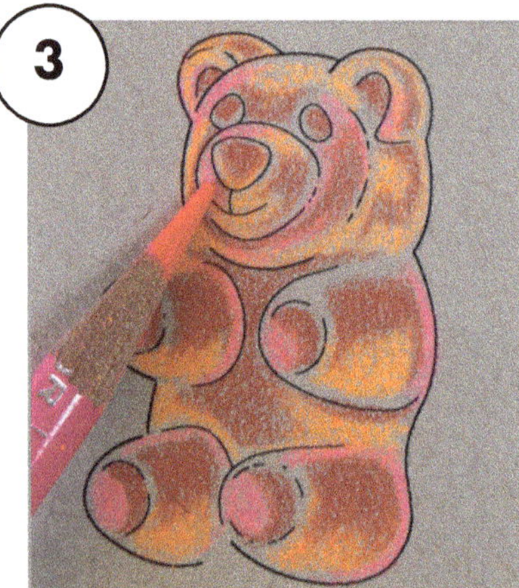

I fill the right edges of the conical shaped legs and the feet (inside the C-shape red areas) and small areas on the bear's face with 1038 Neon Pink to create *variety*.

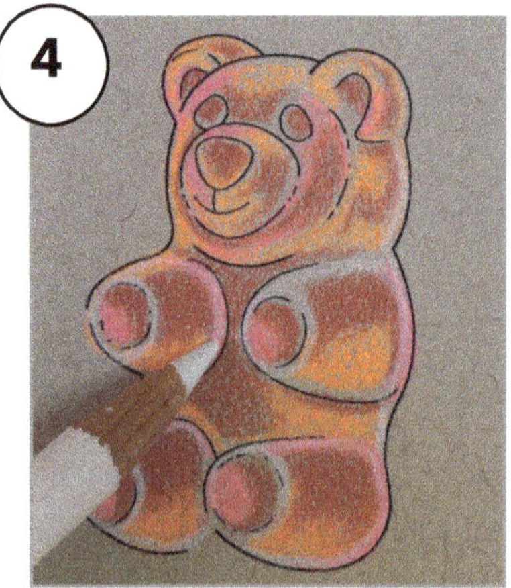

Now I use the 938 White or Lumi 001 around the edges on the legs to lighten them more than the insides and blend the Neon Pink.

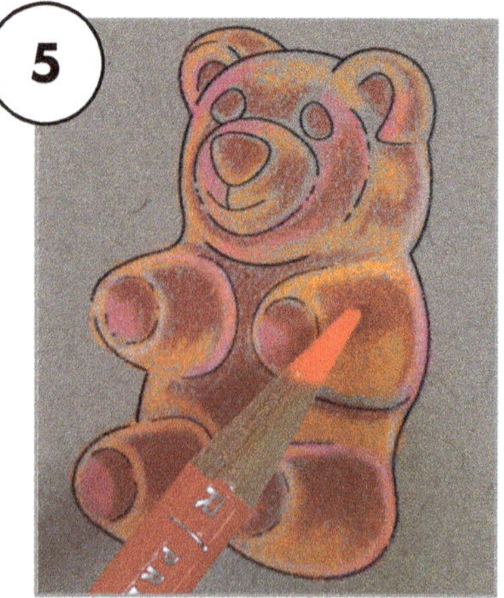

Next, I use the 1036 again to cover the top and bottom edges of the legs and I use it over all of the 923 to brighten, blend and smooth it.

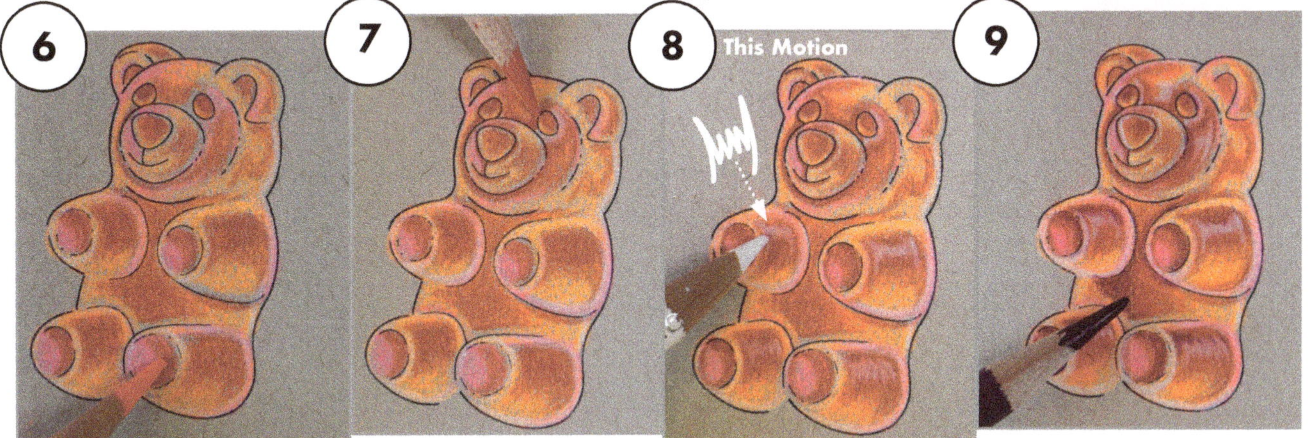

6. I add more of the 1038 to the red on the feet to smooth those too – this process of neon color over dark, dull color does two things at once! It gets rid of the scratchy texture and saturates the color below. Use your colorless blender at this point, lightly, to smooth out any other imperfections, if needed. 7. Next, I go around all of the facial features with the 923 again, sharpening it first. This makes the eyes, nose, mouth and muzzle look more dimensional. 8. I am adding a white "reflection" right along the middle of the darkest part of each leg, in sort of a scribbly "H" shape, using short, curved up and down motions – and on the darkest parts of the face and forehead too. You can see this more clearly in the next photo. 9. My last pencil is 931 Dark Purple. I apply it very sparingly, only to the tops of the white reflections and to one side of the belly to create *contrast*.

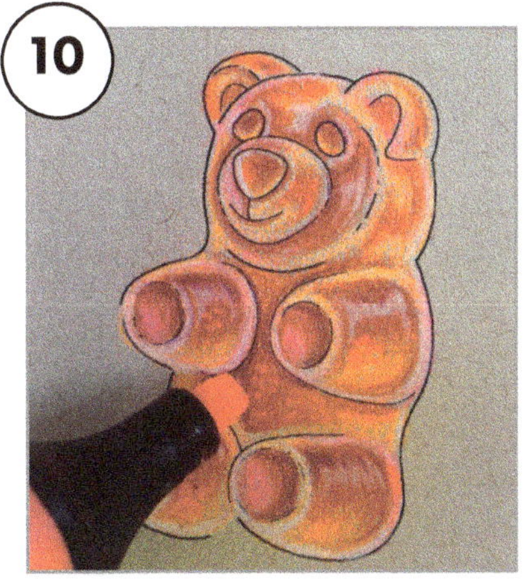

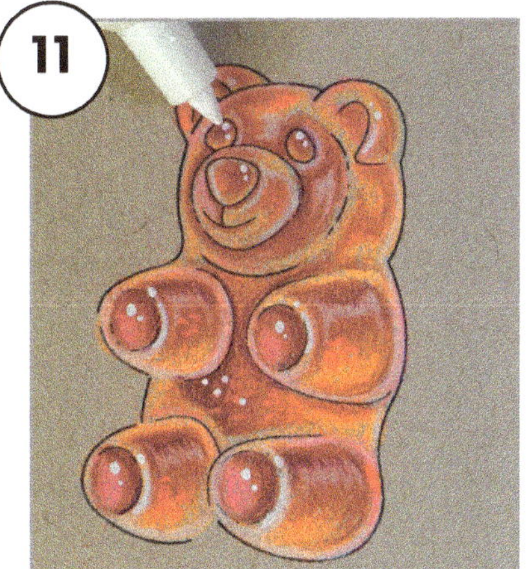

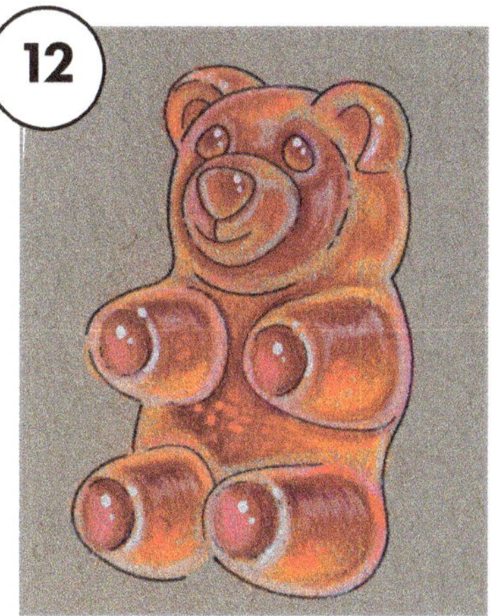

Make it Pop! The magic begins with the Stabilo Flourescent markers! Here I'm adding "glow" to the legs and tummies using just the tip of the marker to make little dots. I'm careful not to overdo this. I will also add a few brighter ones on top in the next step.

Before calling my gummy bear complete, I add Posca white "high shine" highlight dots to the nose and each of the eyes and feet – the only glossy areas. I also add some to the belly but I don't want these to be white in the end, but rather to appear as inner glowing air bubbles. The brightness needs to be toned down.

To tone down the dots, I wait for the Posca to dry (to avoid damaging my fluorescent marker) and then dot the marker on top. Use another coat after the first dries if the dots are still too bright.

Try 'em in different flavors!

Stabilo Fl.Grn	
Stabilo Fl.Ylw	
PC 908	
PC 1004	
PC 910	
PC 913	
PC 901	

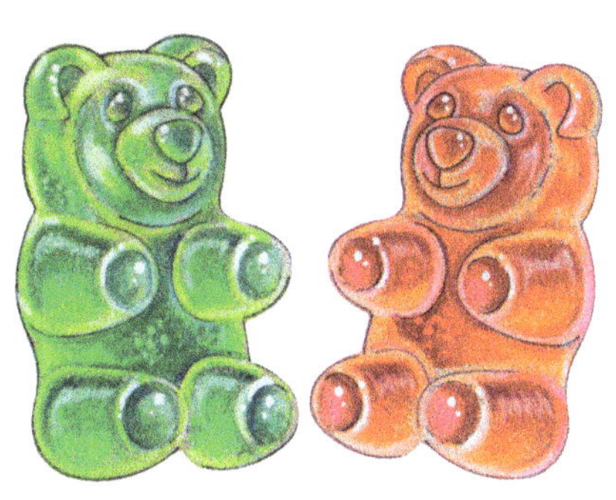

Tip: Swap your fluorescent marker color to match any set of dark tone primary or secondary colored pencils, as long as you have fluorescent pencils to match! It may take one extra marker or pencil to get the exact varitions you want so test them out on the practice page! *For a limited time* use your secret code, found towards the end of this book on one of the page backs, to access free coordinating bonus printable PDF files at ModernColoring.com/freebies

Purple it is!! Fabrics have all different chracteristics. It's important to undertsand the features of each. The following three shoes can be recreated by using the same handful of mixed media coloring supplies for very different effects! It's all about color placement and amount. You may choose to alter the combinations used to create your own version. Keep in mind that every type of marker has its issues. I will say that when I set out to design "purple" boots of different leathers, I was shocked that I had a such a difficult time finding purple markers in the same temperature family from the same manufacturers, so I have chosen several brands here based on the best color match! Sometimes I do mix brands, and it's easy to find less expensive ones to go with the more expensive. The bottom line is "when in doubt, test them in a store" before buying open stock, if you are trying to create your own specific color grouping. Of course you can trust my suggestions in these tutorials because I've done all of the legwork!

You will need:

- The Shoe Department line art page
- Prismacolor Premier pencils: 934, 993, 996, 938, 914, 940, 1076, 1054, 1009, 932, 935
- Winsor & Newton BrushMarkers: V626, V735 + Copic Sketch V04
- White Uniball Signo gel pen and (optional Neon Orange Lolliz)
- White Caran D'Ache Luminance 001
- Black alcohol marker (Sharpie used here)

Patent Leather Bootie

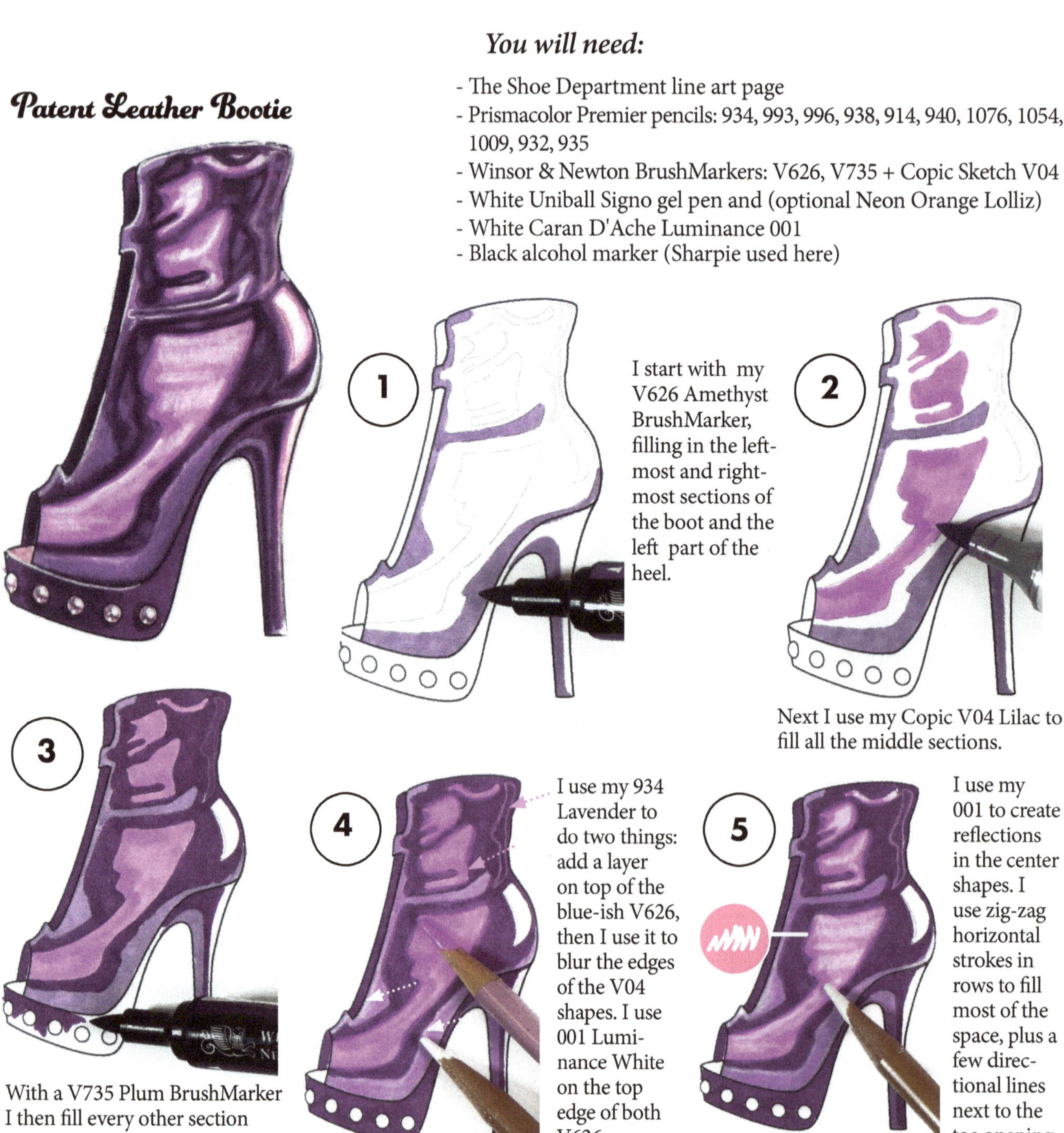

1 I start with my V626 Amethyst BrushMarker, filling in the left-most and right-most sections of the boot and the left part of the heel.

2 Next I use my Copic V04 Lilac to fill all the middle sections.

3 With a V735 Plum BrushMarker I then fill every other section except the toe, heel reflection, back of heel and studs.

4 I use my 934 Lavender to do two things: add a layer on top of the blue-ish V626, then I use it to blur the edges of the V04 shapes. I use 001 Luminance White on the top edge of both V626 areas.

5 I use my 001 to create reflections in the center shapes. I use zig-zag horizontal strokes in rows to fill most of the space, plus a few directional lines next to the toe opening.

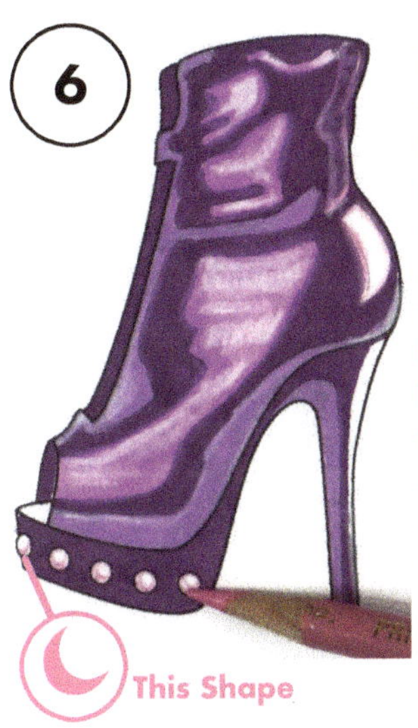

6 I use a sharp 993 Hot Pink to blur the edges of the reflections towards the back of the bootie, fill the insole, and create a crescent shape for the bottom left of each stud.

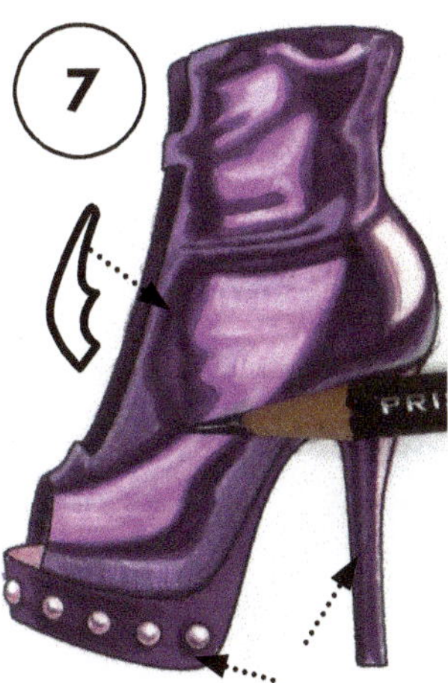

7 Drama is added to the glossy look using 996 Black Grape to outline some of the dark areas of Plum, leaving the middles alone. I add a stroke up the heel, smaller crescent shape core shadows to each stud and cast shadows to the left.

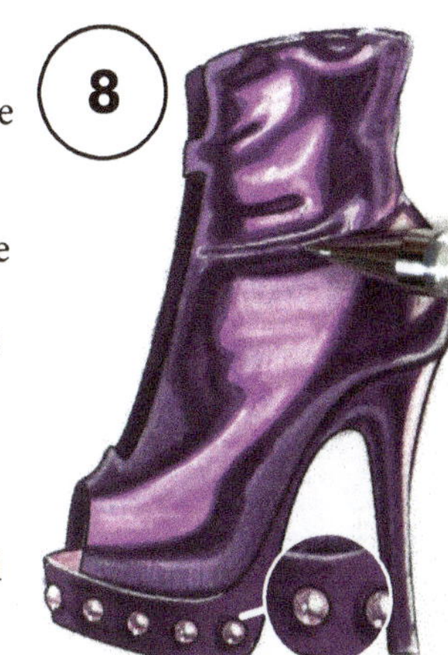

8 Finally, I use a white gel pen to create skinny highlights all around the shoe: a few on the upper center shapes, a fine line where the platform meets the leather, and on each stud. Add a few details with 934 and vôila!

Leather Cowboy Boot

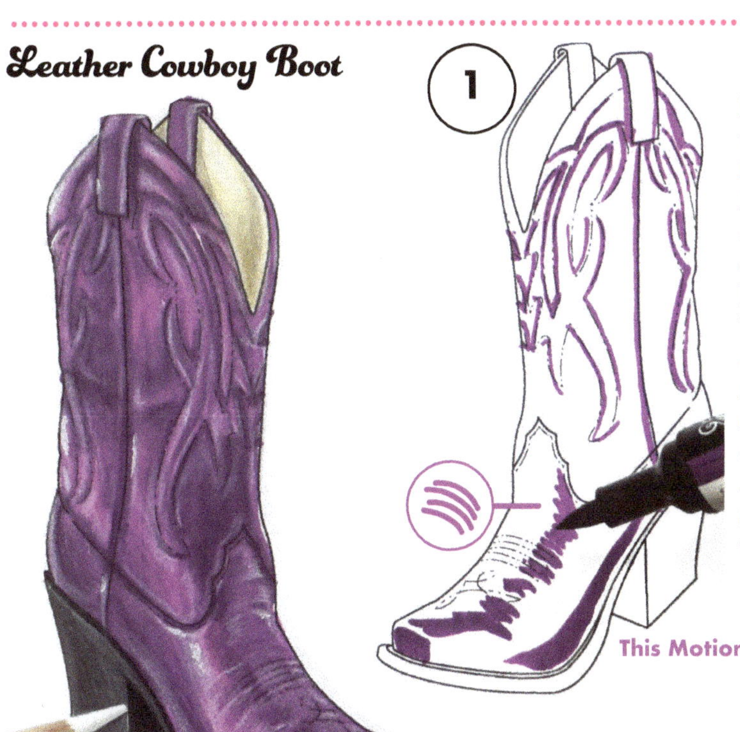

1 First, I begin with a V735 Plum Brush-Marker. I lightly accent the dotted stitching lines and seams. Then I add two shadows, one made of hatch marks and the other a long stroke. I add a rectangle to the toe area.

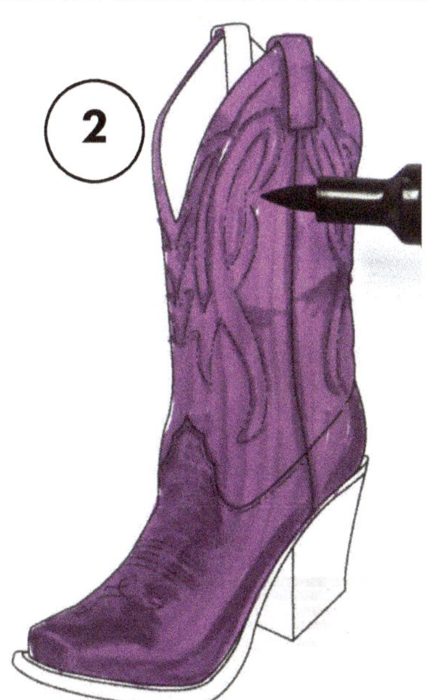

2 Next I use the marker to draw swift vertical strokes with no gaps over the whole surface of the boot.

3 Now I create dark gradations and details around the stitched decorations to make them pop out more, using 996 Black Grape. I avoid darkening the raised areas. Instead I add a single stroke inside each stitched design as a core shadow.

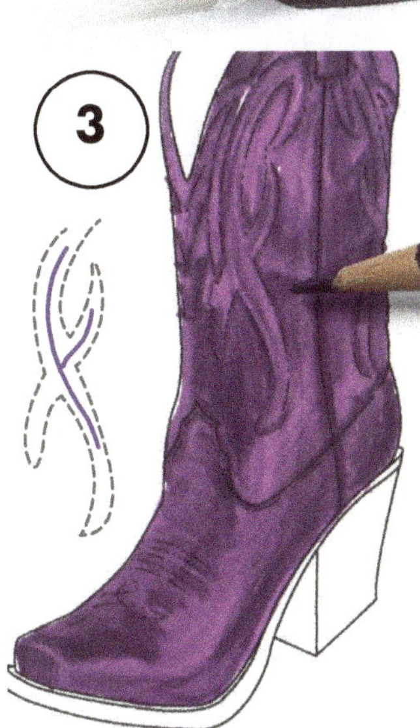

4 Lightly I add 938 White highlights around the main curve of the lower boot, in between the stitching on the toe, and on the raised detailed designs towards the top.

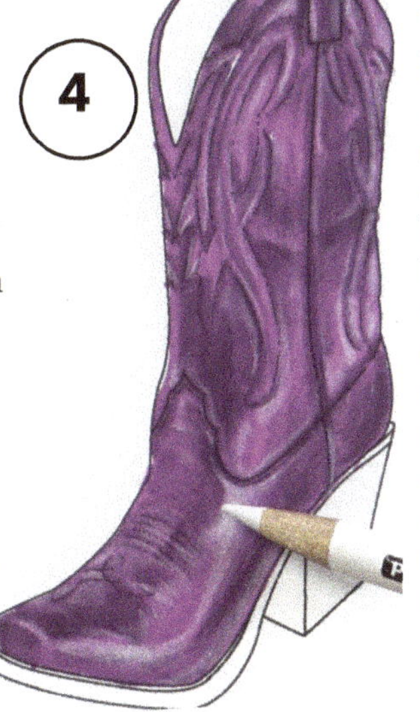

5 Then I introduce some 993 Hot Pink on top of most of the white highlights to create warmth and a pop of color.

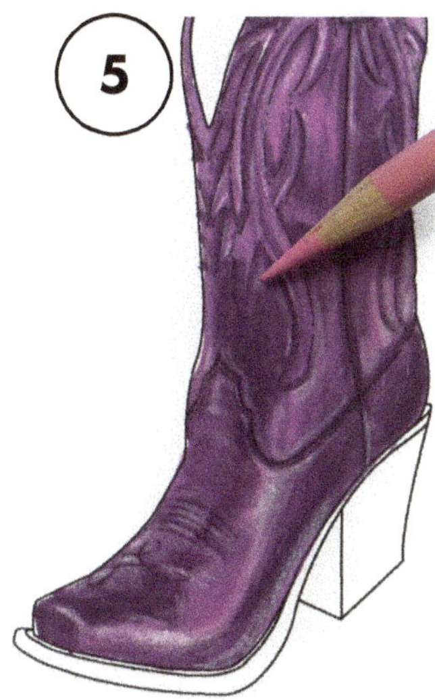

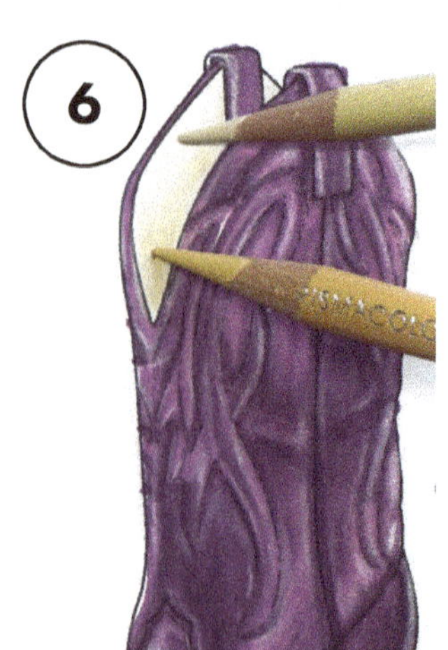

6 I use a light coat of 914 Cream to the inside lining of the boot and then a layer of 940 Sand to the bottom half, gradating downwards to the end.

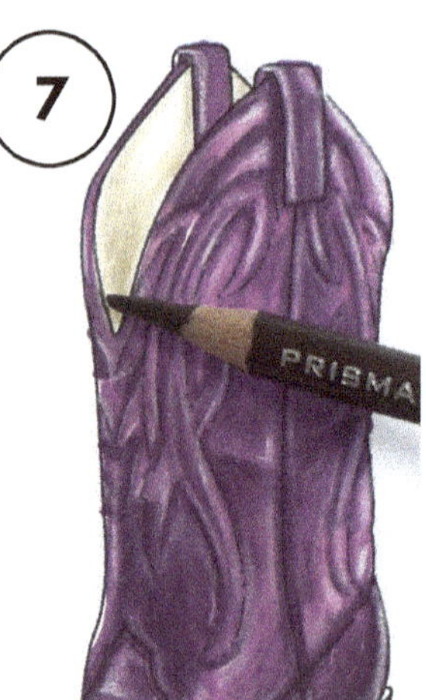

7 With a very light hand I add some 1076 90% French Grey to the lower part of the inside lining of the boot.

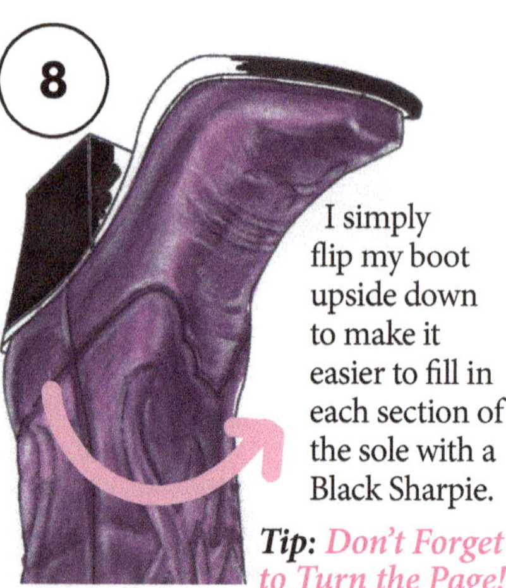

8 I simply flip my boot upside down to make it easier to fill in each section of the sole with a Black Sharpie.

Tip: *Don't Forget to Turn the Page!*

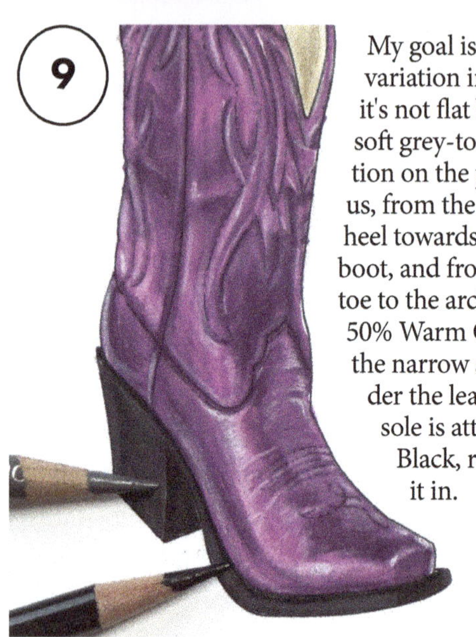

9 My goal is to create some variation in the sole, so it's not flat black. I create a soft grey-to-black gradation on the part that faces us, from the corner of the heel towards the back of the boot, and from under the toe to the arch using 1054 50% Warm Grey. I get into the narrow strip right under the leather where the sole is attached with 935 Black, really grinding it in.

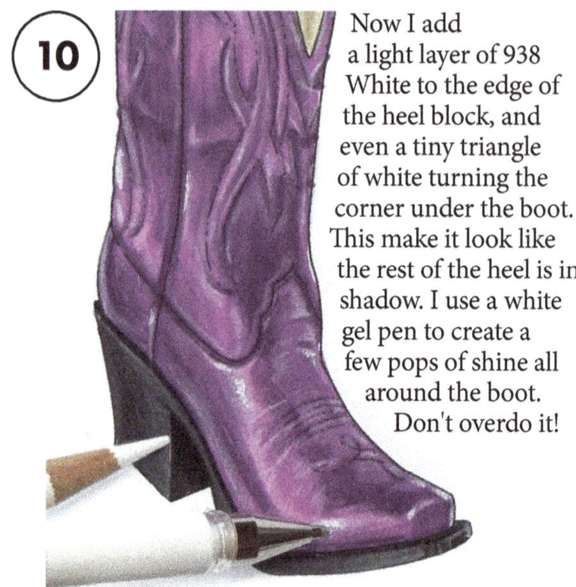

10 Now I add a light layer of 938 White to the edge of the heel block, and even a tiny triangle of white turning the corner under the boot. This make it look like the rest of the heel is in shadow. I use a white gel pen to create a few pops of shine all around the boot. Don't overdo it!

Slouchy Suede Boot

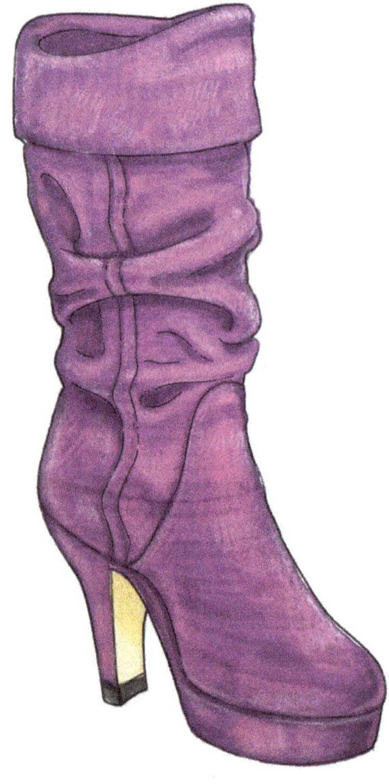

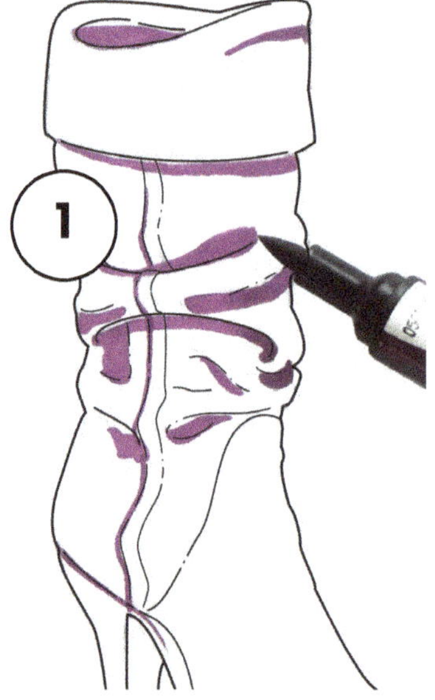

1 First, I begin with a V735 Plum BrushMarker creating the shadows between the folds of fabric and emphasizing some of the seams.

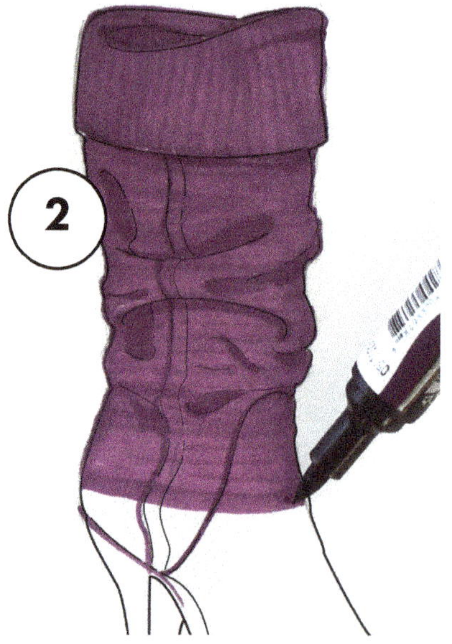

2 Then I add a layer of V735 over the whole boot. I did the top cuff vertically and the rest horizontally, being sure not to leave gaps.

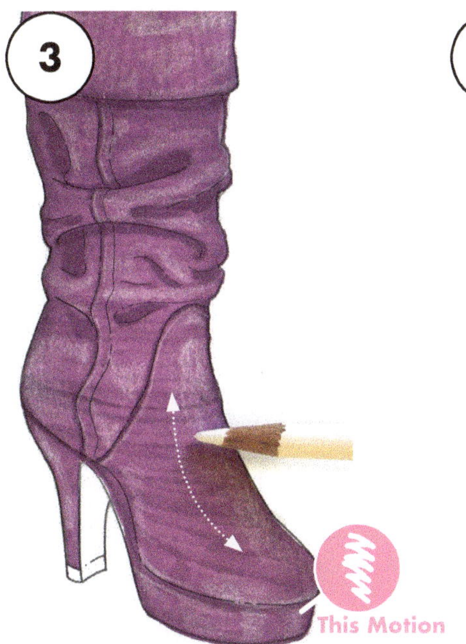

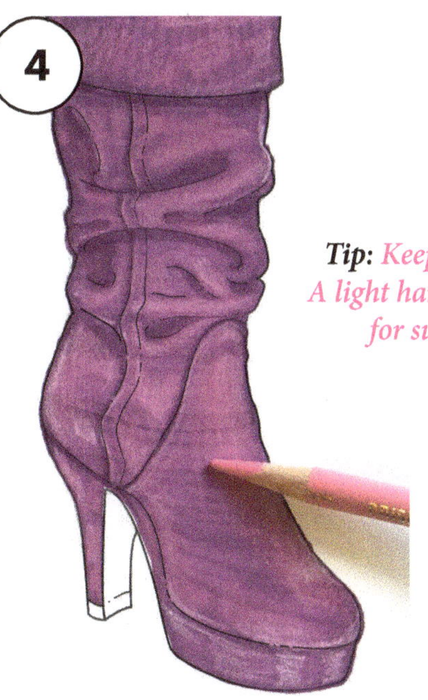

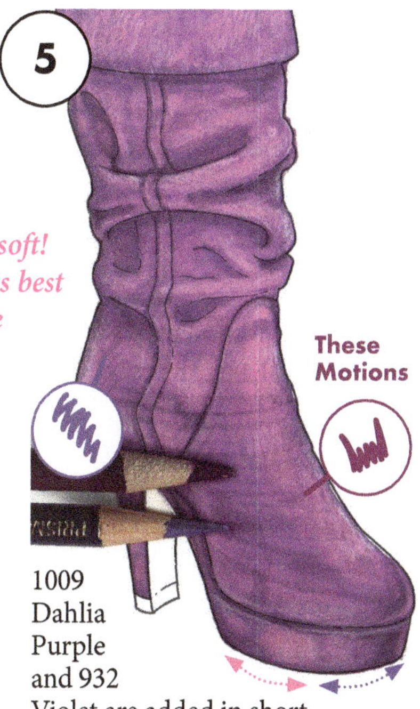

Now I add a light coat of 938 White pencil to the tops of each of the folds, directionally down the center of the lower part of the boot, and three vertical columns of horizontally scribbled lines on the front of the platform.

I blend a layer of 993 over most of the white, softening the texture of the suede. In the next step you can see how the front of the platform is softer with the addition of horizontal strokes of 993 and other colors.

Violet are added in short scribbly patches all over the boot. I vary the angle of the strokes to keep it soft – suede has subtle transitions. Don't overdo it! I darken above the platform with the 932 and blend the columns from Step 3 horizontally.

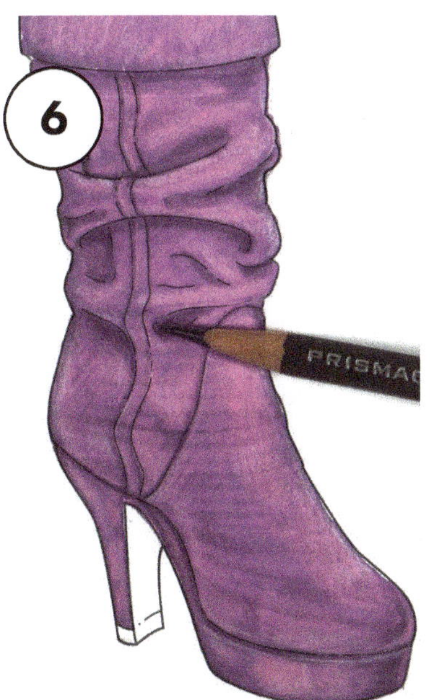

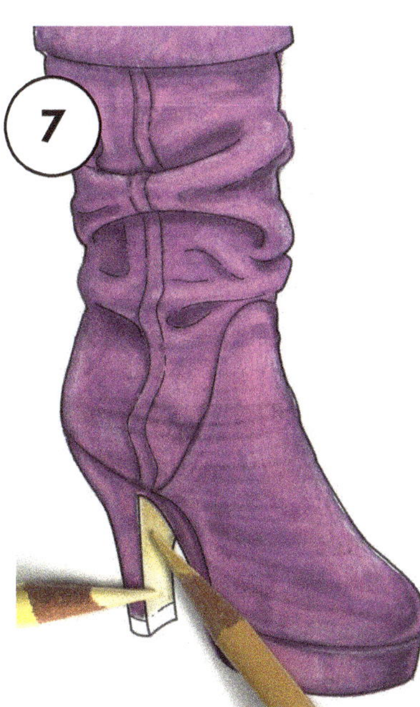

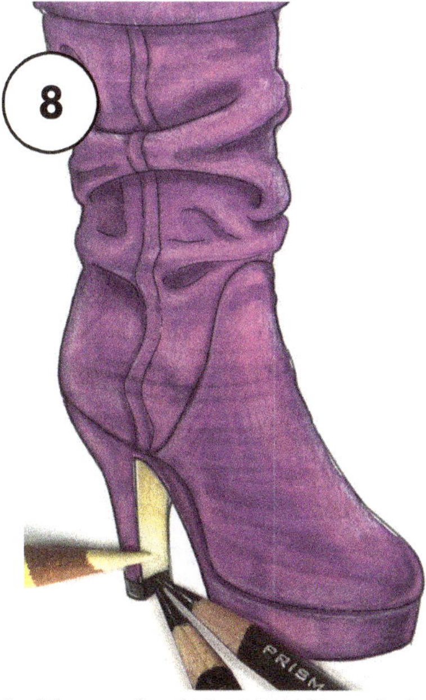

I introduce a subtle layer of 996 Black Grape in the folds to deepen them against the lines, and use it to create a little focus on the seams. I've also added a few more touches of 938 again on the folds (not shown).

I create the underside of the boot using 940 Sand on top and gradating it into 914 Cream downwards.

I add a touch of 1076 90% French Grey at the very top, over the some of the 940. I also use it to fill in the bottom piece of the heel and darken the longest side with black. I use the 914 to blend the colors and smooth the texture.

What did you learn?

Which fabric is the shiniest? Which is matte? Glossy surfaces are characterized by high contrast between lights and darks within close proximity to one another, whereas matte fabric has subtle shadows and almost no bright highlights.

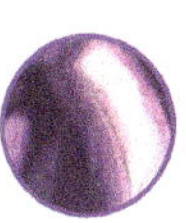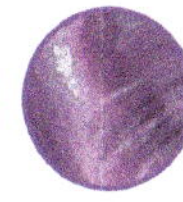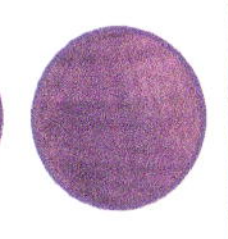

Chapter 8: Holiday Cheer

Get into the spirit of the holidays by coloring glistening decorations! You can almost smell the gingerbread!

A Complete Gift Package

You will need:
- The Holiday Gift line art page
- Prismacolor Premier: 1034, 918, 945, 922, 916, 935, 928, 940, 938
  - A white gel pen or paint marker
- A colorless blender pencil (optional)
- A Tombow Mono Zero eraser pen (optional, as needed)
- A TouchNew dual-end marker in 12 Coral Red or any Copic marker in R27 Cadmium Red

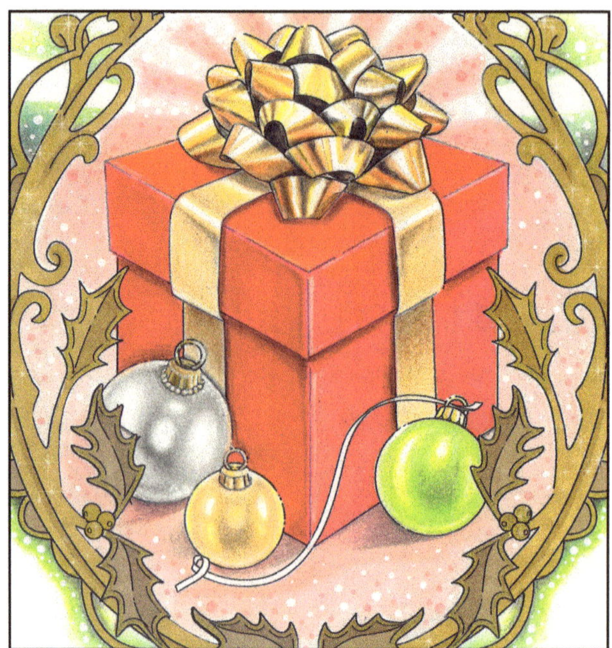

Gold Metallic Gift Bow

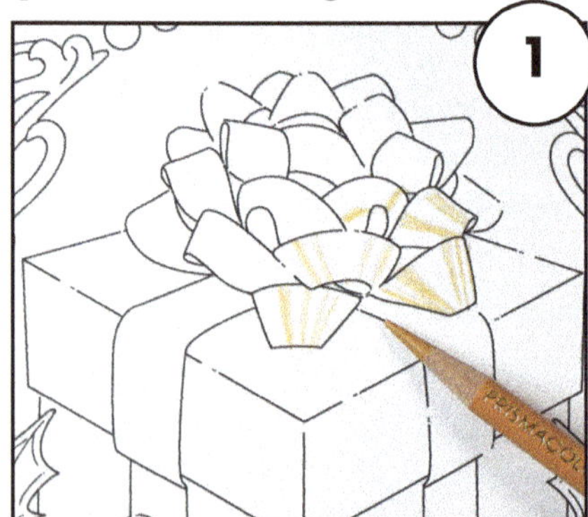

I begin creating a bow by using 1034 Goldenrod, drawing tapered lines that run from the front of each loop towards the back. Wider towards the back, narrower towards the front.

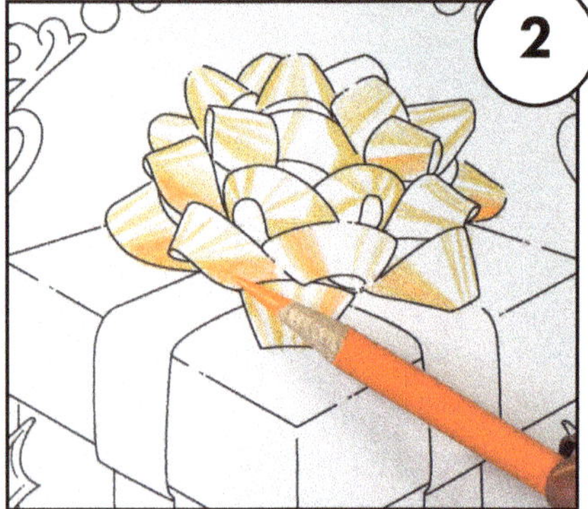

I add 918 Orange only to the lower portion of each loop closest to the box. This is the reflected light from the box (that is going to be red). The top/back loops are left alone.

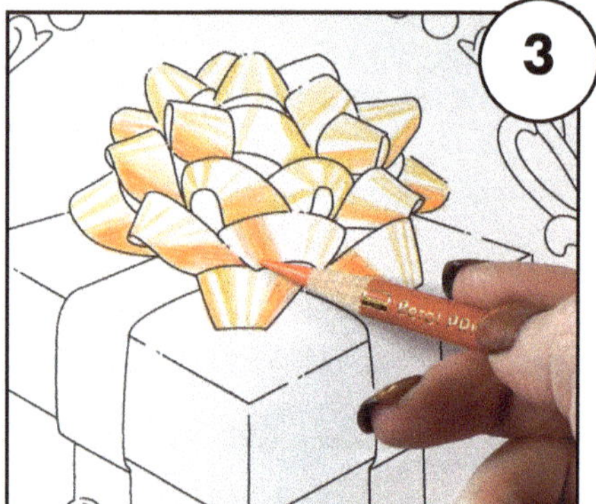

The box color will "bounce" back onto the bow! To create this effect I add 922 Poppy Red streaks on one edge (or center) of each 918 section, darkening it slightly, but leaving a lot of it showing.

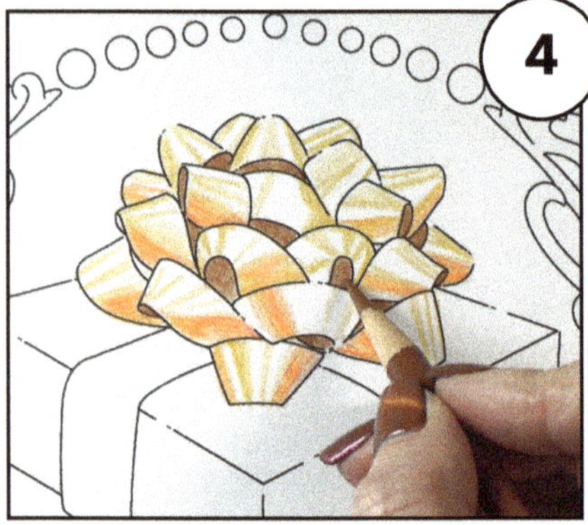

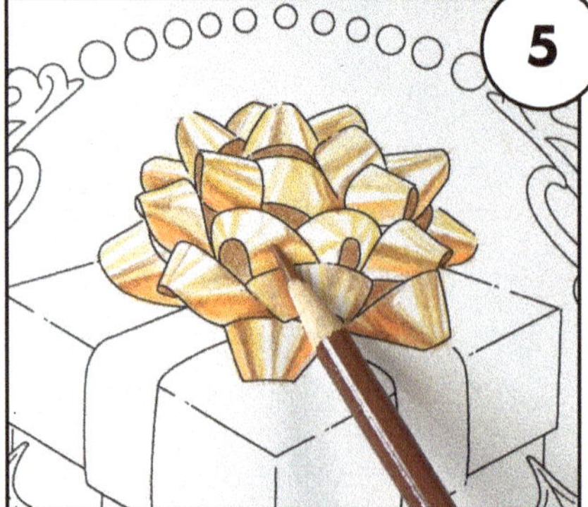

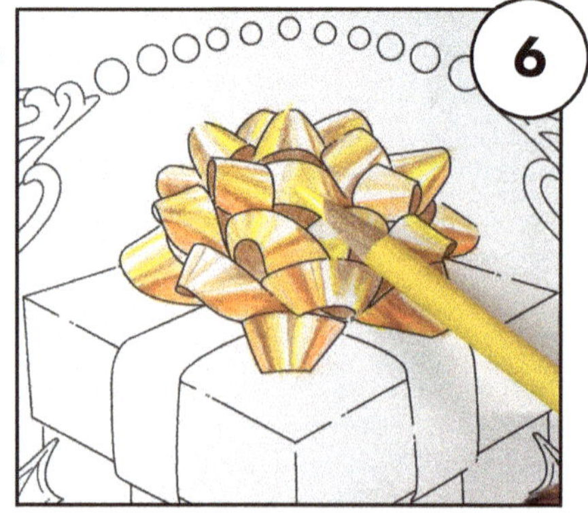

4. Then 945 Sienna Brown is then added to the inside of each loop that is facing me to create darkness to start to convey where contrast will lay in this picture.

5. I then use 945 to darken the core shadow of each loop but because this is a metallic material, some loops will display more than one "secondary" core or dark line. Next I use 916 Canary Yellow to add warmth in the areas that stay mostly light, to create a true gold tone.

I leave some areas white for highlights, but burnish (push a little to blend) some of the places where there is a transition of light to darker colors so that it looks smoother.

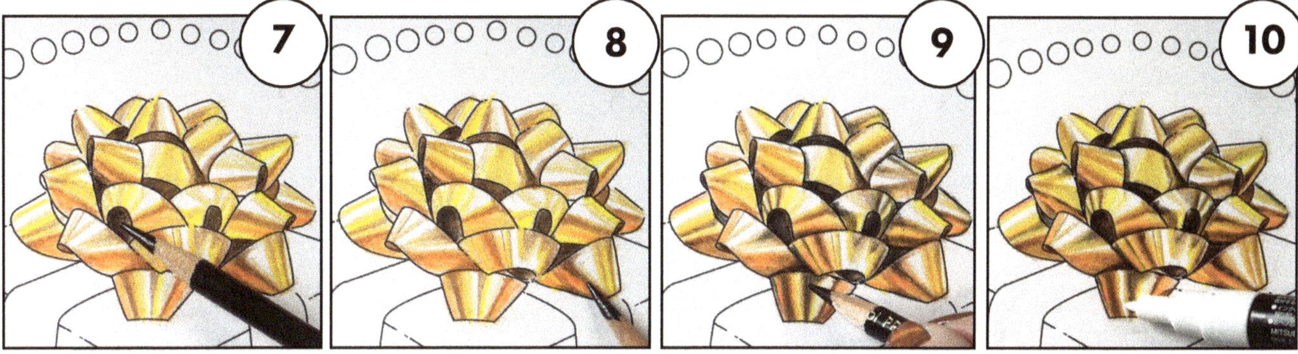

Here I may use a colorless blender (not shown) to smooth some of the colors in small patches. I then start kicking up the contrast! This is where this bow comes to life – adding 935 Black creates drama and depth. Steps 7-9: I color over the the middle of original 945 core shadows to deepen, and along the edges of the inside of each loop to darken. I then refine everything – going back into all of my colors to blend a little, using my blender sparingly. **10.** I add white gel pen on each loop, as needed!

Ribbon Ties

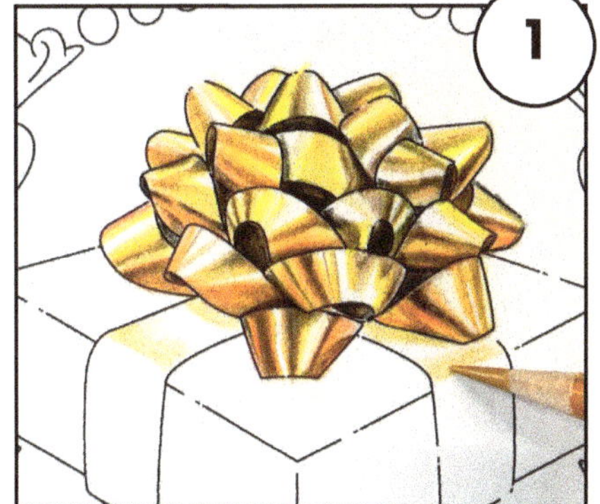

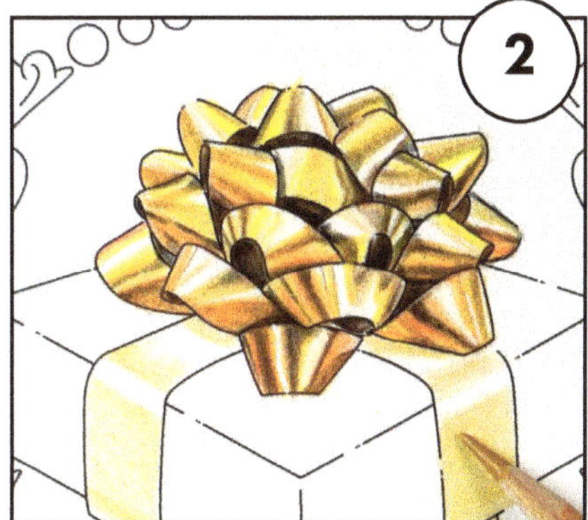

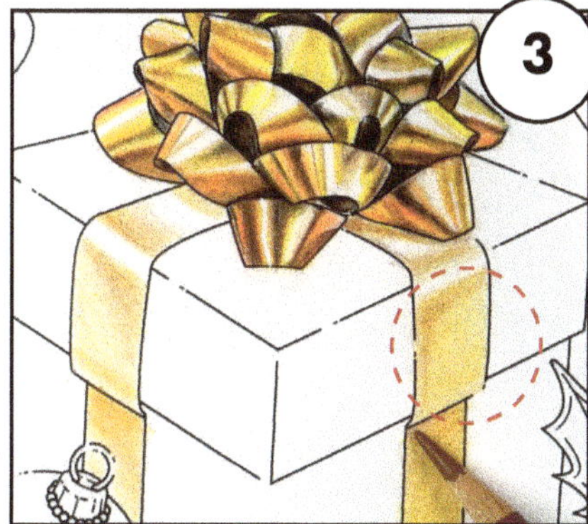

I begin this process by using 1034 GoldenRod, coloring parallel to the edges of the box where the ribbon is bending. Starting with the top plane I create a couple of bands.

Next, I shade from the side down, leaving a white space at the very top where the ribbon bends. I gradate my color as I complete the entire ribbon, darkest at the bend and under the lid of the box.

Following Step 2, I use 945 Sienna brown to start to create more shadow under the lid of the box on the ribbon and in a sideways "L" shape at the top of both left and right bends.

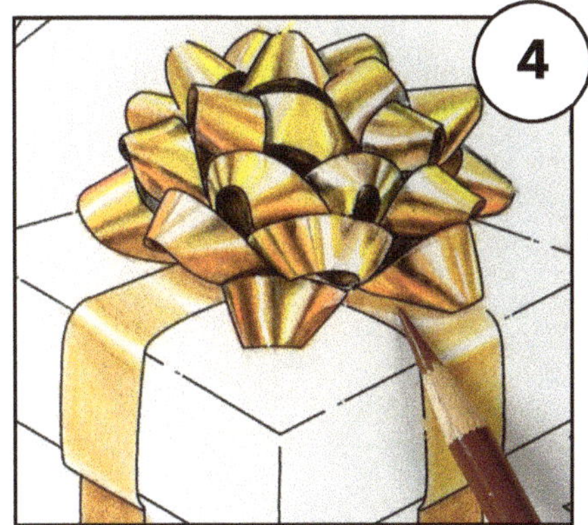

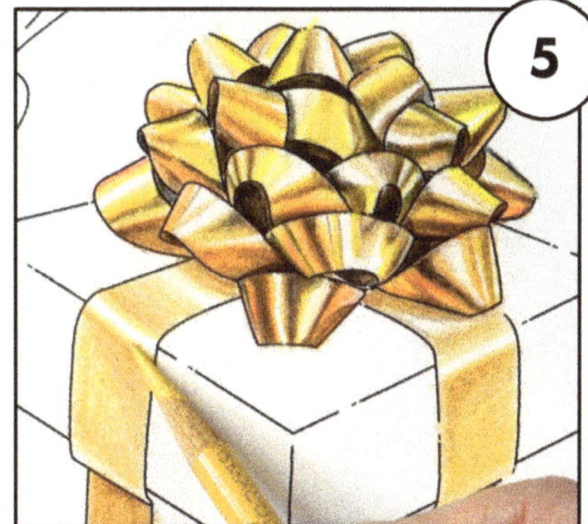

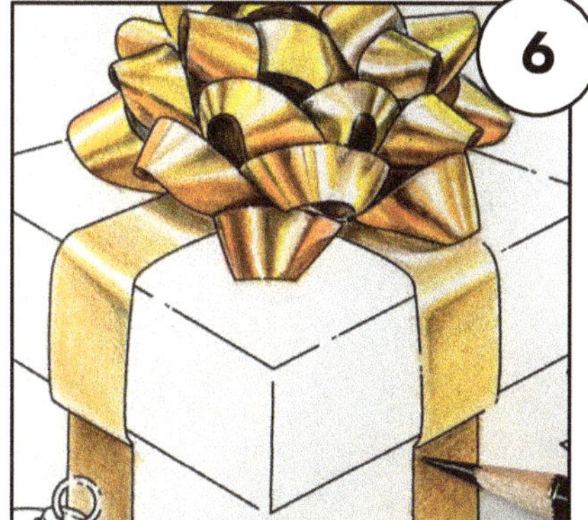

I then use the same 945 to create cast shadows underneath the loops of the bow that are sitting on top of the ribbon ties.

It's helpful to blend the harsh line of the Sienna Brown with some 940 Sand Prismacolor. This helps to soften the transition of the metallic ribbon. I also use the 940 in a thin layer over all of the 1034 to blend out the paper tooth.

Under the box lid and ever so lightly on the "L" shapes, I then blend with a Black 935 pencil to deepen – it's important to have the 945 underneath as it so that the Black sitting on top of the Goldenrod does not turn greenish.

Remember! Before you begin the next step...

Red Gift Box

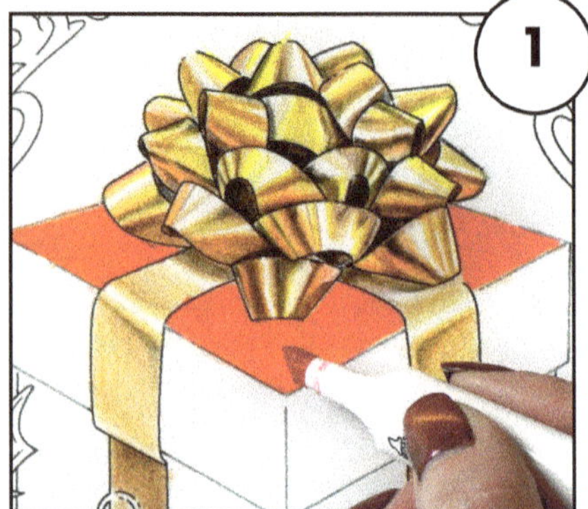

I use the chisel tip of my TouchNew marker in 12 Coral Red, covering the entire surface of the top plane of the box, with swift parallel motions using the wide side of the tip.

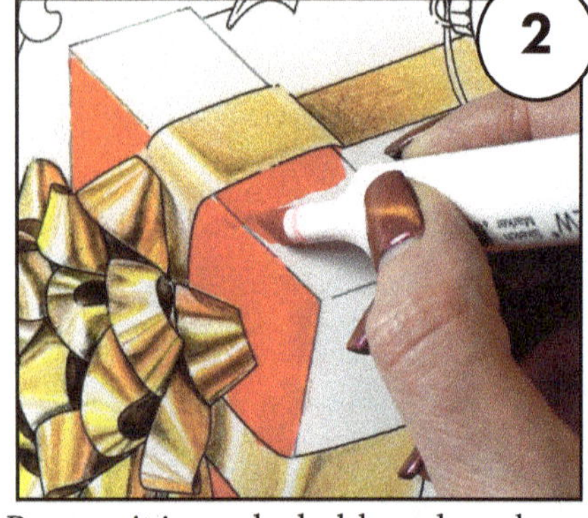

Because it is an alcohol-based marker, I'm careful to make a little "bleed room" by leaving a bit of space before the edge. It makes it easier to continue if I rotate my paper 90 degrees – this way I am

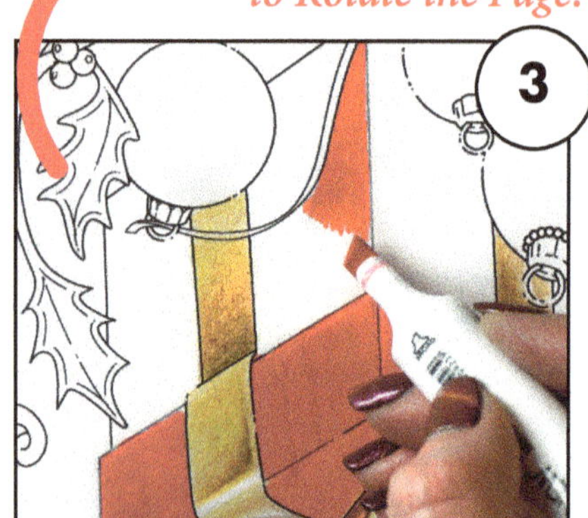

able to get my marker to cover evenly. After completing the lid, I turn the page again using the tip of the marker to get into smaller spaces more easily. Quickly, I use the side to fill in the rest.

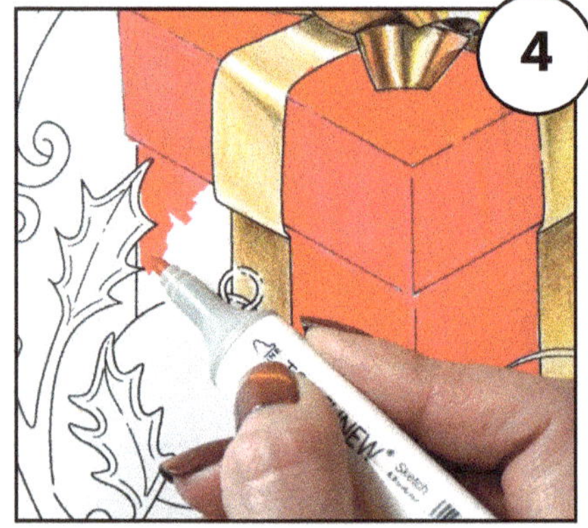

I then use the smaller fine point end of the dual-end marker to get into tight spaces that wouldn't be possible with the chisel tip.

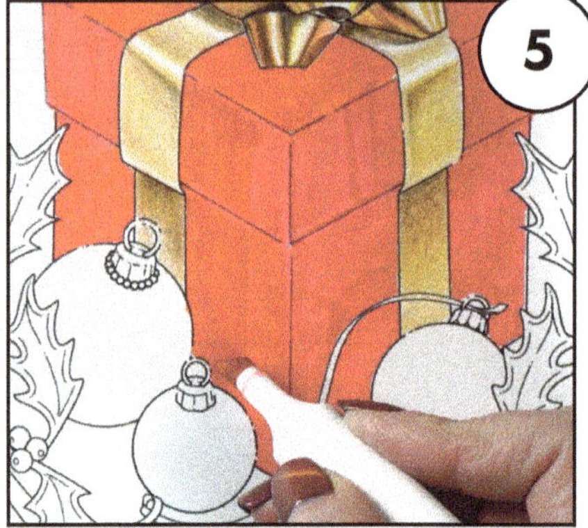

After I've completed covering each entire side of the two front planes of the box, I then apply a second coat to the left side only, to make it read as a darker hue than the right side plane.

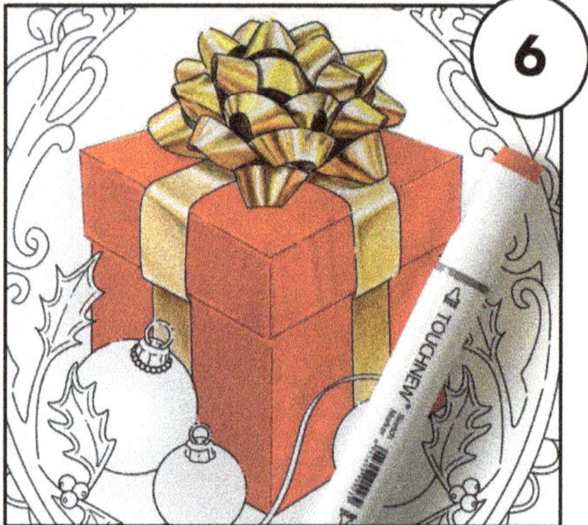

This extra coat "pushes it back" and creates depth. *A time-saving option would be just to use one coat of a darker marker in the same family.*

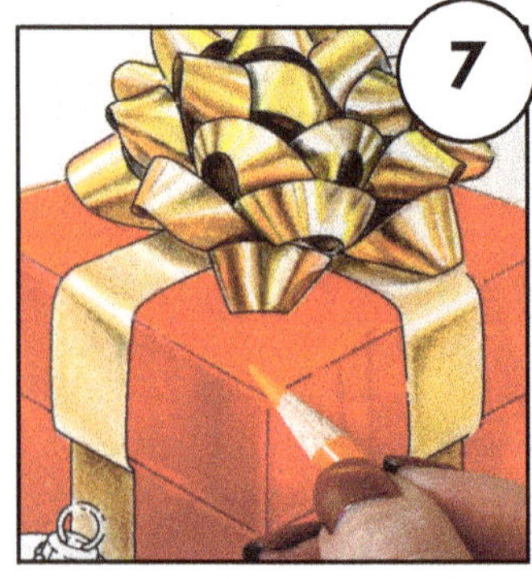

I use a 918 Orange pencil, just to apply a feather-light coat in the front corner to make that edge jump forward because of its warmth.

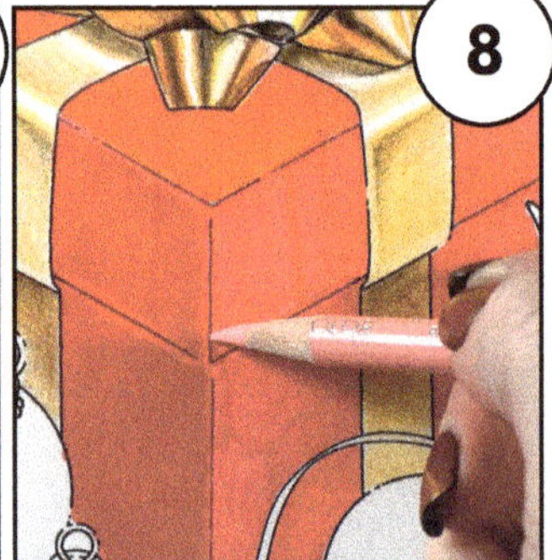

928 Blush Pink is then added to the right hand side of the box from the very edge, gradating right lightly – only up to the ribbon. I add a White 938 highlight on very edge.

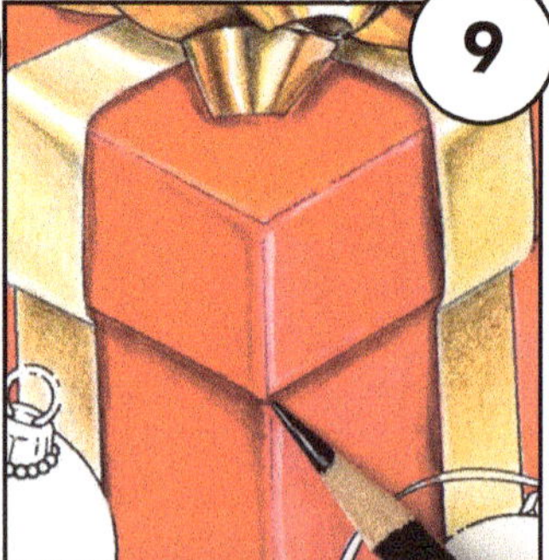

Black 935 is used to get underneath the lid of the box, to the left and right of the ribbons, and underneath each bow loop that sits directly on the box – to create cast shadows. The darkest area is right underneath each object and I very subtly blend the pencil until the transition is seamless into the box. Now I just blend and refine everywhere as needed. Vôila!

Want to color the ornaments right now? Skip forward two pages!

Iced Gingerbread Man

You will need:

- The Holiday Plate line art page
- Copic Marker E37 Sepia (or Arrtx Terra Cotta 21) + Salad YG05*
- Prismacolor Premier pencils: 945, 940, 140, 1026, 996, 909, 938, 992, 907 (optional 913)
- White Posca

1 I use my Copic E37 Sepia marker to block in solid color. I add strokes under the iced or candy decorations (and at the arrows) as cast shadows.

2 945 Sienna Brown is used to create small dashes and dots around the surface of the gingerbread. These will be become the cracked, dimpled *texture*.

3 To create a 3-D look I add a heavy stroke of 940 Sand under each dimple, following it's particular contour. Most are a "U" shape.

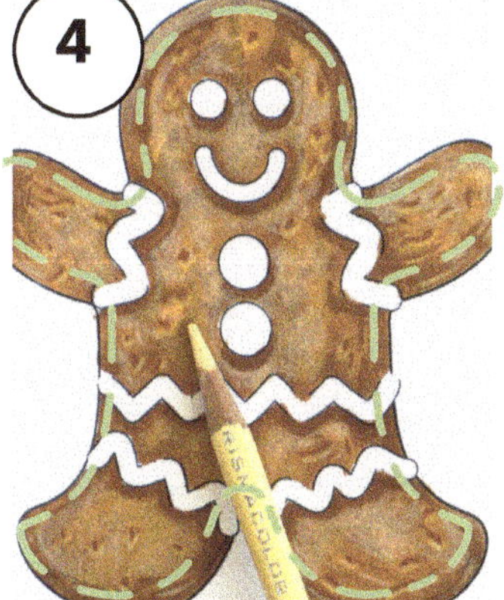

4 Now I use a layer of 140 Eggshell in between all of the dimples to lighten the surface. I keep it away from the edges, except a few dashes on the feet.

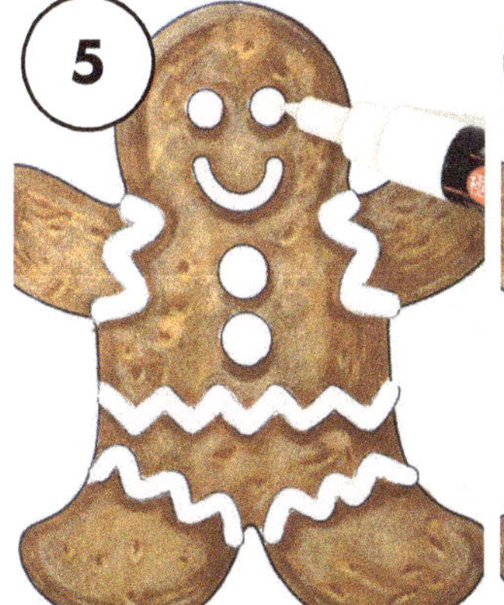

5 I'm using a Posca here to "erase" the black line art around the white shapes. In the end it will look less flat and more convincing.

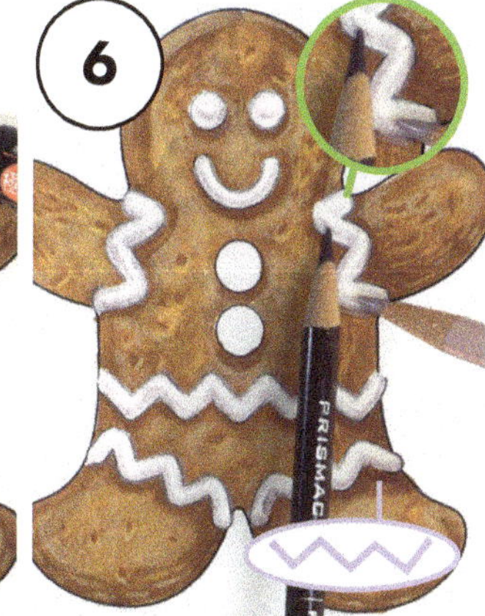

6 To give the icing dimension/shadow I use 1026 Greyed Lavender as a stroke on each bottom side, then 996 Black Grape just to darken the turns.

Candy Details

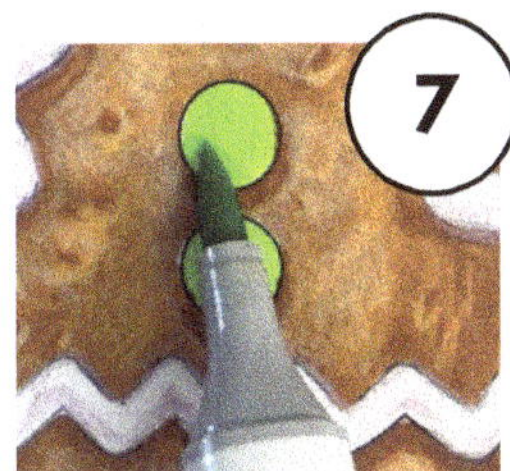

7 *I'm using an YG05 Salad Copic to fill in the circles. If you don't have one, a Prismacolor Spring Green pencil or marker is your best bet.

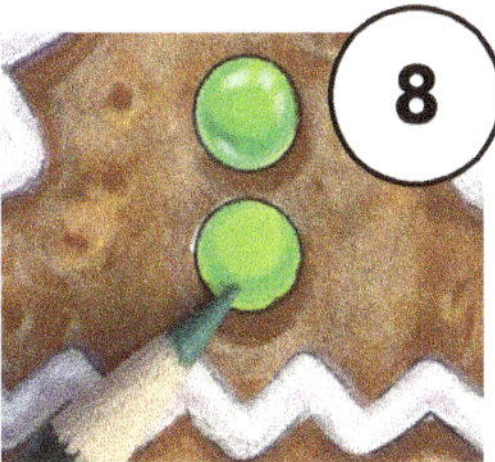

8 Now I use a 909 Grass Green to make a crescent shape close to the bottom of each circle.

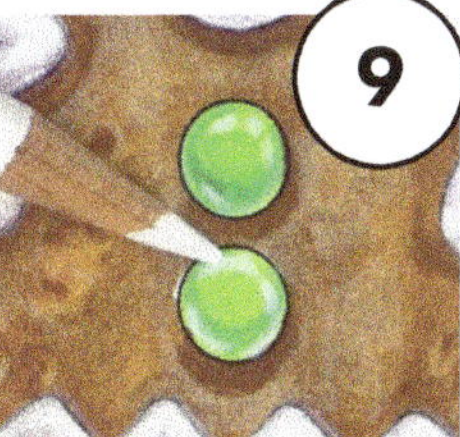

9 White 938 is used to create a highlight along the top edge, in one long stroke or a few segmented ones. I add just a hair to the bottom edge as well to lighten it before Step 10.

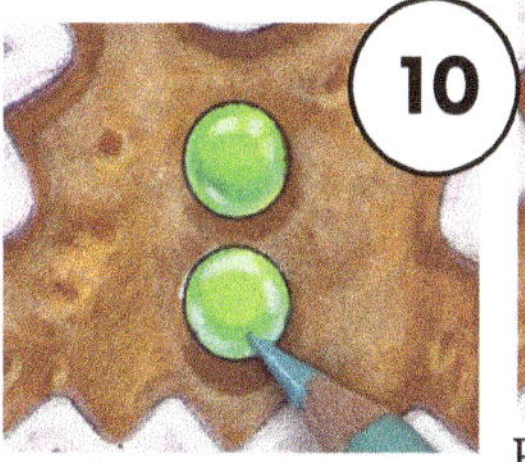

10 I color over the White with 992 Light Aqua to create some cooler reflected light on the bottom edge.

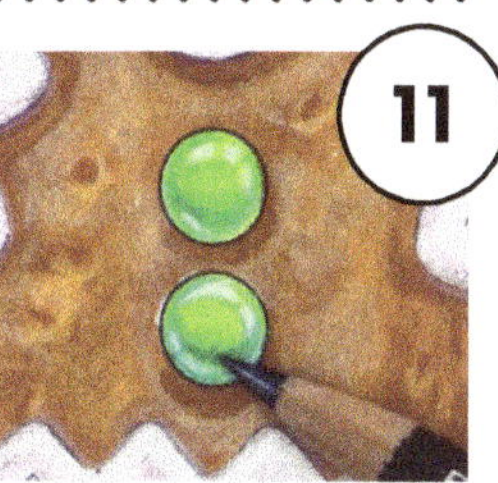

11 Finally I deepen the core shadow (crescent) slightly, in the center, with 907 Peacock Green. (You may wish to refine the edges of each of your shapes with a black Verithin.)

Holiday Ornaments – Silver Bauble

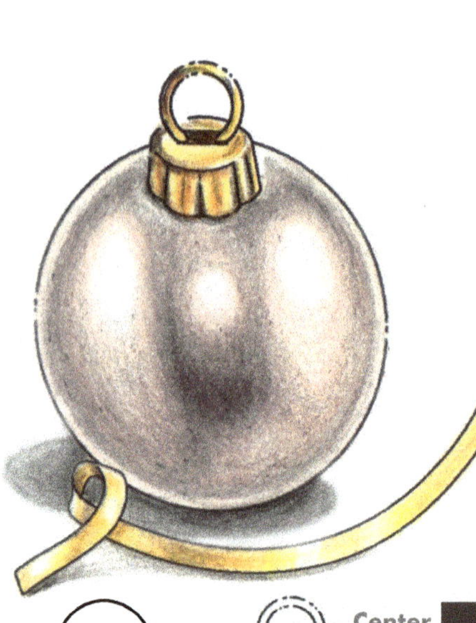

I begin **mapping** out the reflection outline in 928 Blush Pink. Think of them as a rounded "U" with a bean-shape in the middle, that don't quite fill out the circle.

Next I fill 1051 Warm Grey 20% in **between** the bean and the "U" and surrounding it (except the very edges) circling outward from the bean.

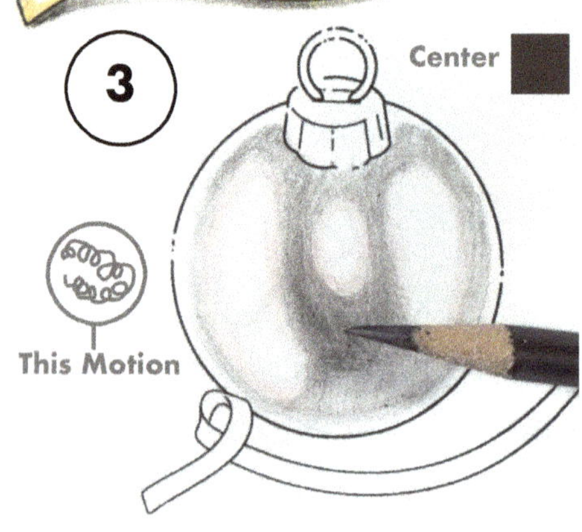

Then *very* lightly, with tiny circles I fill in the **center** and around the "U" with the darkest color, 1058 Warm Grey 70%, heaviest under the bean-shape in the middle.

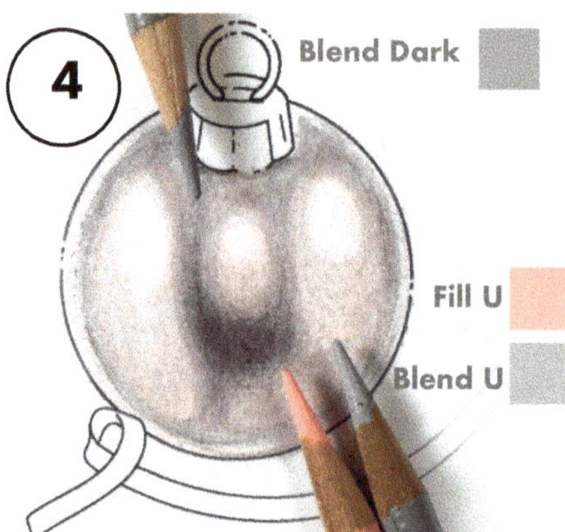

Next, I **blend** the darkest part with 1052 Warm Grey 30% until smooth. I **fill** in the edges of the ball and most of the "U" and the bean (leaving 3 white highlights) with 928. I **blend** a layer of 1051 on top.

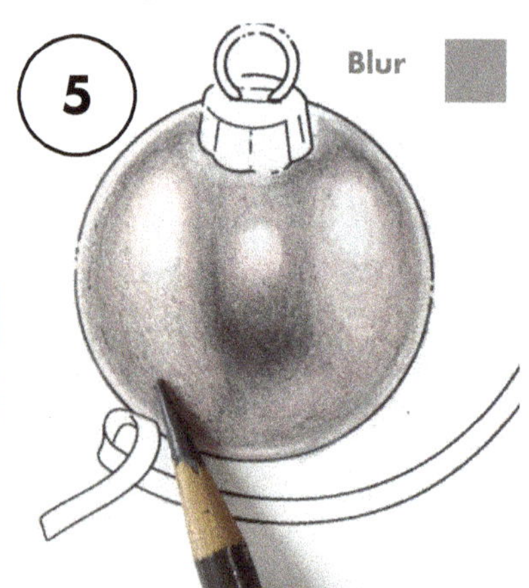

I leave the edges of the ornament itself alone, but with a light hand I darken and "**blur**" around the outside of the "U" and blend the pink parts into the rest with 1054 Warm Grey 50%.

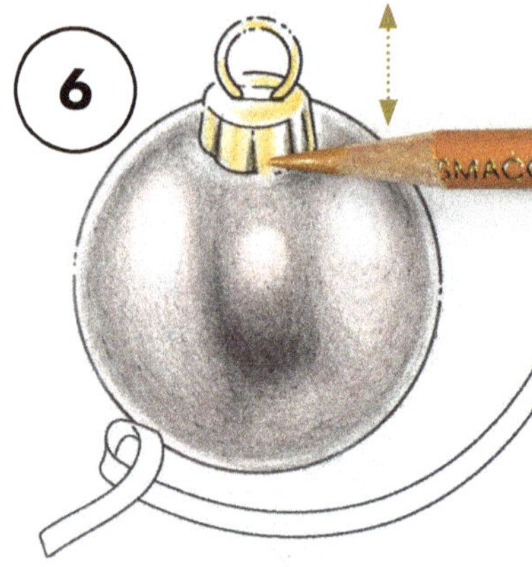

For the gold I use 1034 GoldenRod to fill in a vertical stroke in the center of each section of the ornament cap. I also fill in the right side of the top plane of the cap and most of the ring.

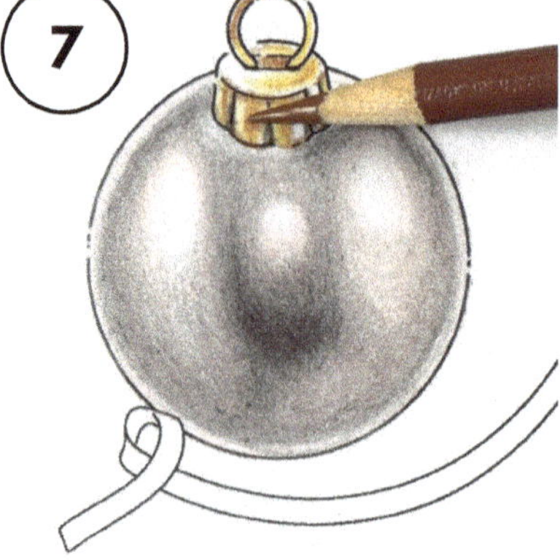

I deepen the vertical stokes with 945 Sienna Brown, as well as the left side of the ring and I fill in the notch where it attaches to the cap.

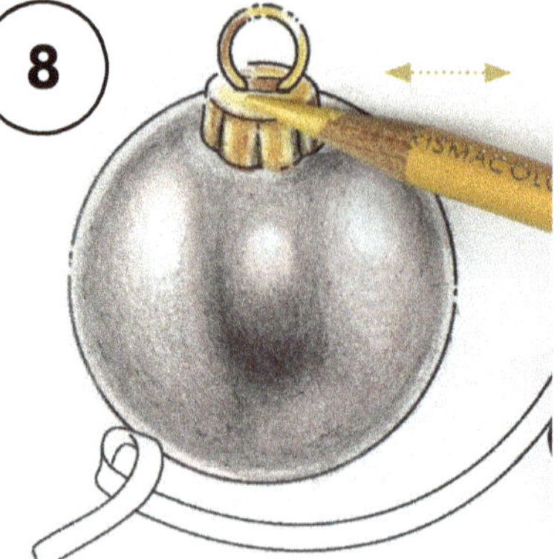

To complete the bauble I fill in the cap top horizontally + burnish with 940 Sand, I leave a few white highlights. Optional: 916 Canary Yellow may be added for more warmth.

Holiday Ornament Blends

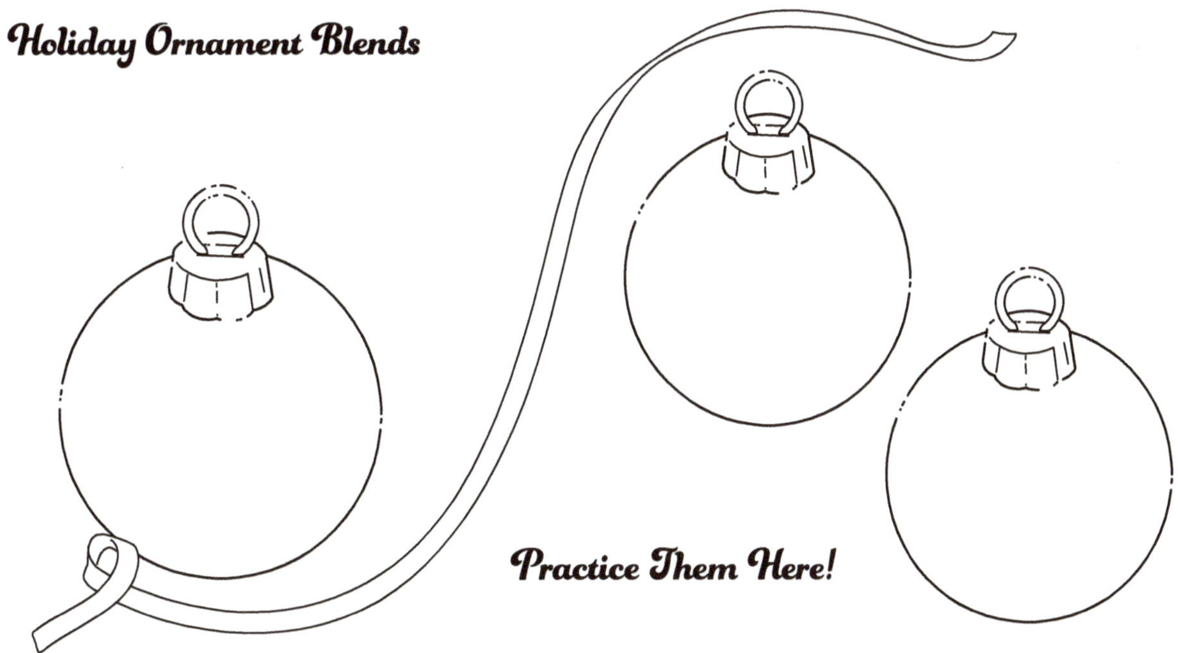

Baubles are lustrous so the approach is very similar to creating a pearl. To make them look reflective, keep the darkest tones light-handed and in the center under the "bean" the darkest. You may even use a little black to deepen the center, if need be! Remember to leave a glow at the edges! Follow the guidelines for the Silver Bauble and swap out the colors below to create ornaments in different hues! A similar Ribbon tutorial is in The Secrets of Coloring Volume 1.

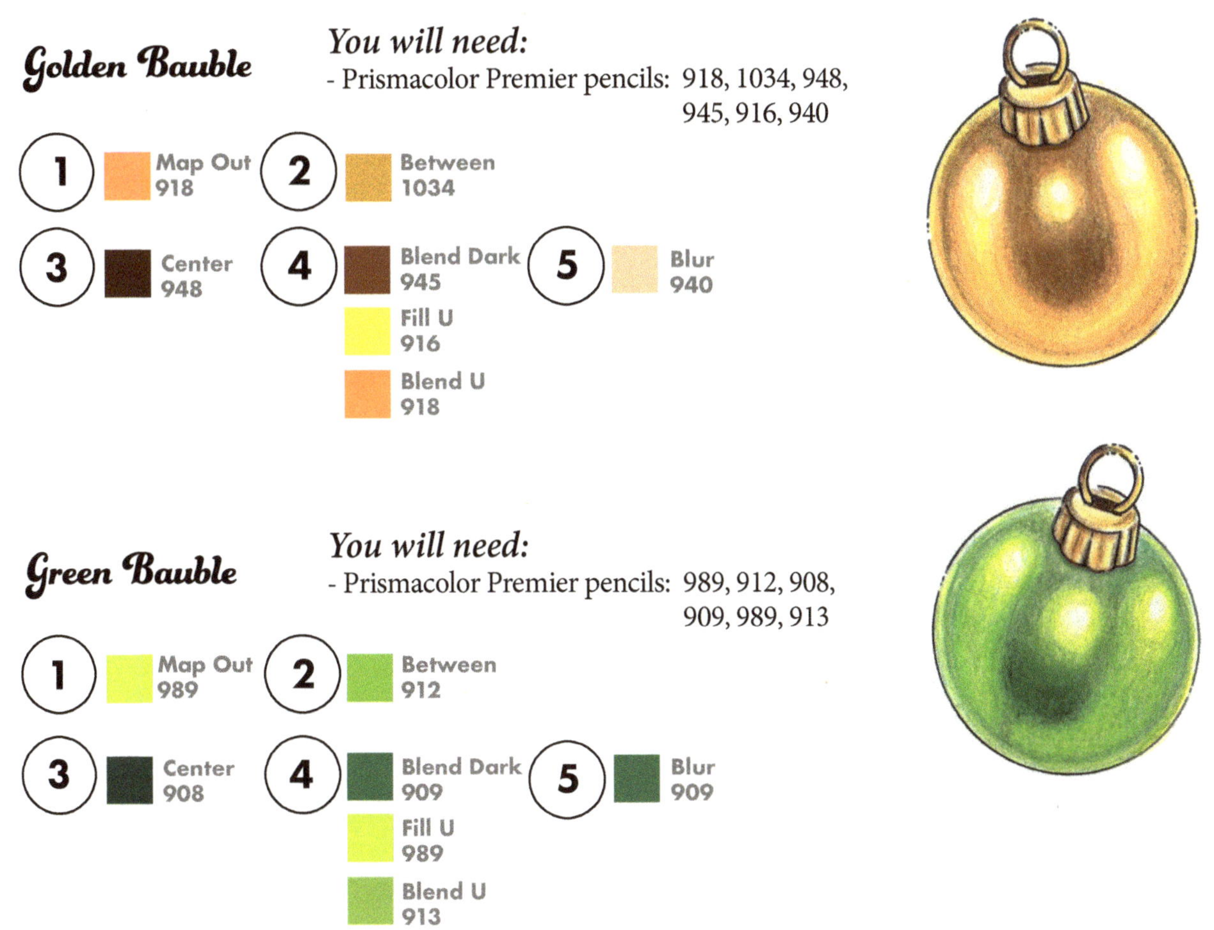

Golden Bauble

You will need:
- Prismacolor Premier pencils: 918, 1034, 948, 945, 916, 940

1 — Map Out 918
2 — Between 1034
3 — Center 948
4 — Blend Dark 945 / Fill U 916 / Blend U 918
5 — Blur 940

Green Bauble

You will need:
- Prismacolor Premier pencils: 989, 912, 908, 909, 989, 913

1 — Map Out 989
2 — Between 912
3 — Center 908
4 — Blend Dark 909 / Fill U 989 / Blend U 913
5 — Blur 909

Chapter 9: Adding Shimmer and Pizzazz - Make It Your Own

Why not make something your own, personalized version? You can easily turn your coloring pages into next level art or even custom holiday cards. Add your own details to make them shimmery and extra festive! Use real glitter here!

Before these steps I added a few background elements to this page. A green marker was used to fill the background, then abstracted snowflakes were hand-drawn with a white pencil. A darker green pencil was added around the shapes to make them stand out. Finally a thin white line of gel pen was used to top the snowflakes off. Then I took it to the next level...

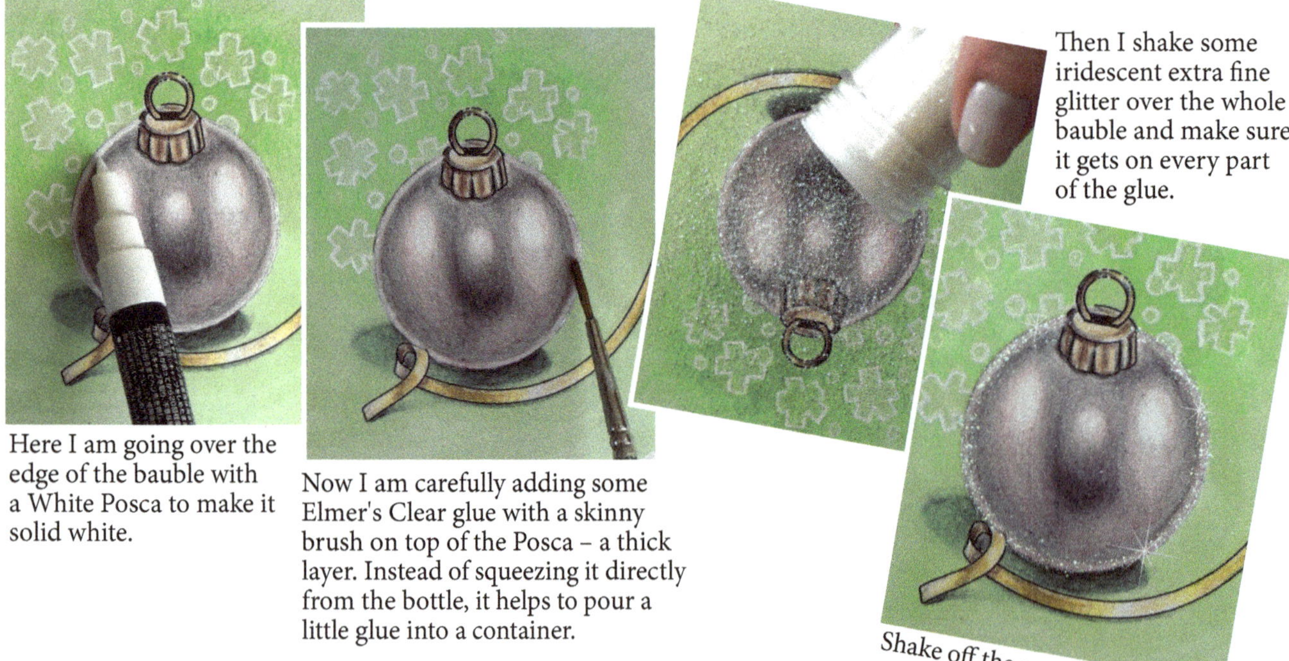

Then I shake some iridescent extra fine glitter over the whole bauble and make sure it gets on every part of the glue.

Here I am going over the edge of the bauble with a White Posca to make it solid white.

Now I am carefully adding some Elmer's Clear glue with a skinny brush on top of the Posca – a thick layer. Instead of squeezing it directly from the bottle, it helps to pour a little glue into a container.

Shake off the excess...and Voîla!

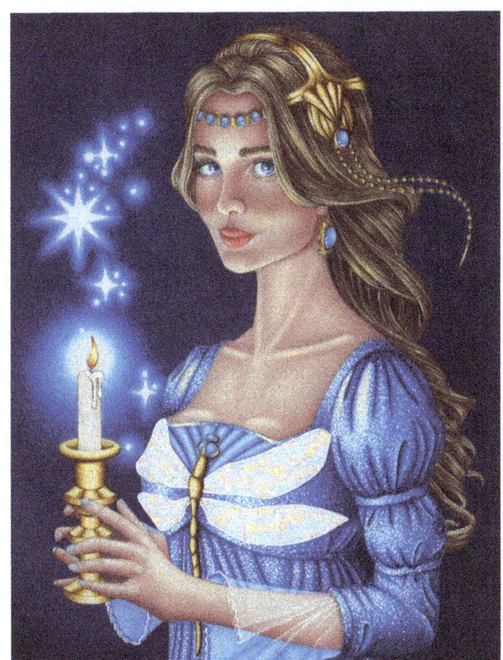

You can apply this look to any fabric you've colored by matching a few glitter colors to a pencil base color family (in this case, blue)! To create this effect, Selina does a complete pencil drawing first, then coats the pencil with several layers of gel pen for the magical finish! Check out her amazing Instagram account for her trademark technique video tutorials.

You will need:

(A base of 4-6 pencils in a color family. Used: Polychromos - Blues 145, 152, 110, 151, 157 + 108 Dark Cad Yellow + Luminance White 001)
- Glow Princess line art (printed on optional toned paper)
- Gel pens similar to the base color (light/dark/white). Used: Copic AtYou Spica pens in Baby Blue and Sky Blue + White Gelly Roll

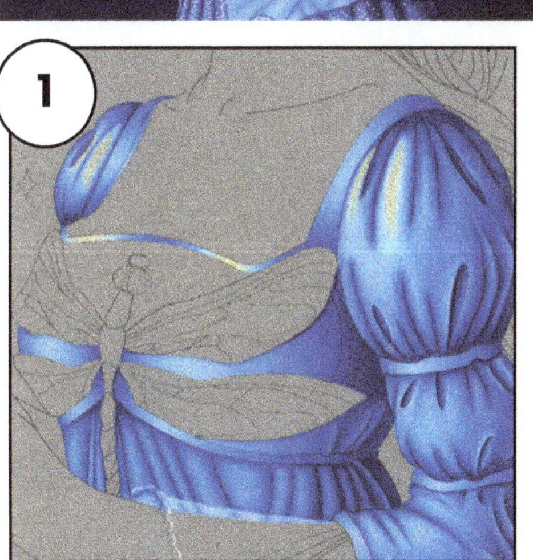

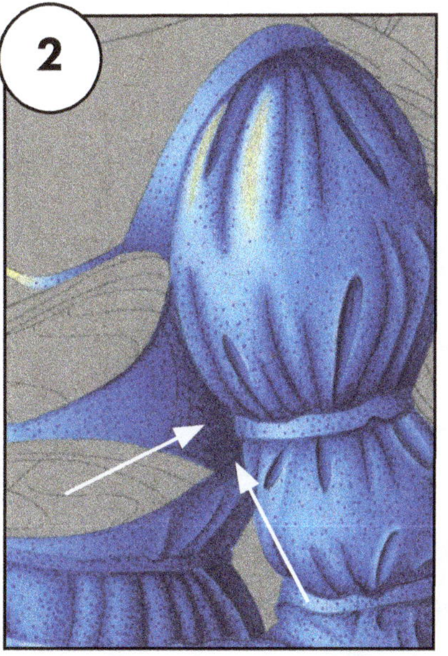

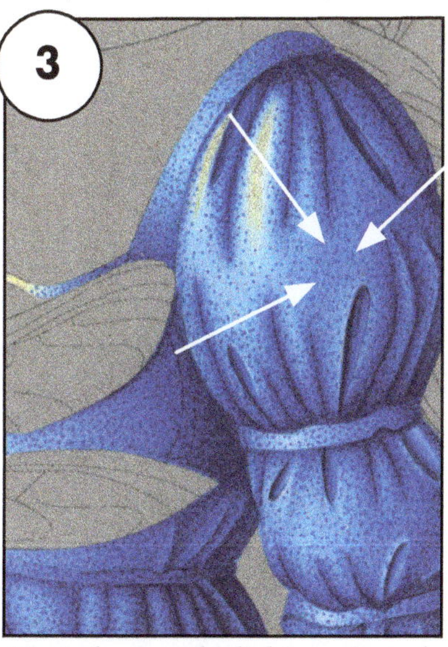

Selina begins to create this look by coloring the bodice and sleeves of the dress entirely in a colored pencil base of blues where she intends to overlay a glittery effect. She works from light to dark while developing *contrast*, to carefully create a realistic *form*. The areas that are sunken in (creases) will have more shadow, while the parts that pop out are rendered with light value tones. A few of the brightest highlights have a touch of yellow. White Luminance pencil is used to blend it all.

(The focus will be on the sleeve detail to best demonstrate this technique, but you will want to apply it everywhere you'd like a shimmering sparkly effect.)

She starts the glittering process by "stippling" dots close together in the darkest gel pen color first. These dots are concentrated in the areas of shadow, such as the creases and bends. She applies the darkest color of glitter less densely (futher apart) on the areas of fabric that start to advance towards us.

Next, she uses the lighter color gel pen, stippling over some of the darker dots into the mid-range area. The dots become less densely applied (further apart) as she covers the lightest areas, leaving some of them without the dots at all.

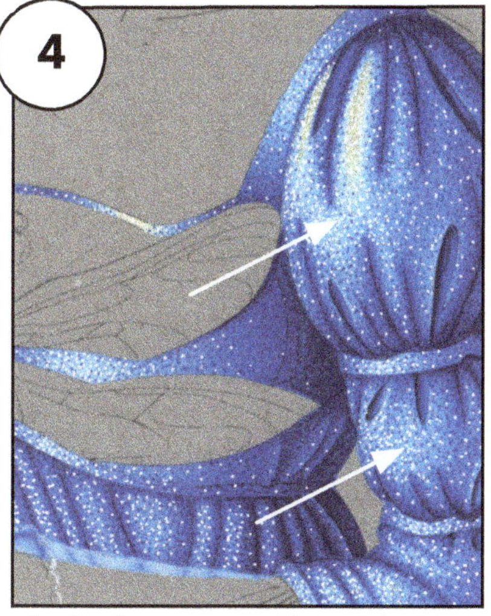

The final step is to add the white gel pen. It is used very sparingly in the darker areas and concentrated on the areas that advance most.

Chapter 10: The Living World

It's All in the Eyes! Realistic Eyes & More Color Combos

Please revisit the in-depth eye tutorial in The Secrets of Coloring Volume 1. It's based on a light, very transparent iris. The iris in the Dark Brown tutorial below is quite different. In addition I've included extra eye color combinations: Complex Blue-Green, Baby Blue and Gold-Green. These use a similar format to the original tutorial in Volume 1, with the "spokes" – just use razor sharp pencils and swap out the colors! Once you get the hang of both approaches, you can easily try other color combinations and customize the eyes!!

Dark Brown Eye

You will need:

- White Signo Uniball gel pen
- Caran D'Ache Luminance pencils: 495, 571, 030, 065, 069, 009, 001
- Optional: colorless blender pencil

Complex Blue-Green Eye

Lumi 495		Lumi 180	
Lumi 571		Lumi 159	
Lumi 030		Lumi 906	
Lumi 069		Lumi 001	
Lumi 820		Lumi 009	
Lumi 470		Uniball Signo	
Lumi 181			

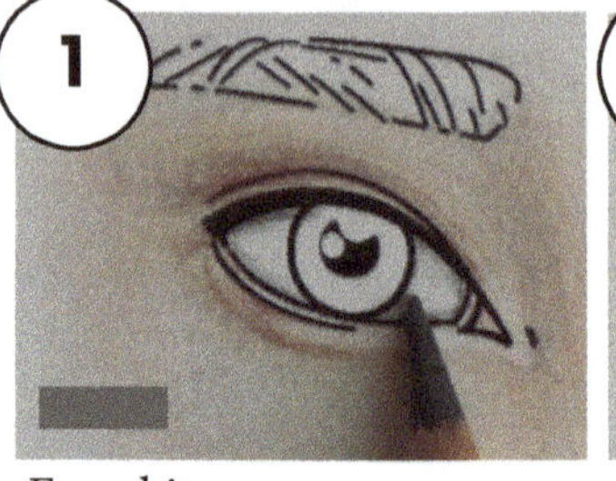

1 Eye whites are never pure white! I add 495 Slate Grey shadows under the upper lash line and above the lower one.

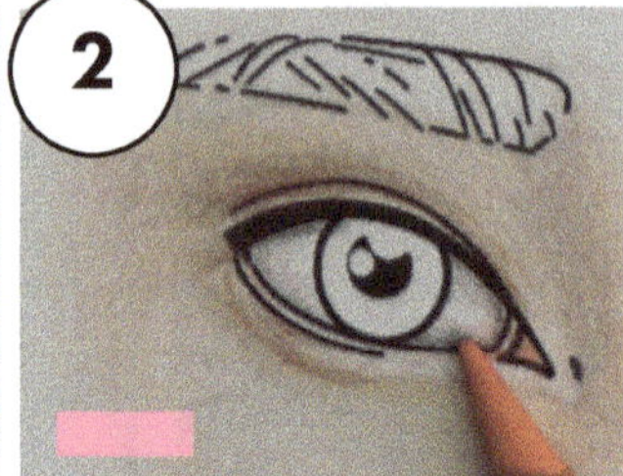

2 Next, in the inner corner I use 571 Anthraquinoid Pink, and a little on the eye white itself.

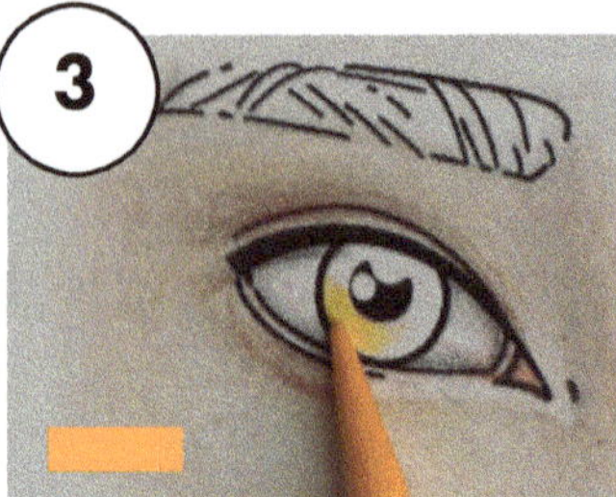

3 In the lower left area of the iris I add a layer of 030 Orange (across from the designated highlight/reflection spot.)

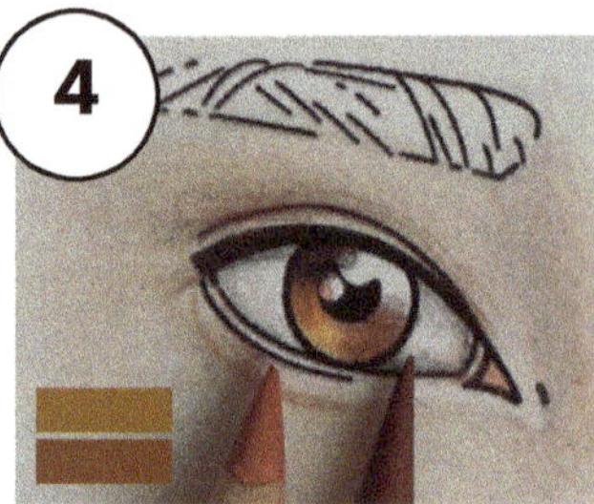

4 Then I add a touch of 065 Russet just to the left and 069 Burnt Sienna to the right, leaving a small white area.

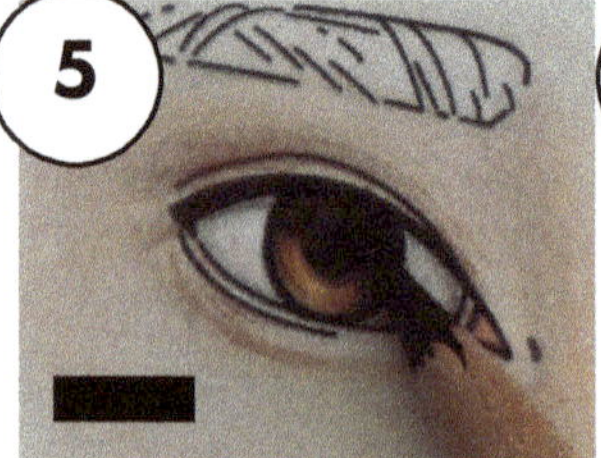

5 Now I use a heavy coat of 009 Black to fill in the whole blank white area.

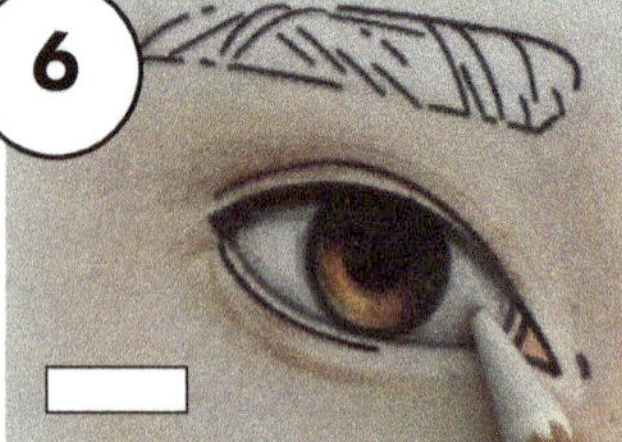

6 I use 001 White to blend and smooth the eye white, blend the black outline of the iris and later the upper eyelid.

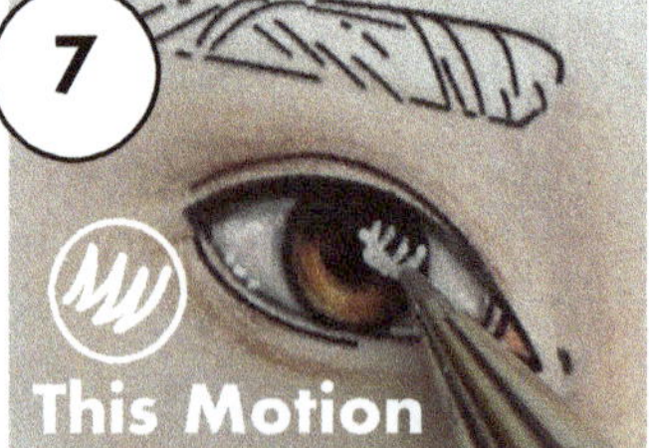

7 A thin white gel pen is used to draw in a reflection of lashes! I use a colorless blender to shape and scrape away extra.

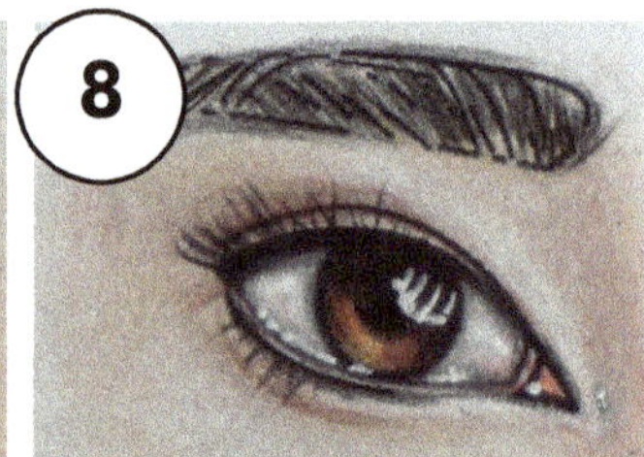

8 I use a flicking motion for lashes, from the base up and base down. A sharp 009 is used for both lashes and brows.

Did you know?

A light iris (the colored part of the eye) is transparent, meaning the light passes through it and the color is intensified. Some eyes are so dark that the pupil (the center of eye) is barely visable, making the eyes look like a solid black color. The darker the eyes, the more prominent the reflection!

Baby Blue Eye

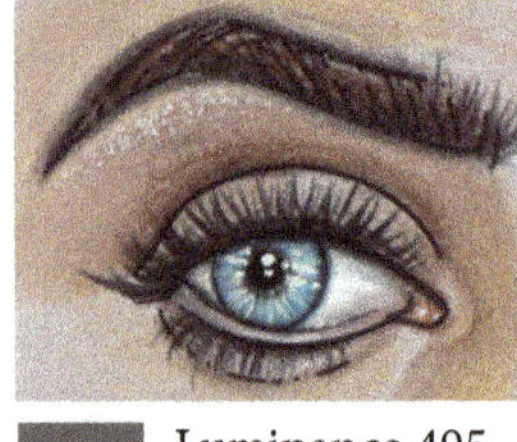

	Luminance 495
	Luminance 571
	Luminance 181
	Luminance 185
	Luminance 159
	Luminance 001
	Luminance 009
	Uniball Signo

Gold-Green Eye

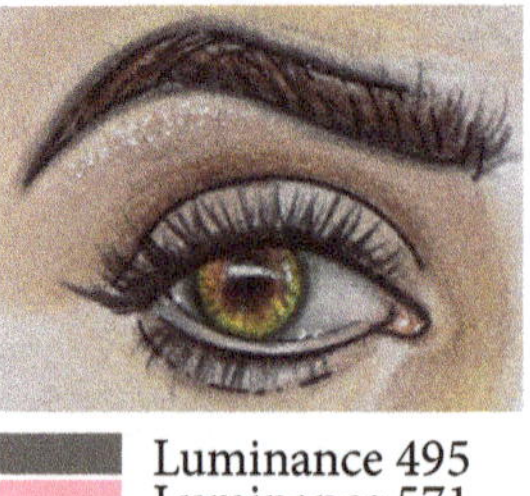

	Luminance 495
	Luminance 571
	Luminance 030
	Luminance 065
	Luminance 820
	Luminance 470
	Luminance 220
	Luminance 001
	Luminance 009
	Uniball Signo

Try an Eye!

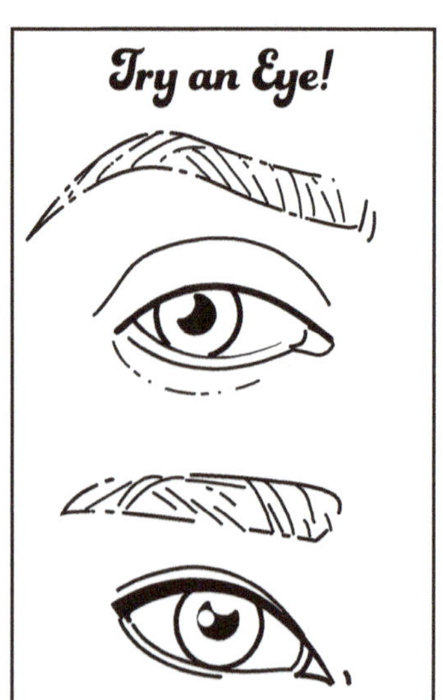

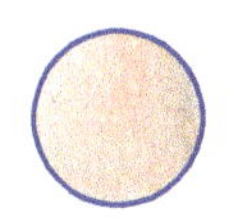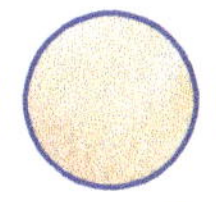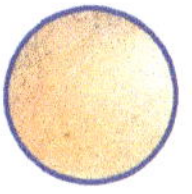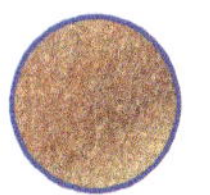

There is so much to know about skin tones: temperature, undertone, degree of darkness... and everyone is different! Skin ranges from fair to deep in pigment, and in hue from pinkish to olive. Here I have simplified skin tones using Caran D'Ache Luminance four ways: Cool, Neutral, Warm 1 & 2.

Customize your skin by warming, cooling or darkening with more pinks, greens & browns. I will focus on the skin itself in these tutorials but you may also want to refer to The Secrets of Coloring, Volume 1 for basic eye & lips tutorials to apply here.

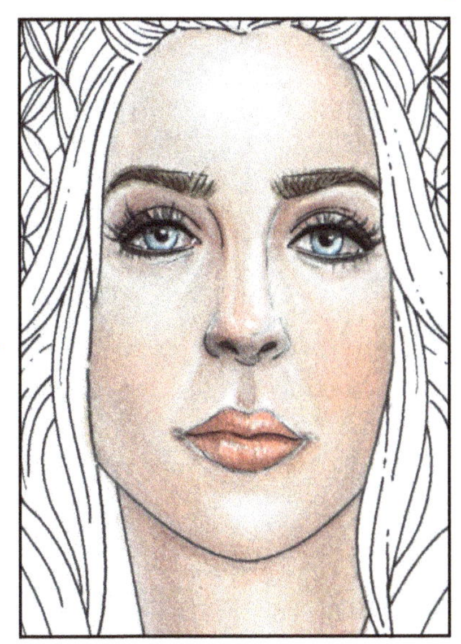

Luminance pencils will work similarly to Prismacolor. Don't have them? Get a free conversion chart with your secret code at ModernColoring.com

Cool Tone

You will need:
- The Portrait Practice line art page
- Caran D'Ache Luminance: 862, 661, 571, 872, 866, 001
- White gel pen & optional Mono Zero eraser

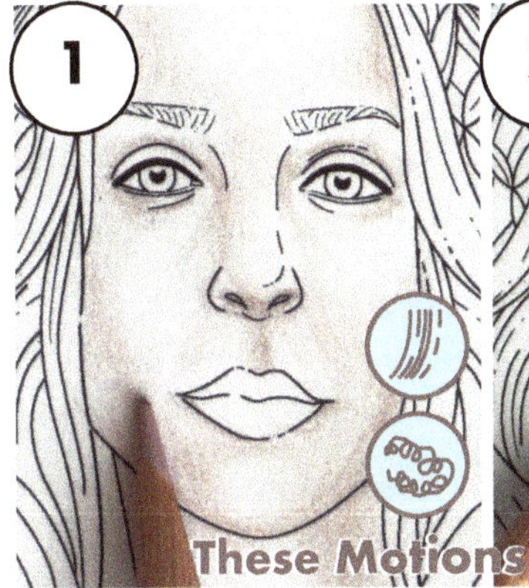

Starting with 862 Burnt Sienna 10%, I darken under her cheekbones, the underside of her nose and sides of her nose, in her eyelid creases, on the outsides of her forehead and sides of her neck – using tiny circles and light directional strokes.

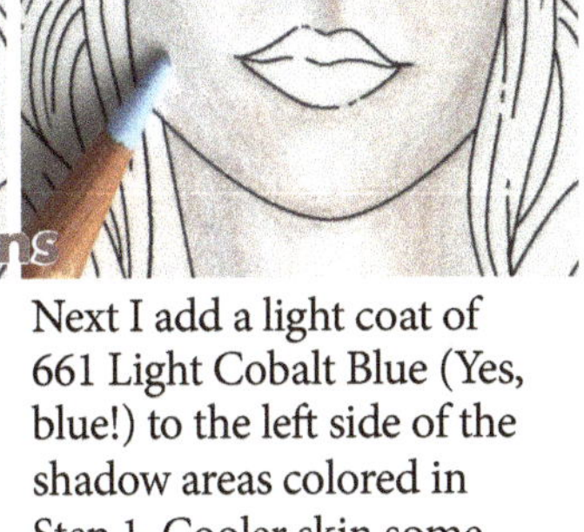

Next I add a light coat of 661 Light Cobalt Blue (Yes, blue!) to the left side of the shadow areas colored in Step 1. Cooler skin sometimes reflects blue, but don't worry, it will be very subtle in the end!

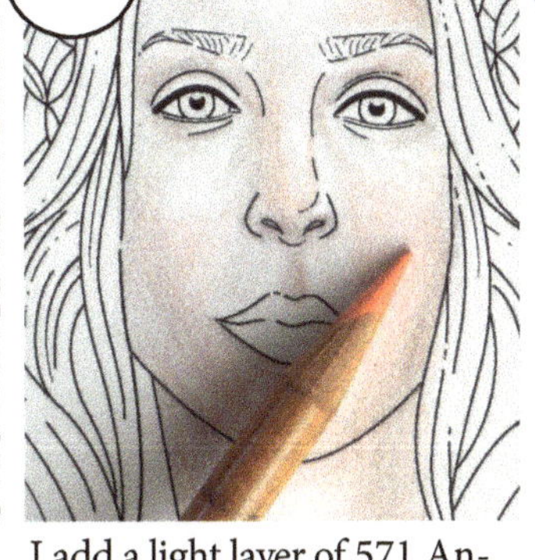

I add a light layer of 571 Anthraquinoid Pink all over the cheeks, outer forehead, chin and neck – and to the bridge of the nose more heavily.
I am mindful to leave white highlights in areas of each feature (under the eyes, right side of nose, above lips, etc.)

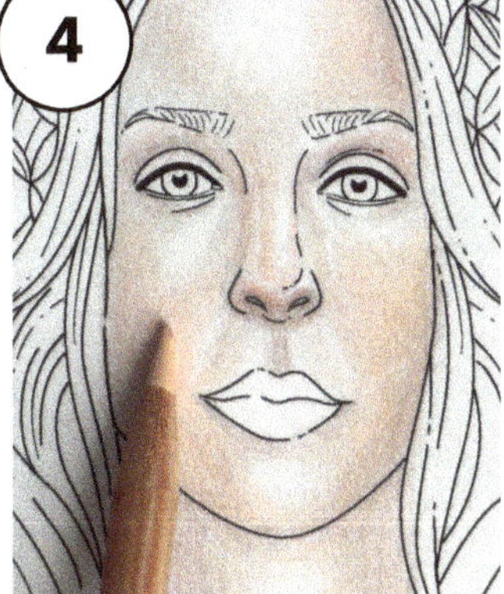

It's time to blend all of these colors and fill in some of the paper tooth with a sharp 872 Burnt Ochre 10%, again leaving some areas mostly white. Notice the highlight areas getting smaller and smaller and her skin is starting to shine!

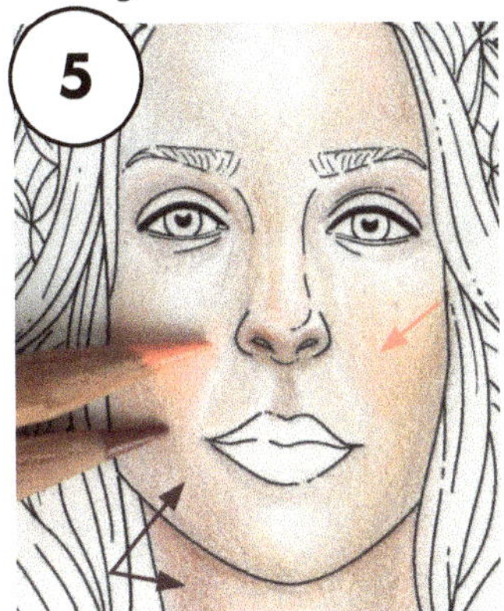

Now I am giving her rosy cheeks with more 571. I add more plus a little 866 Burnt Sienna 50% to her lower face and sides of her neck.

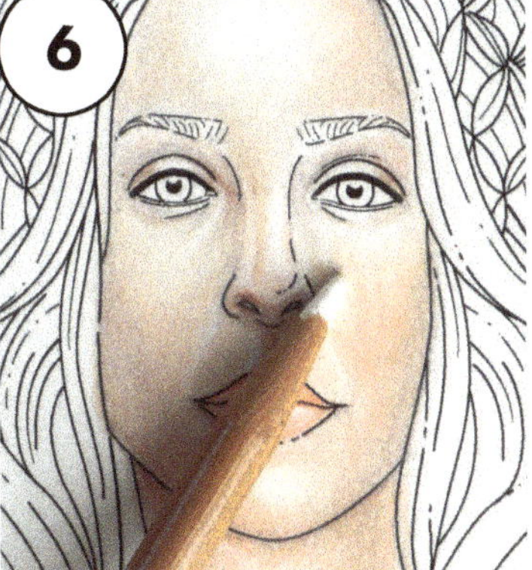

I really smooth everything out and blend it all with 001 White. I take time to blend one area into another and it really polishes the look of her skin.

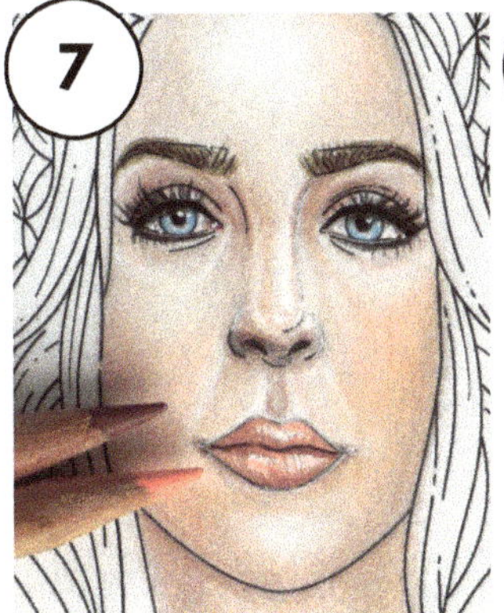

866 helps to define the ridges of the lips while 571 is used to fill them, except for a highlight I left white. These colors are also on her eyelids. The "Baby Blue Eye" color combo was added here.

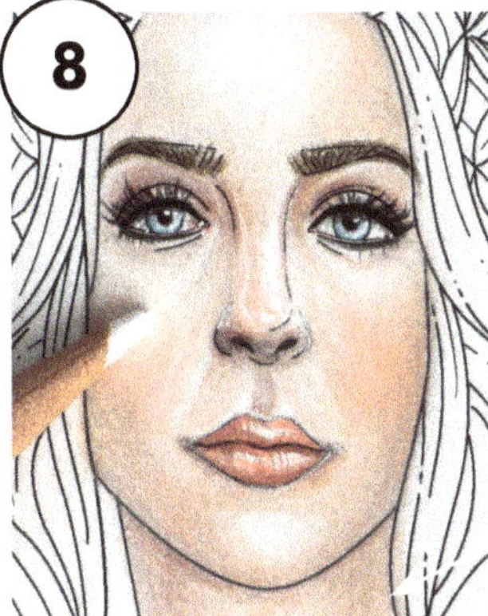

Finally, 001 is used once more to lighten everything and to strengthen the highlights. I push a little harder to make this overall skin tone a lighter one.

Neutral Tone

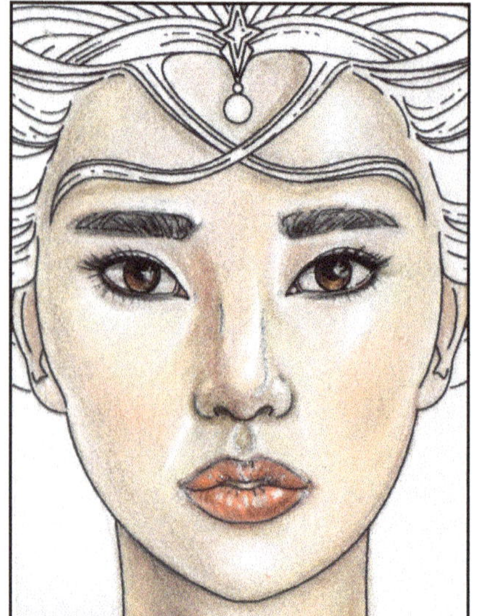

You will need:
- The Portrait Practice line art page
- Caran D'Ache Luminance: 732, 846, 872, 862, 866, 571, 242, 065, 001
- White Signo Uniball gel pen
- Optional Mono Zero eraser

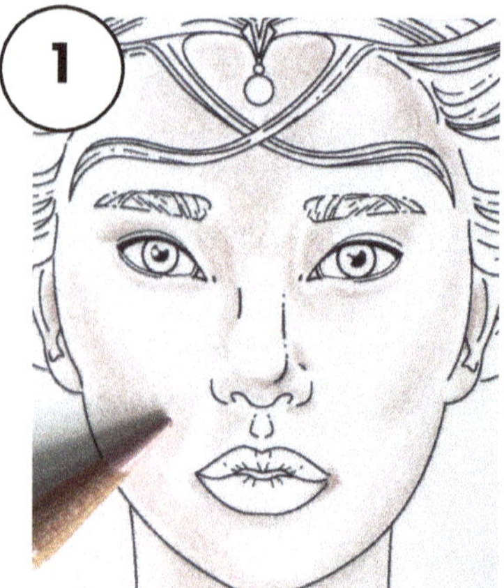

Before starting, a few things to think about:

I use a very light hand for every step and leave a few paper-white highlights. Use a Mono Zero eraser if you mess up or want to add more highlights! Add more 846 and 732 for a more distinct olive complexion!

I begin using a 862 Burnt Sienna 10% to carve in the features. I add shadow under the cheeks and the tip of the nose; in the central part of the forehead; under the eyes and eye brows; under the lower lip; in the corners of the mouth, and along the jawline and under the chin, onto the neck.

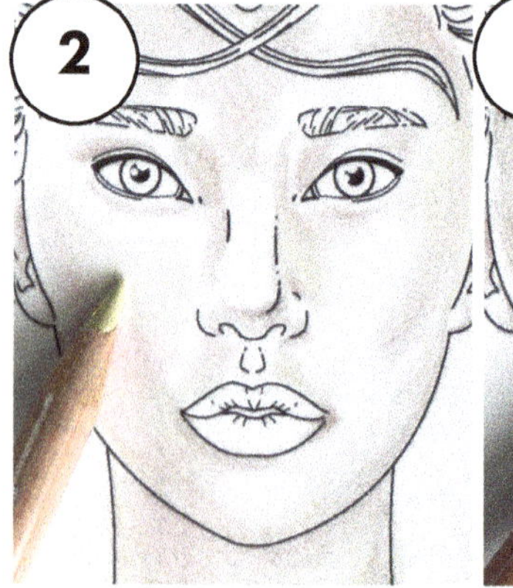

Now I use 732 Olive Brown 10% above the cheeks, on the right side of the nose, above the mouth, the right temple and both sides of the neck.

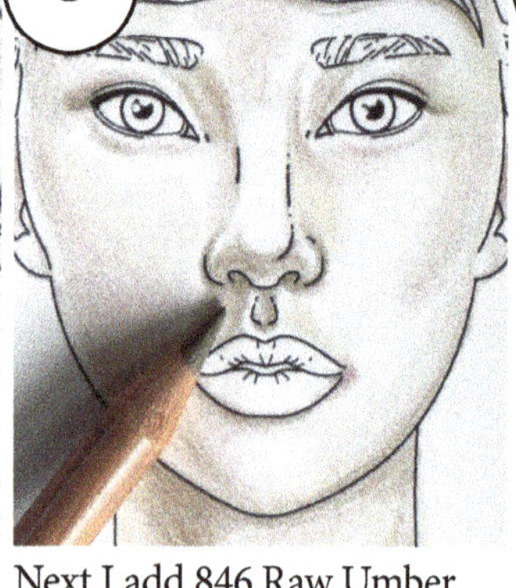

Next I add 846 Raw Umber 50% to deepen around and under the tip of the nose and the locks of hair, the eyelids, the left side of the neck, and the Philtrum (notch above the lip).

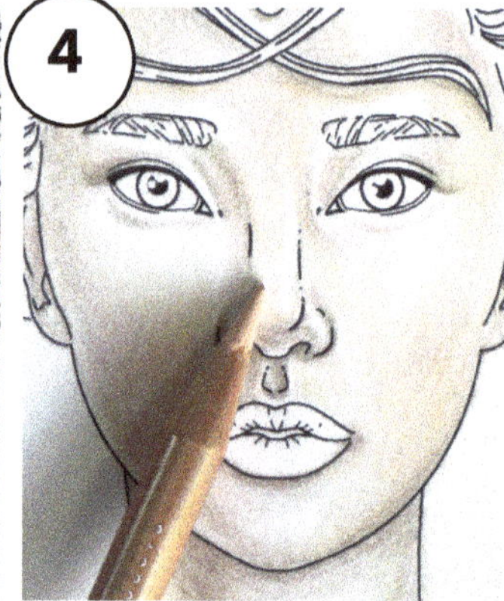

Now I add color to the bridge of the nose with 872 Burnt Ochre 10%. I also use it to blend and smooth all of the other colors, leaving only a bit of white showing as highlights.

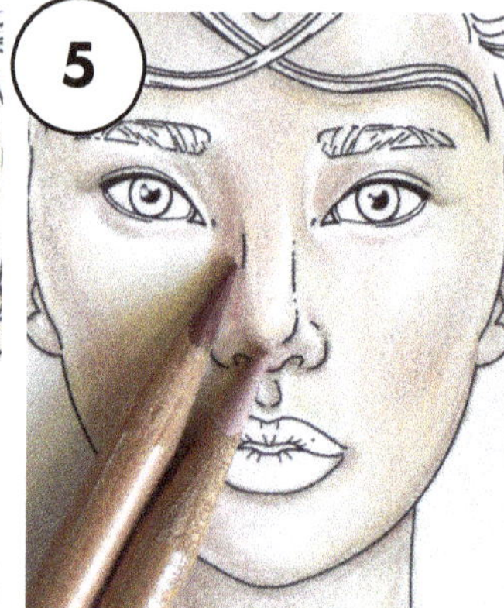

Now I add another layer of 862 under the tip of the nose, temples and in between the eyes mixed with a little 866 Burnt Sienna 50%, also darkening the left side of the nose.

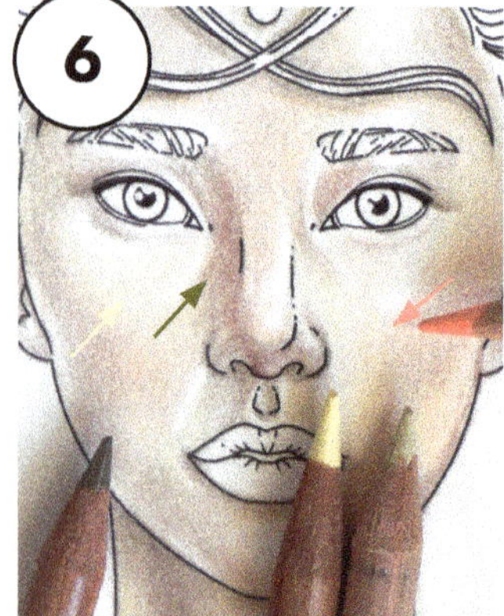

I cool shadows with 846 and blend edges with 732. I add a touch of 571 Anthraquinoid Pink to cheeks and blend all with 242 Primrose.

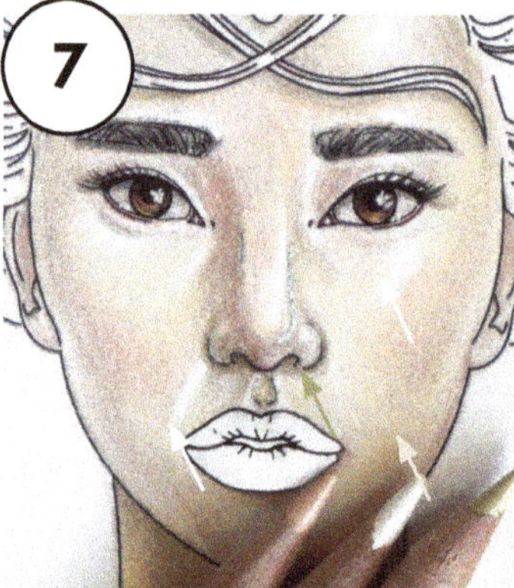

Another round of 872 is used everywhere, followed by 732 on the shadows to smooth them. I use 001 White to add highlights. The "Dark Brown Eye" tutorial is utilized here. Turn back a few pages!

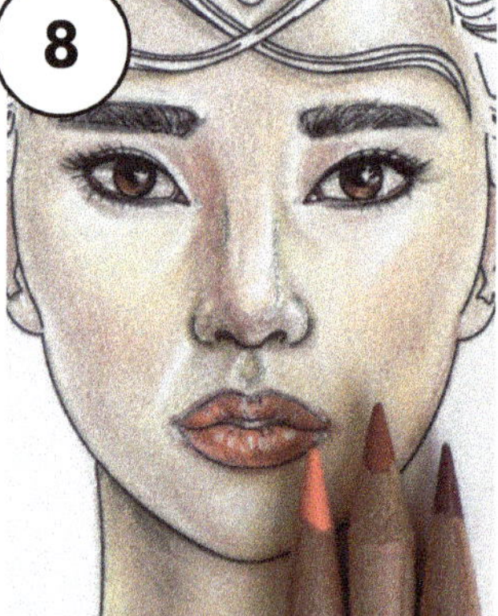

866 Burnt Sienna 50% is used to define the ridges of the lips. 571 and 065 Russet are used to fill them, except a highlight on the bottom lip.

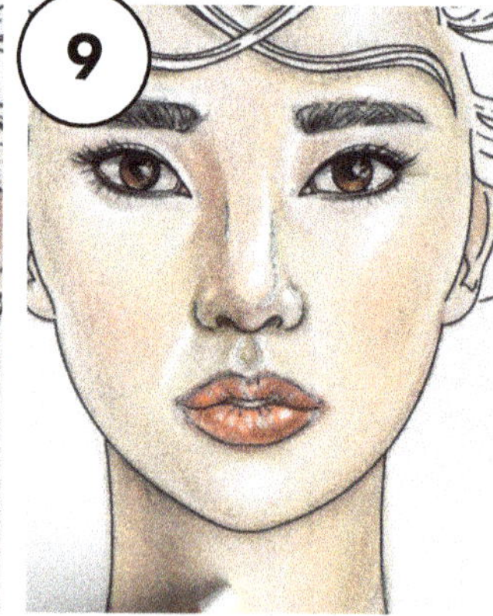

001 is used once more to smooth all transitions on the face and neck. Add highlights, if needed, by erasing with a Mono Zero eraser.

Warm Tone 1

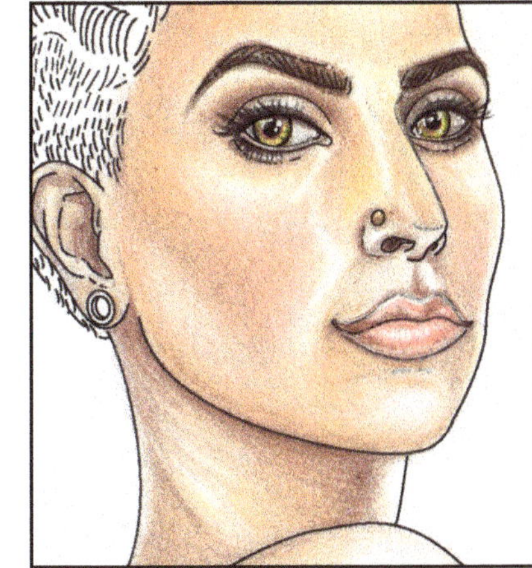

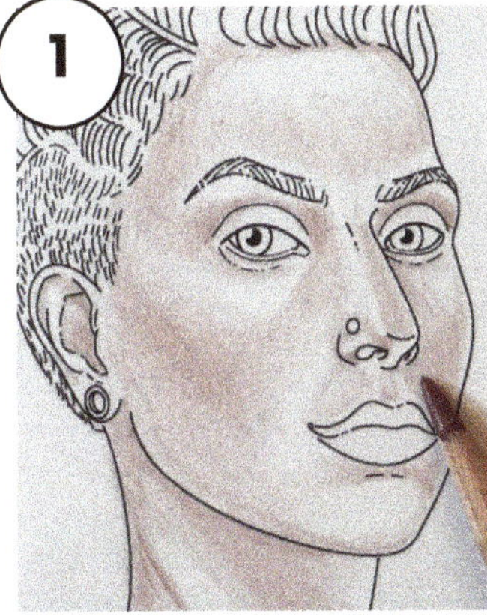

1 I work out all of the mid-tone/shadow areas in one color, 866 Burnt Sienna 50% – I carve in the cheek bones, the creases of her eyelids, the shadow under the hairline and from the jawline on to her neck, and between her lips and chin – all with a very light hand.

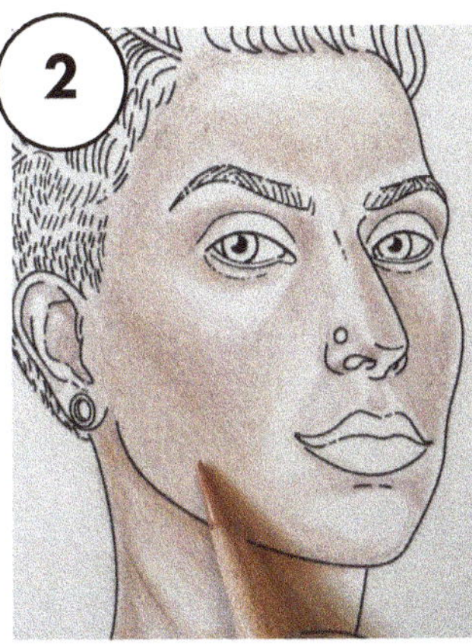

2 Then I add a little warmth all around with a layer of 876 Burnt Ochre 50%, darkest on the neck.

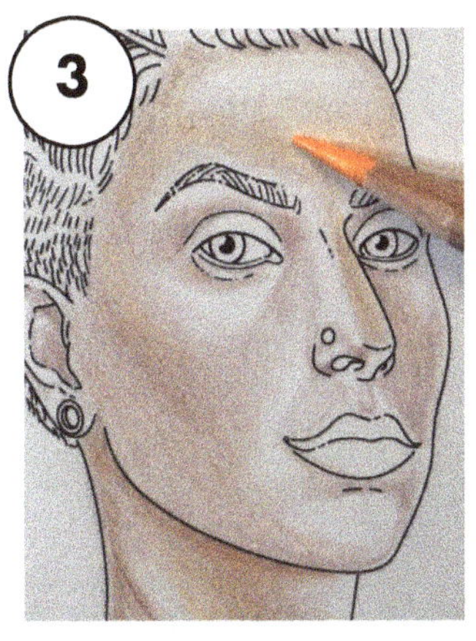

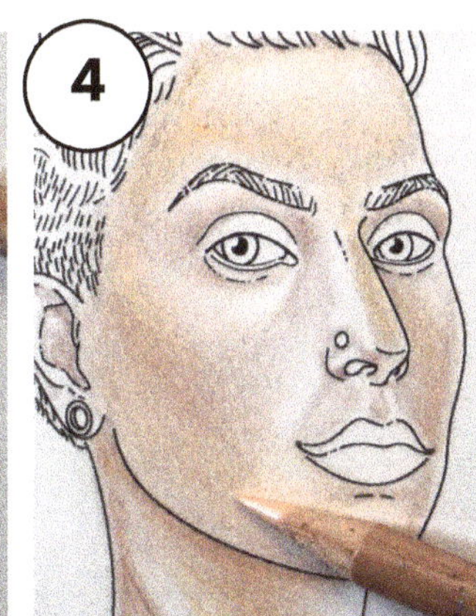

3-4: I use a light coating of 030 Orange on her brow bone, the bridge of her nose, temple and cheeks. I go through my first round of blending the face with a layer of 872 Burnt Ochre 10% to get rid of some of the paper texture. I fill the area under her eyes (but leaving a little white paper showing).

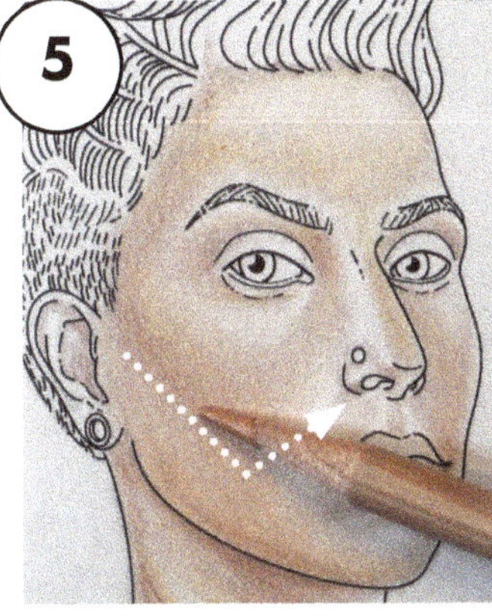

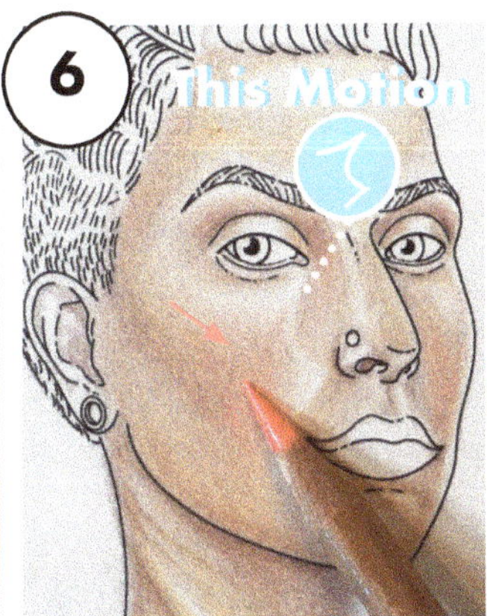

5-6: Then I spread the 876 in a V shape, from the side of her nose downwards to the center of the cheek and back up to the top of the cheekbone. I use some 571 Anthraquinoid Pink on the apples of her cheeks, temple, eyelids, nose and neck. (Optional) I create a white vertical soft zig-zag with my Mono Zero Eraser Pen (not shown), to the left of her nose, to give her skin a glow.

7 I continue deepening with 866 vertically under the chin, on her neck, and use it very sparingly on her cheekbone, the corners of her mouth (and seen in Step 8 to line her lips) along with 876 in the creases of her eyelids.

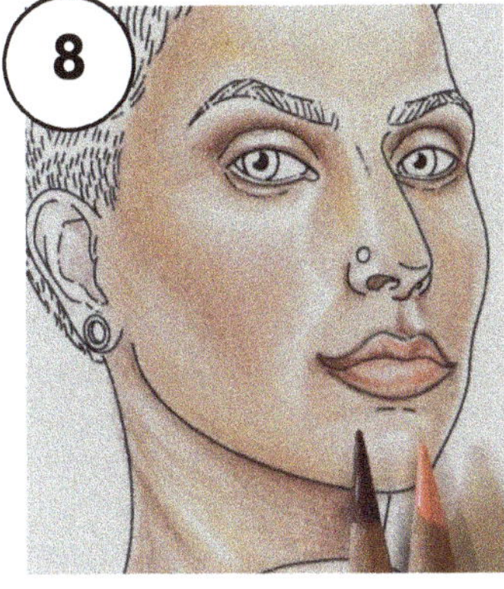

8 I then add 571 to the upper eyelids, hairline and bottom of the chin. I fill in the lips too, concentrating the color on the bottom part, using vertical strokes to define the ridges. I use Burnt Sienna 069 in creases of the face for a final deepening!

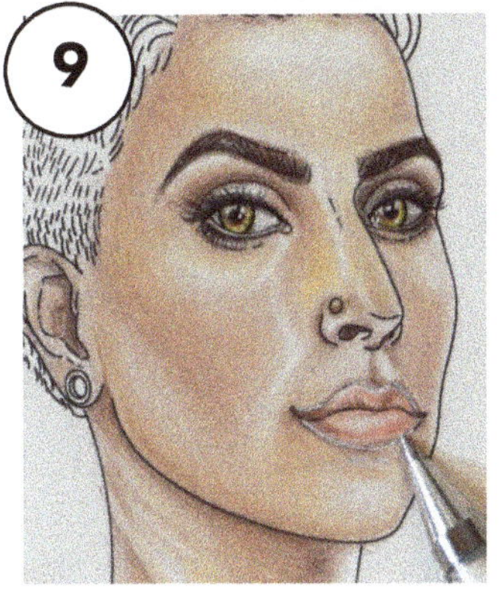

9 I then go back to 876 and 872 to blend everything, round two (not shown) after adding the "Gold-Green Eye" colors (from the "It's All in the Eyes" page). If you need more eye help see Volume 1! I use a white gel pen to "erase" black lines and add highlights to the eyes and lips.

You will need:
- The Portrait Practice line art page
- Copic Marker E30 Bisque or TouchNew 132 Milky White
- Caran D'Ache Luminance: 876, 069, 836, 030, 571, 862, 866, 001
- White gel pen and optional kneaded eraser

To go deeper than this, use another layer of the darkest colors in the shadow areas and increase the value of the midtones – the highlights will stand out more!

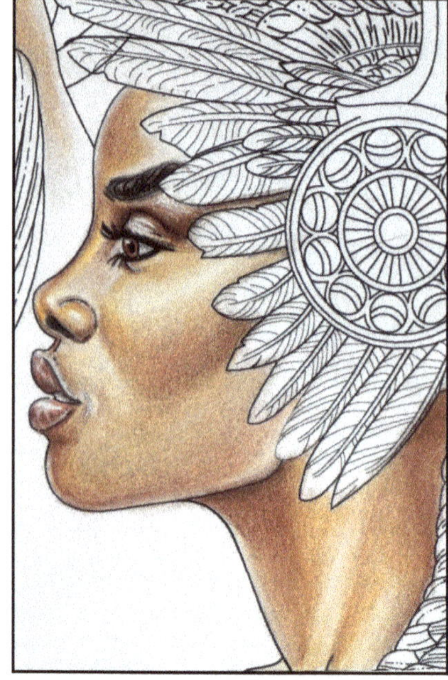

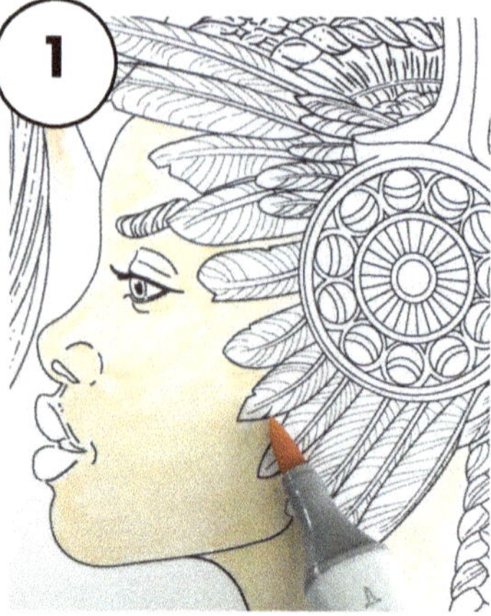

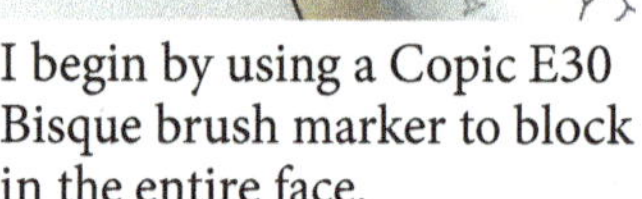

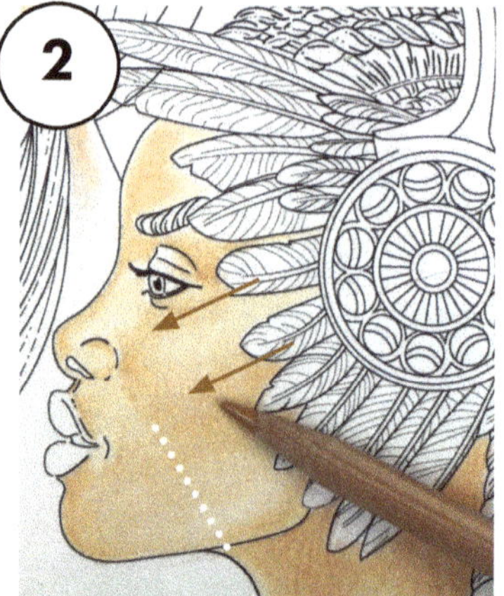

I use a light coat of 876 Burnt Ochre 50% to carve in the details of her face: the front of her forehead, in the creases of her eyes, on the bridge of her nose and edge of her nostril, under

1. I begin by using a Copic E30 Bisque brush marker to block in the entire face.

2. and on top of her cheekbone. I end the gradation as a diagonal that runs parallel to her neck, and I go darkest under her chin – on her neck.

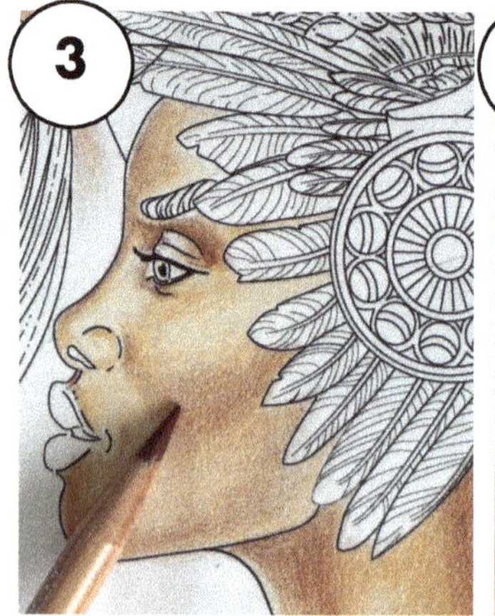

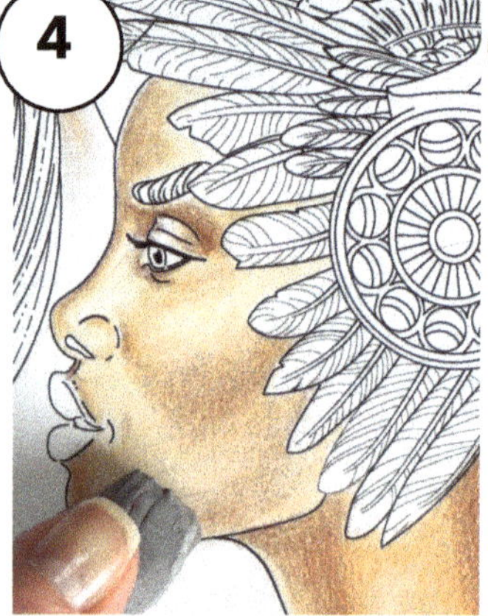

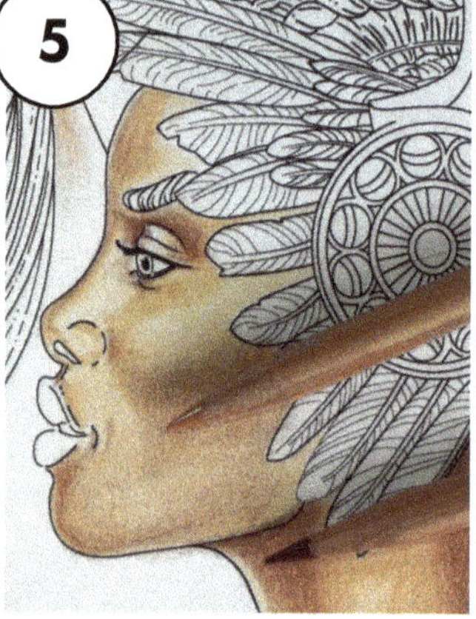

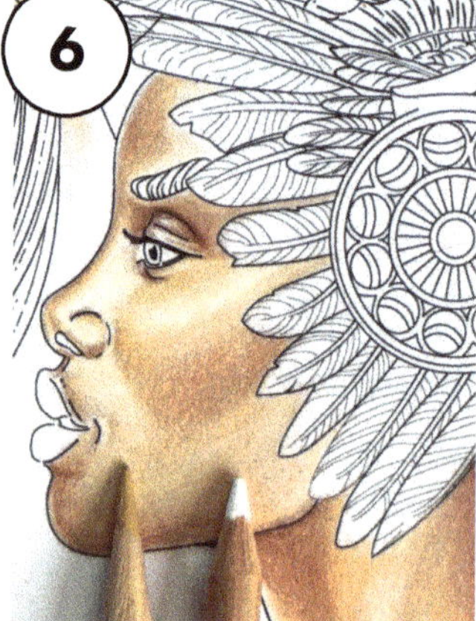

3. I then use a feather light layer of Burnt Sienna 069 to deepen the shadows under the cheekbone, in the eyelid crease, on her chin, forehead and neck.

4. This color is much darker than the last, so since I've gone a little heavy I am "pulling" some off along her jawline with a kneaded eraser.

5. Now I add an even layer of 876 to her face to deepen the color and smooth the texture. I also add more 069 on the front and back of her neck.

6. I use 836 Brown Ochre 50% to blend any grainy areas. I blend with 001 White on top of her cheeks, under her nostril and on the edge of her jaw.

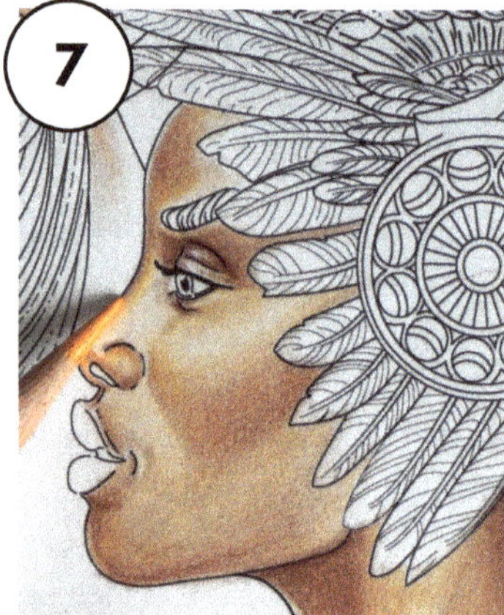

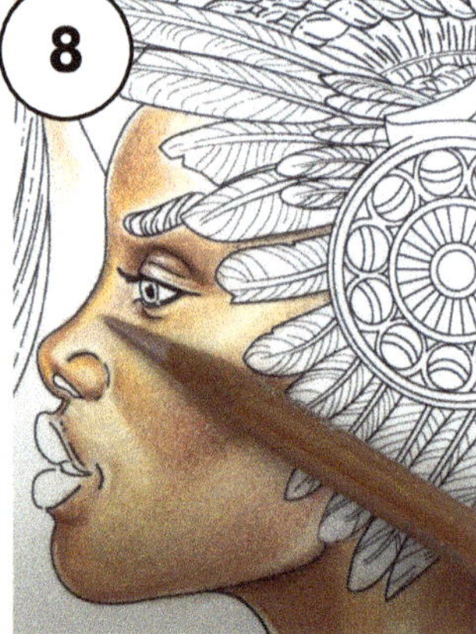

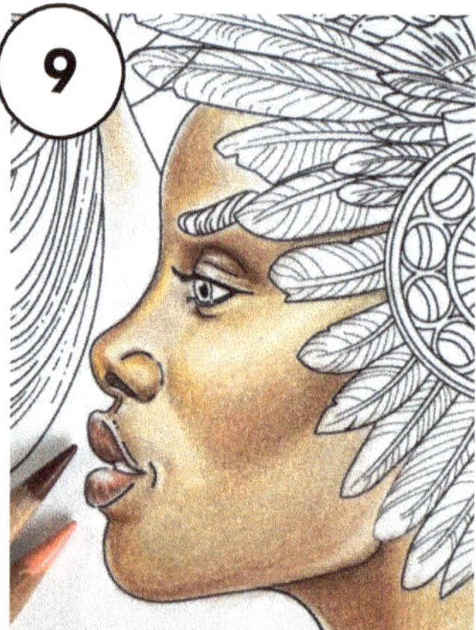

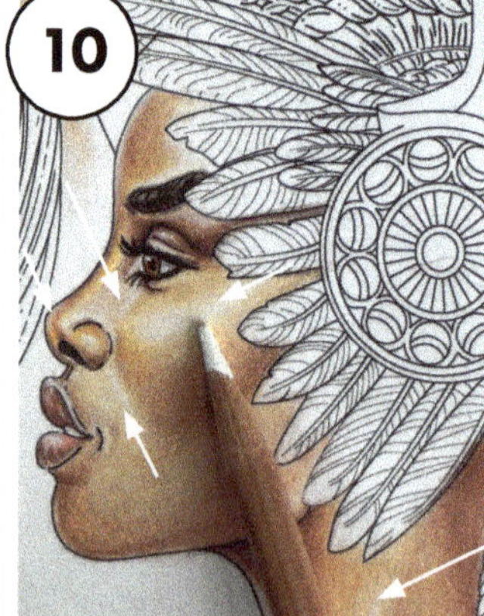

7. Subtle accents in tiny amounts: 030 Orange on her nose – bridge, tip and nostril – and 571 Anthraquinoid Pink on the apple of her cheek.

8. 862 Burnt Sienna 10% is used on the side of her nose and also to blend the gradations on her neck until they are smooth.

9. 866 Burnt Sienna 50% is used to define the ridges of the lips with curved vertical strokes. 571 is used to fill them, except a highlight on the bottom lip.

10. 001 is used again to pump up the highlights. I've also used a white gel pen (see final) to cover some of the lines and add sparkle to her brow bone.

Glowing & Theatrical Skin Tones

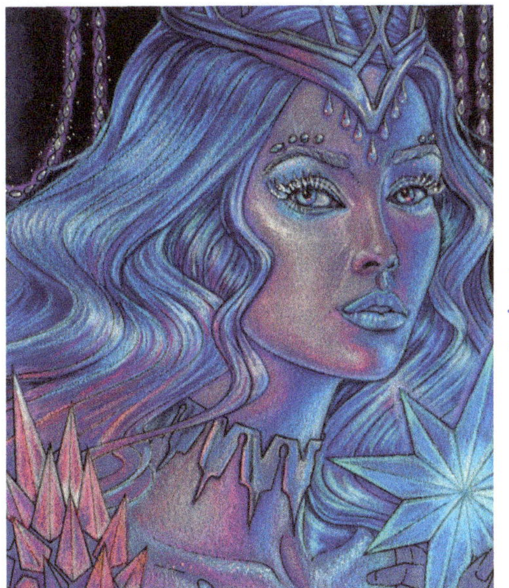

Here I will cover the basics of dramatic lighting with skin tones, but because of the complexity of this portrait, it's impossible to show every step of the process. I suggest that you watch my purchasers-only YouTube video that outlines the skin, hair and crystals (link in back of book). This method uses colored paper and two light sources! I chose acid-free Canson Mi-Teintes paper which is often used with pastels. Canson offers smoother paper too – Colorline. Strathmore's is called Artagain, and there is yet another called PastelMat. Papers have different textures, so be sure to test them to find one that will work best for you. When working on dark paper the process is a little different – layering towards lightness. It works best with waxy, opaque pencils.

You will need:

- Prismacolor Premier 919, 1014, 1038, 956, 1008, 933, 903,1077
- Luminance White 001, Verithin Black (or other hard pencil)
- "Crystal Queen" line art (on real or faux toned Royal Blue paper)
- Gel pens, Uniball Signo White & neon pink/blue for shimmer (Lolliz)

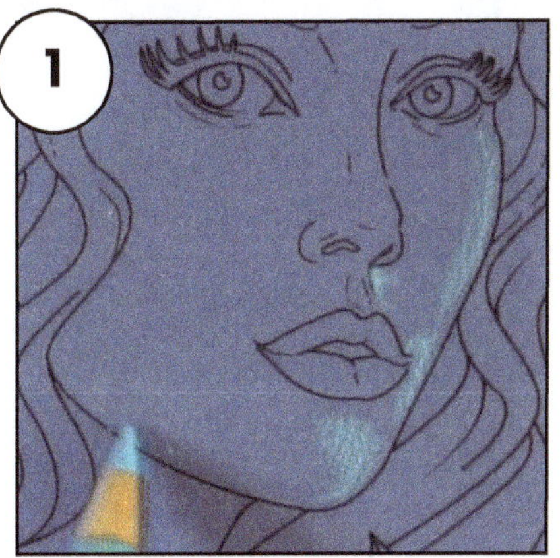

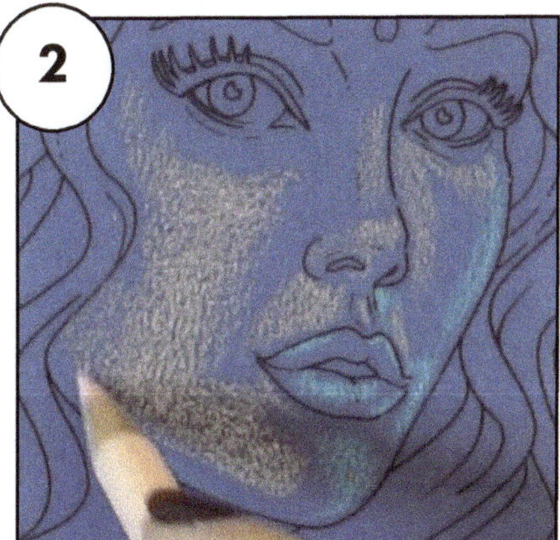

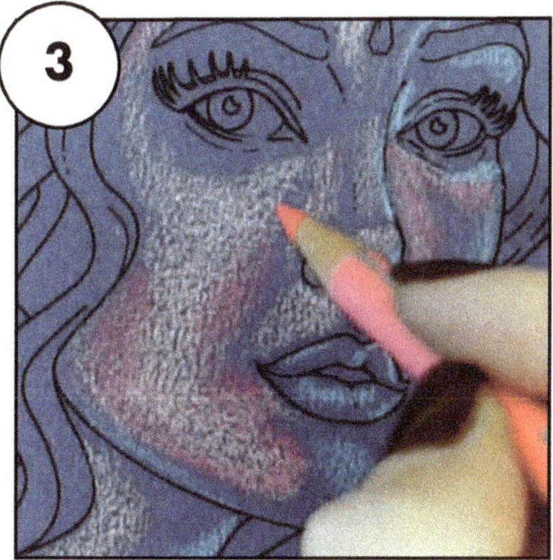

Because this paper is dark, I start out by creating highlight areas on the far side of the face (see Steps 2-3) with 919 Non-Photo Blue where the blue light source would hit. This will include some quick highlights on the lips too.

I create a large shape in 1014 Deco Pink mostly along the close side of the cheek into the jaw towards the chin. I cover the tip of nose (and the close side of the nose and neck – seen in Step 3). I'm using light circular and directional strokes.

I then create a glowing edge of Neon Pink 1038 around the large 1014 shape on the closer cheek and a little on the left part of the other cheek. The texture looks grainy right now, and that's normal.

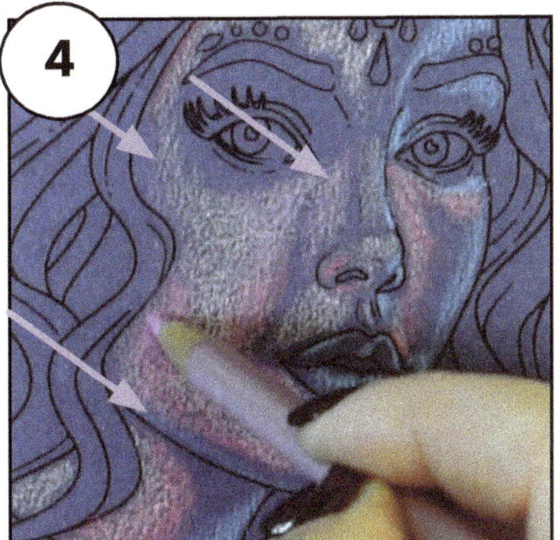

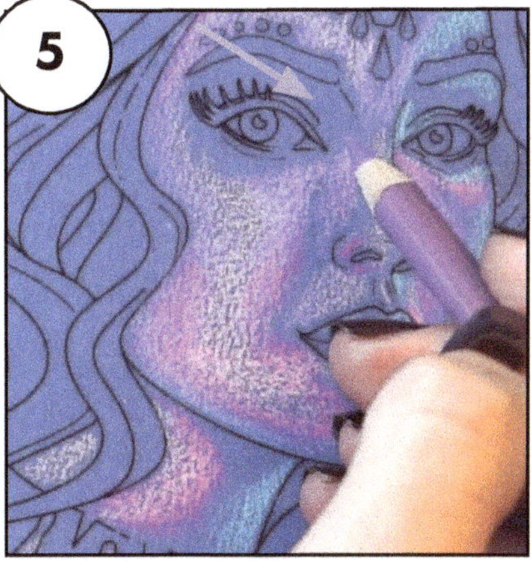

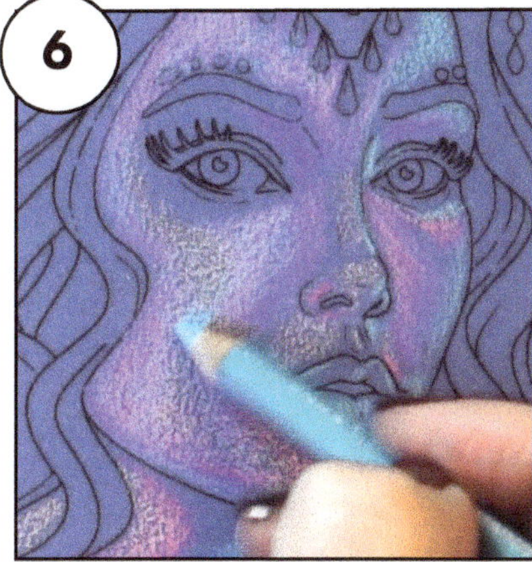

Now I blend over the side of the nose and the cheek area edges into the hairline and jawline with Lilac 956, working my way around the very edge of the face, with a thin stroke of "reflected light."

1008 Parma Violet is a medium violet that is used on the inner corners of the upper eyelids, where they meet the bridge of the nose, down the side of the nose, over the lighter tones.

919 is used again here to "cool down" the overall Deco Pink and plug up some of the paper tooth.

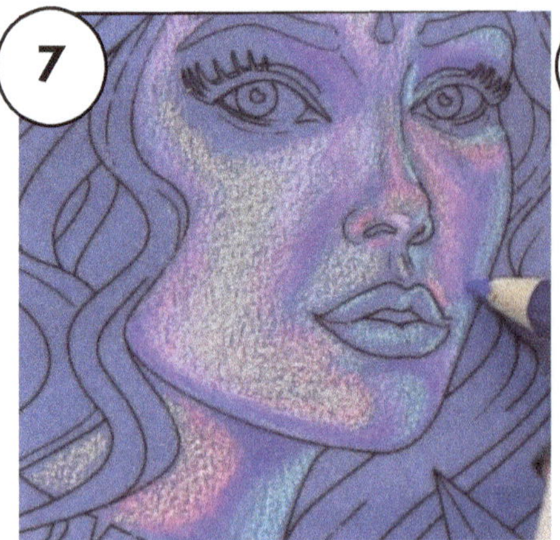

7 Next, 933 Violet Blue is used to darken the core shadows (darkest area between both light source colors). I use a little on far side of face, creases of eye lids, under lips, chin and center of neck.

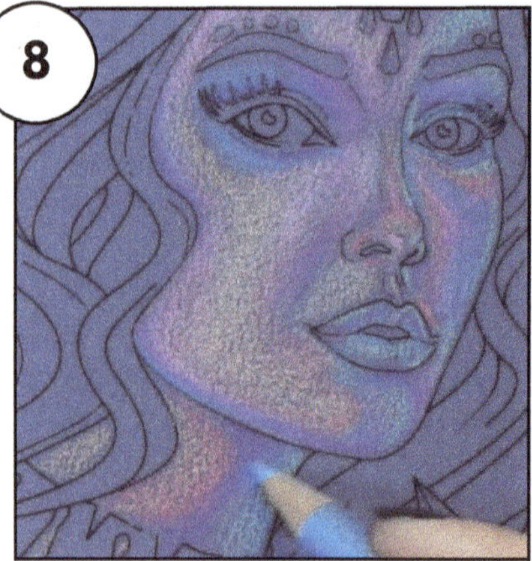

8 I then use 903 True Blue to soften the transition from the dark core shadow into the brightest blue. I add a little to the top and bottom lips and around the eyes as blue eye shadow!

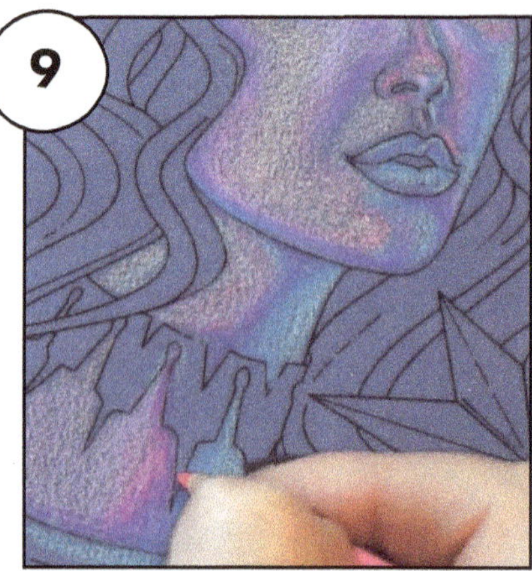

9 Moving downward I extend these colors into the neck, blend back and forth LIGHTLY to get a smoother texture. I've also added a few pink bits to the nose since Step 6.

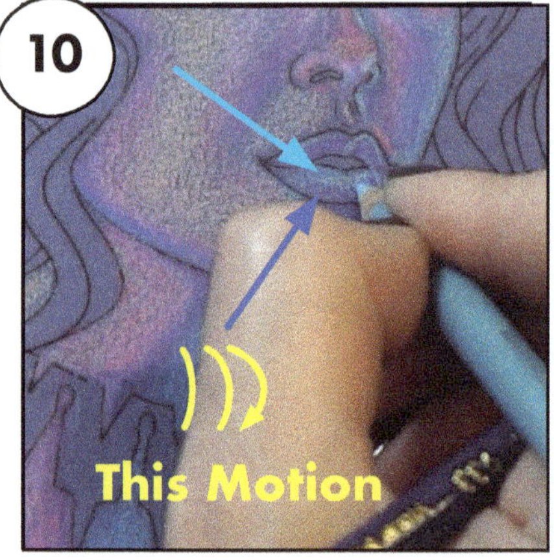

10 Now it's time to add little details – two colors! I add lines on lips using swift downward motions. The 903 on top and the 933 on the bottom. I also emphasize the far side cheek edge and brighten the eye makeup with a second coat of Non-Photo Blue.

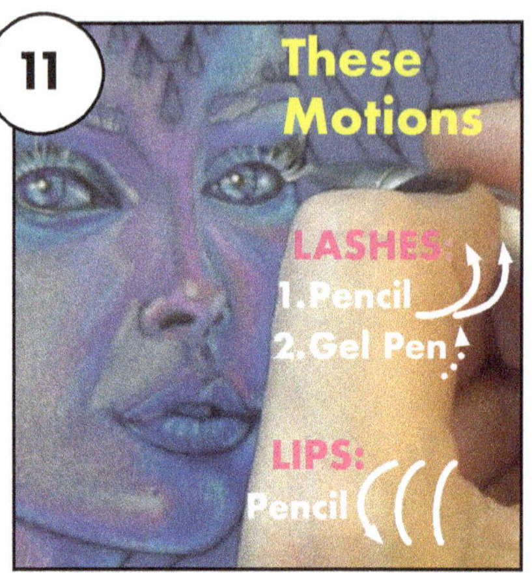

11 Although it isn't shown here, I used the White Luminance to create lashes, brows and to brighten the cheek reflection, tip of nose and lips. I add some flair and sparkle with a white gel pen, DOTTING over the ends of a few of the lashes, and the brow bones, below the eyebrows (next pic).

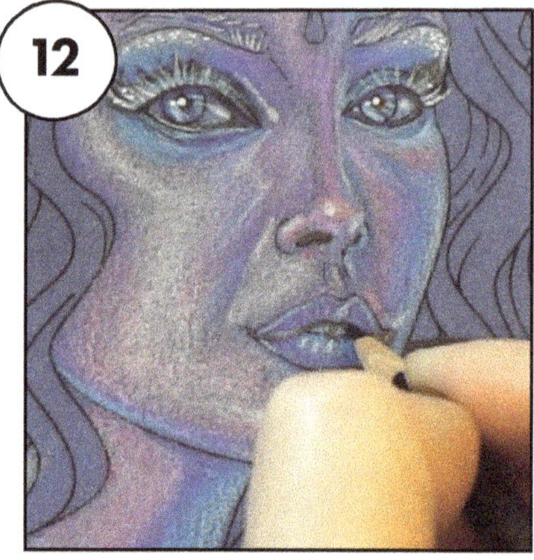

12 The final steps are to use a Black hard pencil, such as Verithin, to add darks to nostrils and inside the mouth and between some strands of hair. I use my 1077 Colorless Blender in small circles (not shown) to smooth everything out and I add definition around all features, as needed. In the detail below you can see use of neon gel pens.

Details for Hair & Eyes

Neon Gels: Brow Bone

White Gel: Lash Ends/ Pupil Highlight

933/ 919: Iris

Lumi 001: White Eye Reflection/ Lashes and Inner Corners of Eyelid

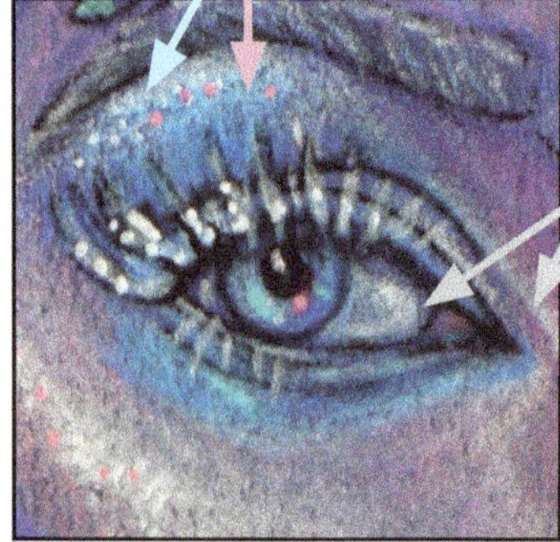

Lumi 001: Highlights in Hair

933: Shadows in Hair

919: Light-Tones

903: Mid-Tones

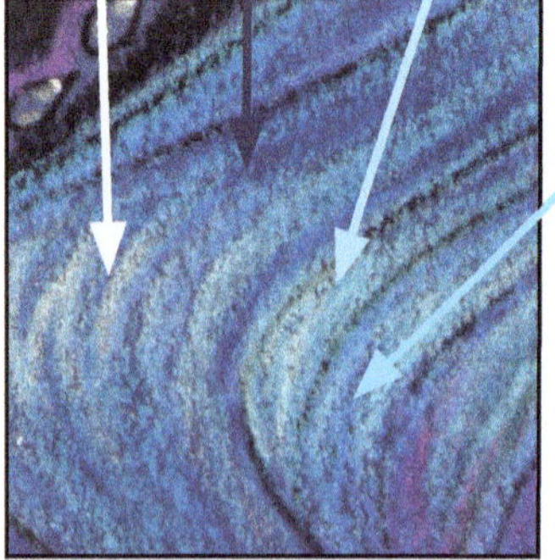

Did you know?

Use harder pencils such as Polychromos and Verithins for fine details such as separate strands of hair, but if you don't have them use a sharp waxy pencil HELD vertically to achieve a sharper line). Canson's paper has two sides and I've chosen the finer texture. On a budget? You can also use individually sold sheets of cardstock from Hobby Lobby!

See the "Advanced Blending Techniques" information in Chapter 1 and "Hacks" in Chapter 2.

One of the beauties of greyscale is in the subtle tonal shifts and the fact that there are no "outlines" showing! To preserve the nuances in the original drawing or photograph — don't overdo it! Consciously remind yourself not to outline the background areas with harsh line. You may even want to emphasize the "depth of field" (like in a photograph) by creating a less "in focus" background. There are several ways to do this: by using fuzzy soft strokes over the background with pencil, or by using PanPastels (or scraping chalk pastels with an X-acto knife) only in those areas. One thing to be aware of – you are coloring over gray. This has a tendency to dull your colors. Use vibrant colors if you want intensity. Also, you may want to use a marker base or add solvent to your pencils to pump up the saturation to its brightest, but remember to use caution when coloring in a book!

Greyscale Tips

- Choose high quality greyscale art wisely. Look for images made of light greys and almost no 100% black

- Choose your supplies: pencil only; pencils + blender or solvent; marker under pencil; Pencil + PanPastel...

- Start with lightest colors first followed by each slightly darker variation. Quickly block in general areas without too much detail, whether pencil or marker. When including pencil, add light strokes with a sharp pencil, and gradually add darker ones, building up the layers.

- Be sure to constantly clean your blender marker/stump if you use one. Otherwise you will contaminate neighboring colors on your page or smudge the line art ink

-Determine a focal point (*emphasis*) in the image. Use crisp line/contrast to draw attention to those areas

Which Will You Choose? There's More Than Just Pencils

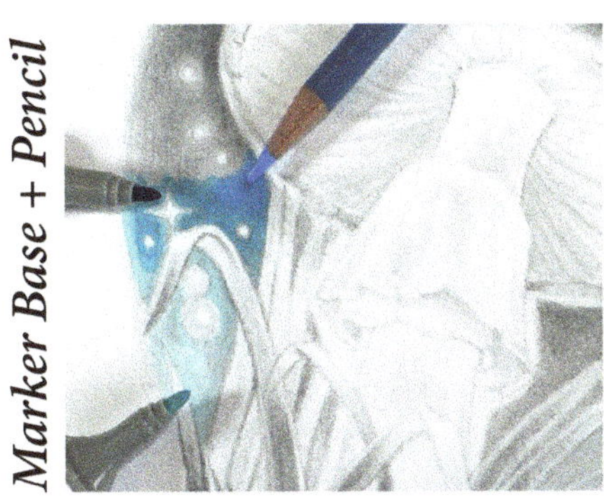
Marker Base + Pencil

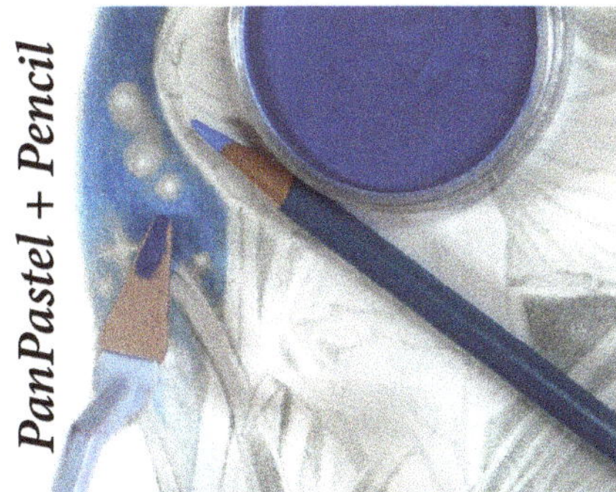
PanPastel + Pencil

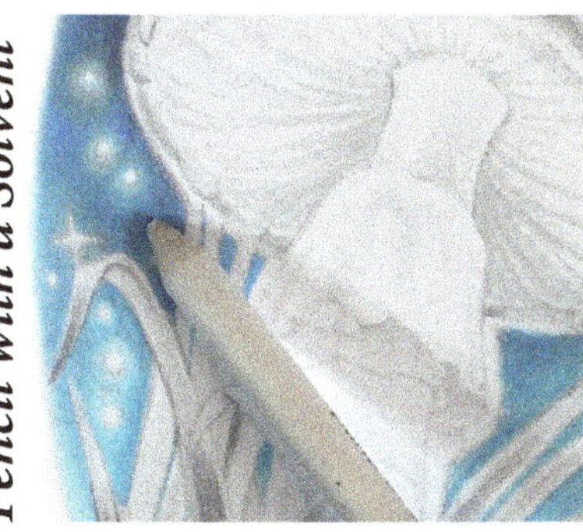
Pencil with a Solvent

Glowing Mushie

For this project I will demonstrate using colored pencils plus a solvent, Bio-Shield, stored in a jam jar (thanks to my friend Lique for reminding me of this hack). It's environmentally friendly and made in the U.S.A. (See the Resource Guide for a link to an inexpensive sample). It works really well to create super-intense color with Prismacolor pencils. There is a similar product made in the UK called Zest-It. Both are made with the same main ingredient – Orange Oil.

You will need:

-The Glowing Greyscale Mushie line art page
-Prismacolor Premier: 992, 903, 103, 901, 935, 1036, 1035, 1002, 916, 1038, 933, 1035, 908 + White Luminance + optional Indigo Verithin
-Mineral spirits or a solvent, such as Bio-Shield or Gamsol
- A tortillion or blending stump

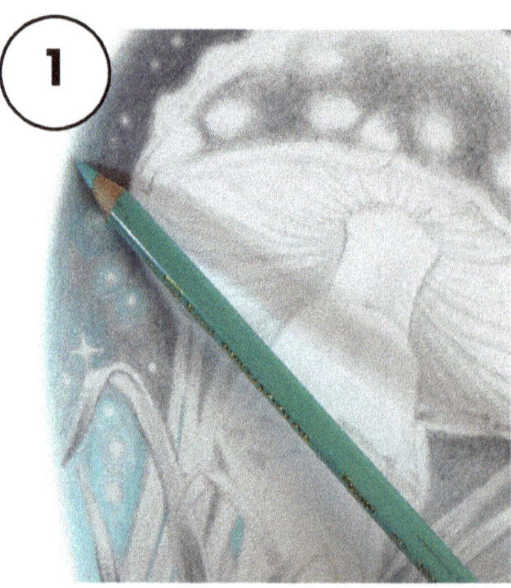

I start out using 992 Light Aqua directionally over the lightest areas and edges of the entire background with a thin coat. I circle around the stars over the entire image.

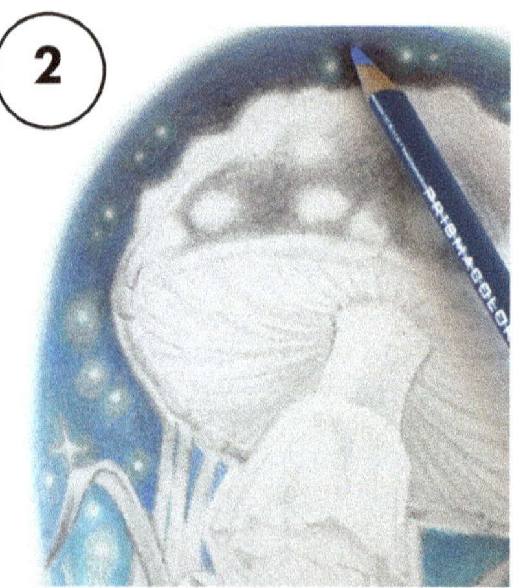

Next, from about mid-mushroom up, I use 903 True Blue to go around the mushroom itself and in between the stars.

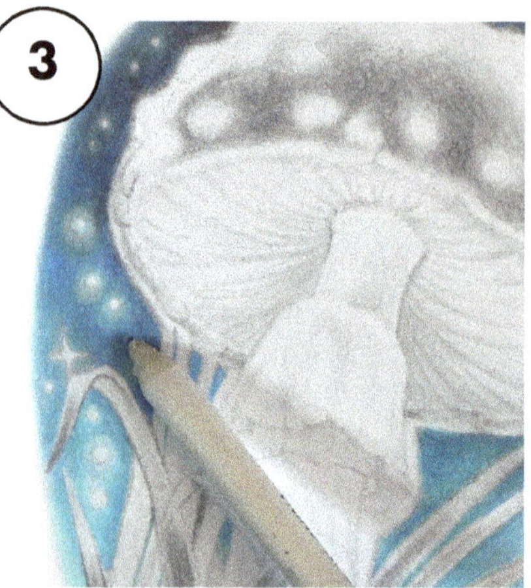

Now it's time to blend! I'm using Bio-Shield today. See the Resource Guide for info. I use a blending stump and just a little solvent on the end to rub over the pencil.

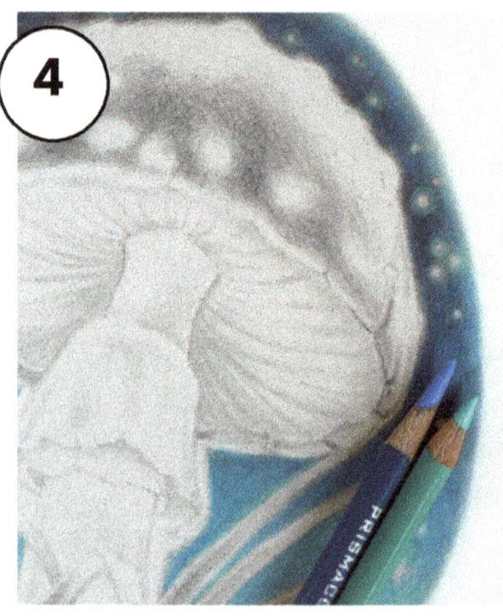

Because the solvent spreads the color into the paper tooth, I go over it again with my 992 and 903, especially around the stars.

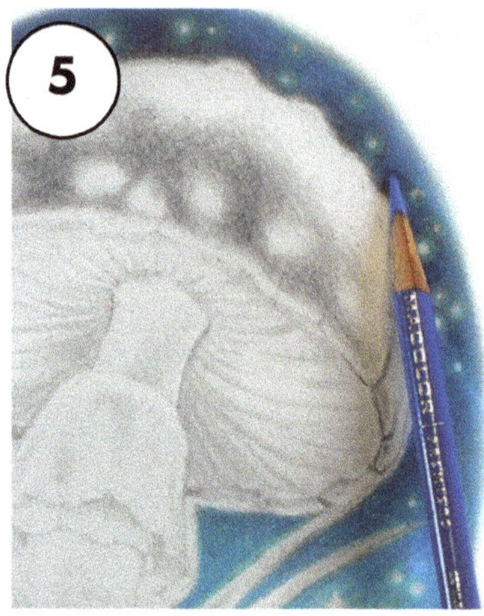

Now I use a little 103 Cerulean Blue on the top half of the background in between all of the stars. This makes it less turquoise.

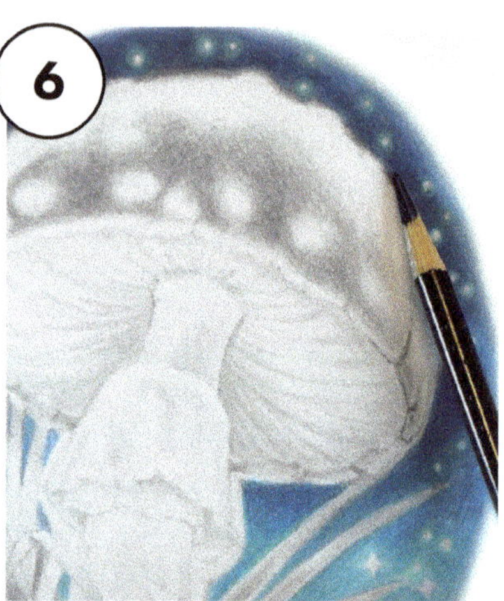

I deepen my blues with 901 Indigo Blue towards the top portion of the image, and just around the mushroom cap as I move down.

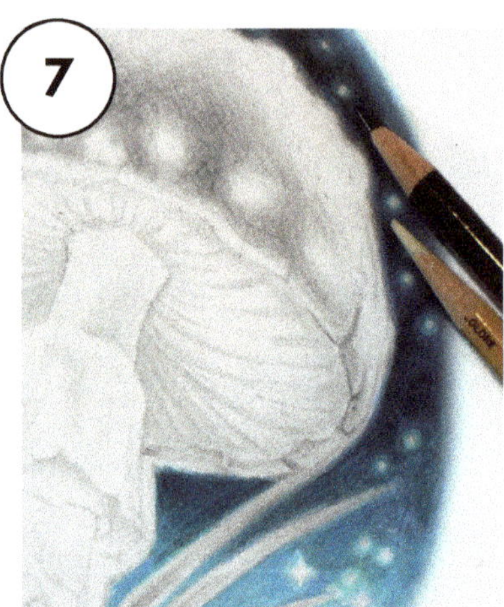

To create a sense of depth, I add 935 Black over the 901 in curved hatching motions in between the stars, but leaving a little space. I use a colorless blender to smooth.

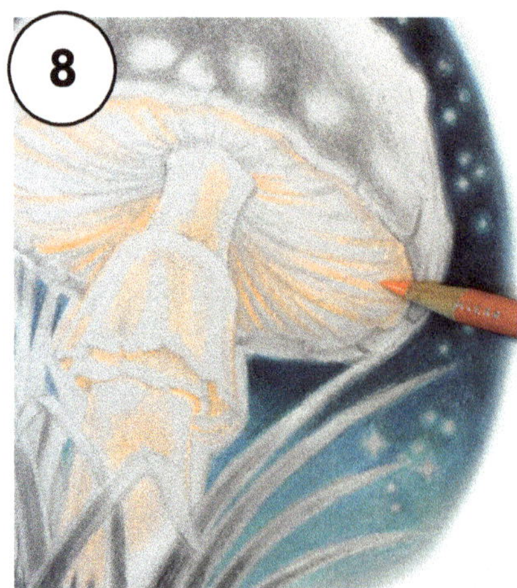

Now I can start the mushroom! I use 1036 Neon Orange on most of the back "gills", in the center of the stem, along the front edge under the cap and under the "ring" ruffles.

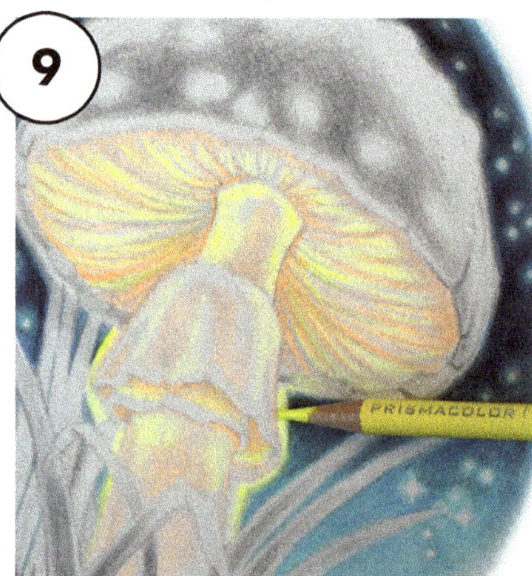

Here is where it really starts to glow! I add 1035 Neon Yellow in between the gills under the cap, on the outside edges of the stem and under the ring. I also add a glow around the mushroom!

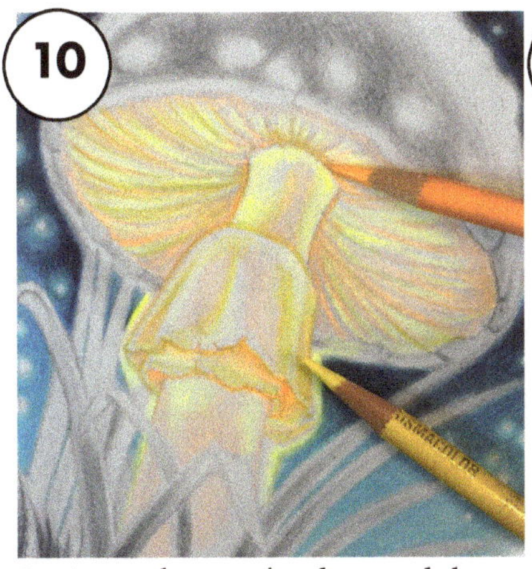

I crispen the stem's edges and the ring's ruffles with 1002 Yellowed Orange. I add 916 Canary Yellow in the creases. I use both to outline the "scales" on the cap (seen in Step 12).

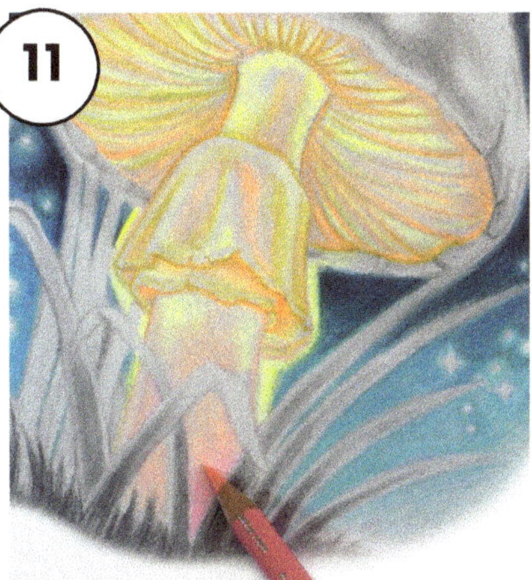

For a little *variety* I use 1038 Neon Pink towards the base of the stem. This will really pop again the complementary green grass.

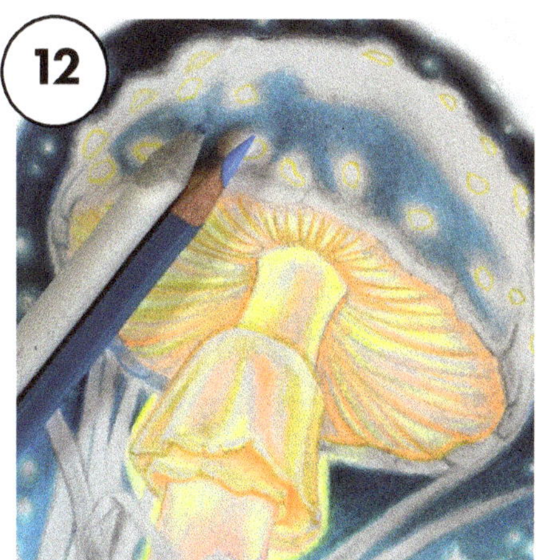

Now I use my 903 again – with some Bio-Shield – over the grey area on the mushroom cap and blend!

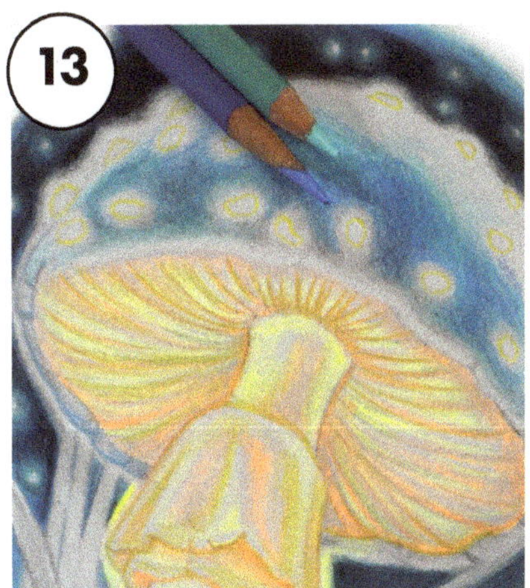

I add some 103 to the bottom of the section I just colored, and some 992 to the top, blending partway into the white of the cap.

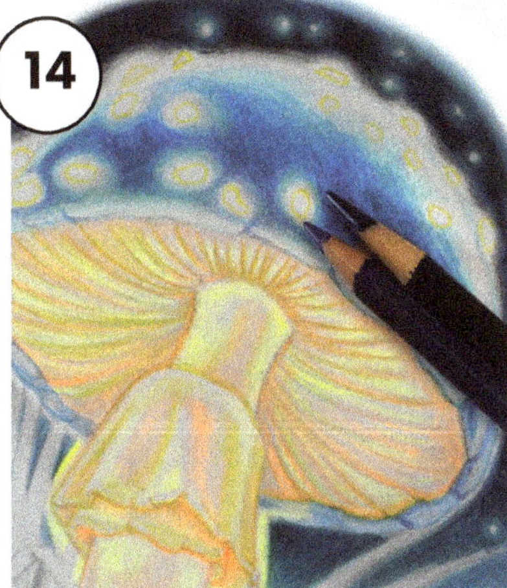

I intensify the color a little with 933 Violet Blue. I create a more pronounced core shadow towards the bottom of the cap, and add details to the cap edges with 901.

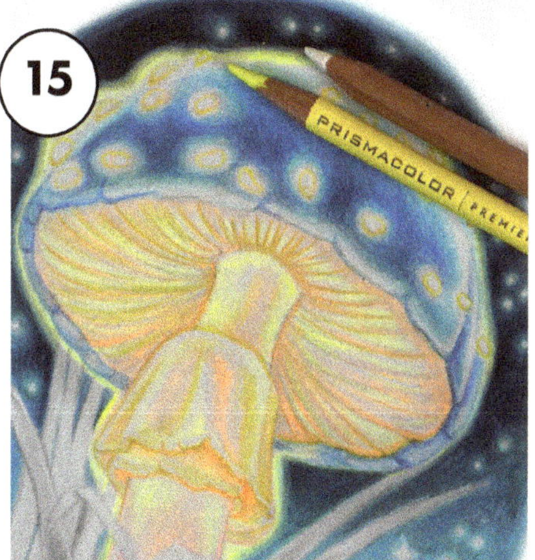

Now I use my 1035 to create the glow around the outside of the mushroom cap and I blend it into the dark sky with my White Luminance pencil.

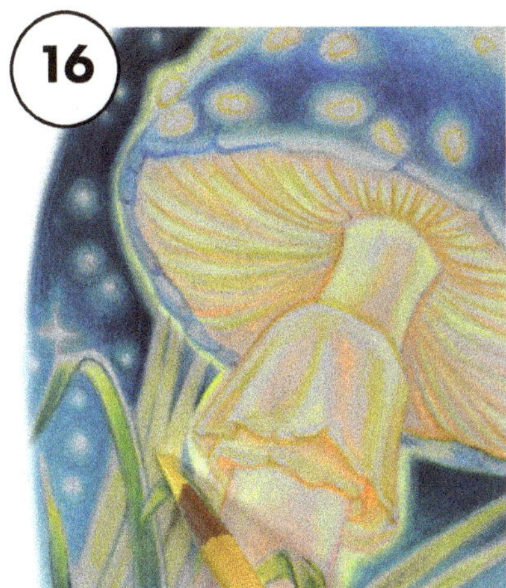

Now I tackle the grass! I use the 1035 on the front blades of grass to illuminate them. The rest are coated in 916 before adding green.

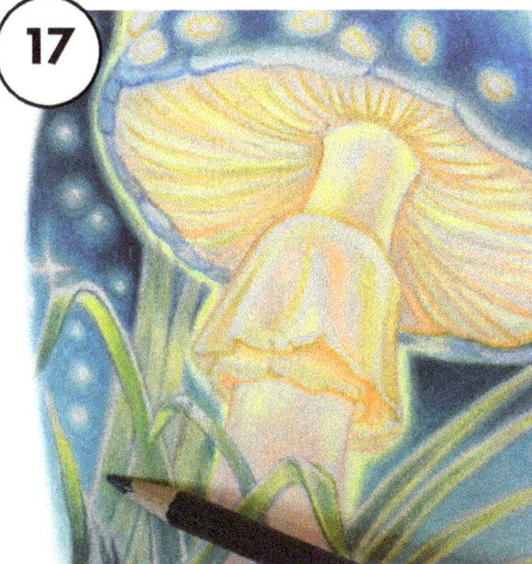

I add 908 Peacock Green to the insides of the front blades and tops and bottoms of the back ones...or where the greyscale art gets darker!

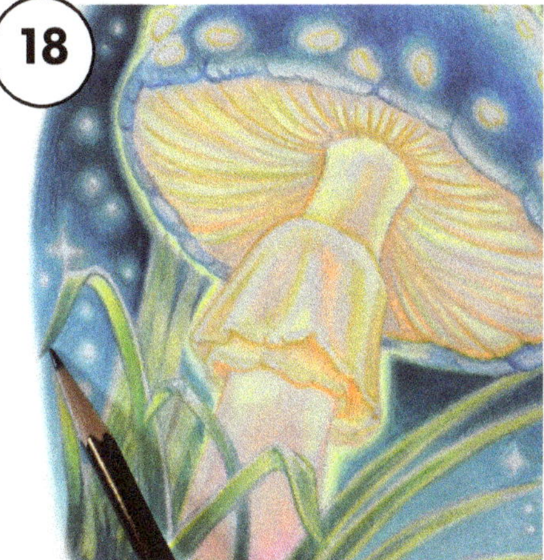

Finally, I sharpen the edges of the very front blades (because objects in the foreground are ususally most in focus) with my Indigo Blue Verithin. :)

Bird of Paradise Flower

You will need:

- The Bird of Paradise line art page
- Copic Marker Y15 (or TouchNew 45) + YG13 (Arrtx 59 is similar)
- Prismacolor Premier pencils: 994, 1007, 920, 918, 922, 907
- White Uniball Signo gel pen (+ optional neon orange gel pen, such as Lolliz)
- Mineral spirits or a solvent such as Bio-Shield or Gamsol and a blending stump
- Luminance pencil 001

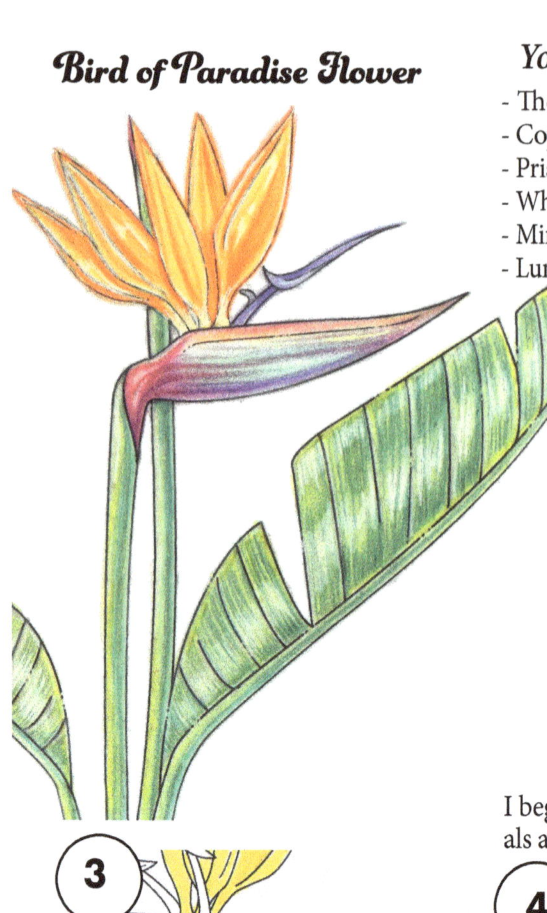

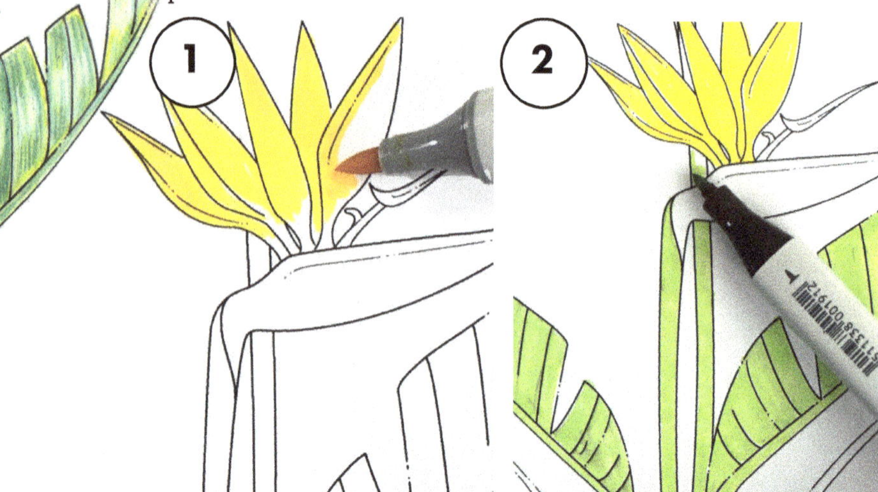

I begin by using a Copic marker Y15 Cadmium Yellow to color all of the petals a solid yellow. I then use YG13 Chartreuse to fill in the stem and leaves.

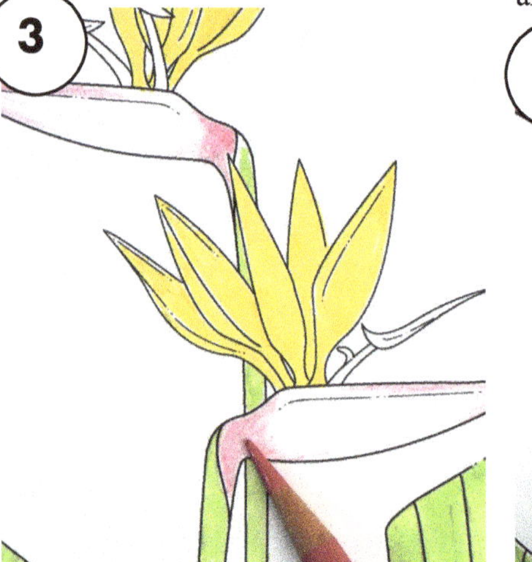

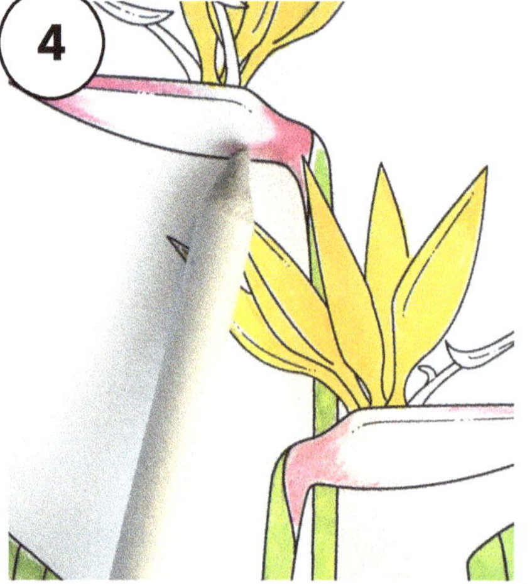

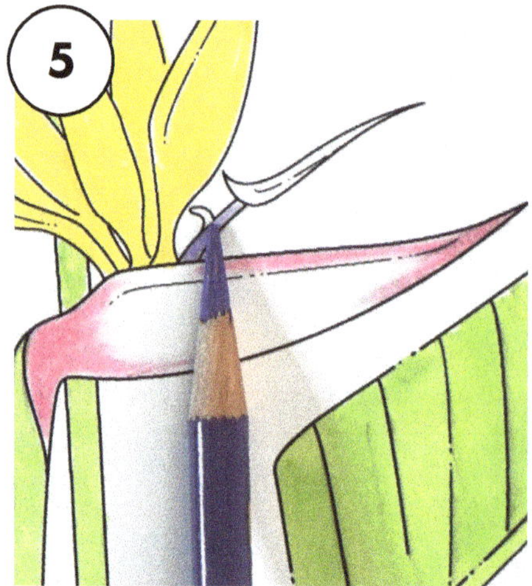

Now I use my 994 Process Red pencil to shade in the left and right edges of the main flowers. I use a single layer with moderate pressure.

To intensify and smooth the color I dip a blending stump in solvent and gently spread the color towards the center. Look at the difference!

Now, I create the base of the single violet petal. With 1007 Imperial Violet I use an upward motion from the base.

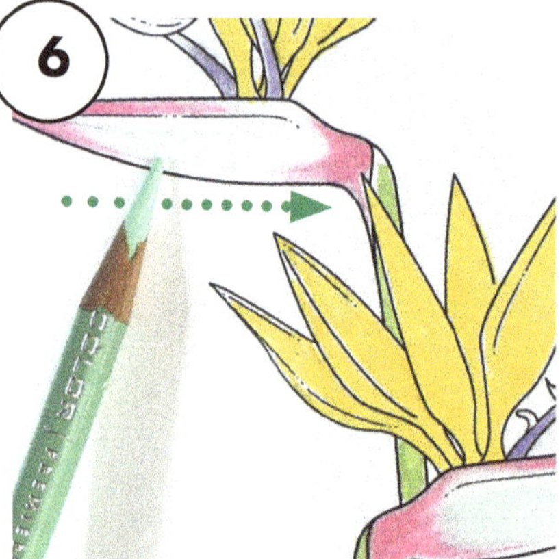

With a sharp 920 Light Green held slightly vertically, starting just past the 994 outside edge, I use horizontal motions towards the stem of the flower, stopping just before I hit the other edge.

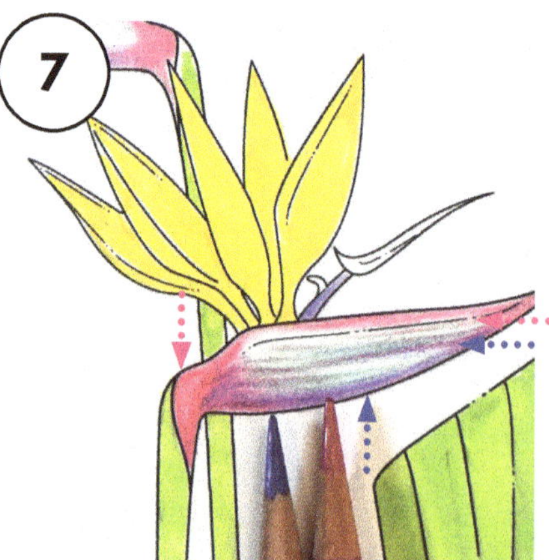

I use a sharp 1007 once again, but this time to deepen the bottom edge of the flower. I darken the "shoulder" of the flower with a sharp 994 again. I add a few feather-light flicks of both colors horizontally into the minty green from the outside edges inward.

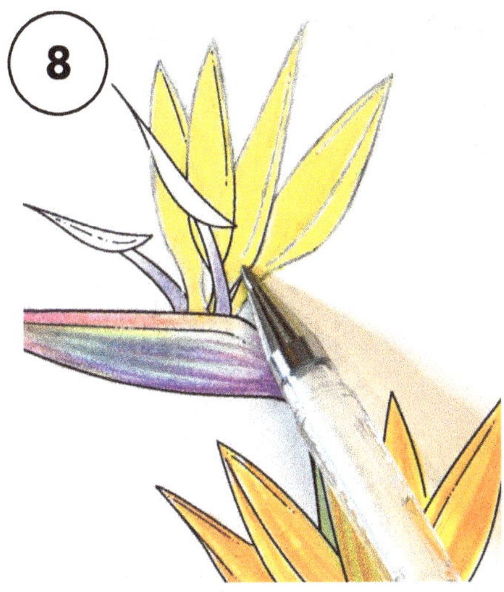

8

Next, I use a gel pen to cover up the black lines around the petals because they really flatten them out! See the "Did you know?" section!

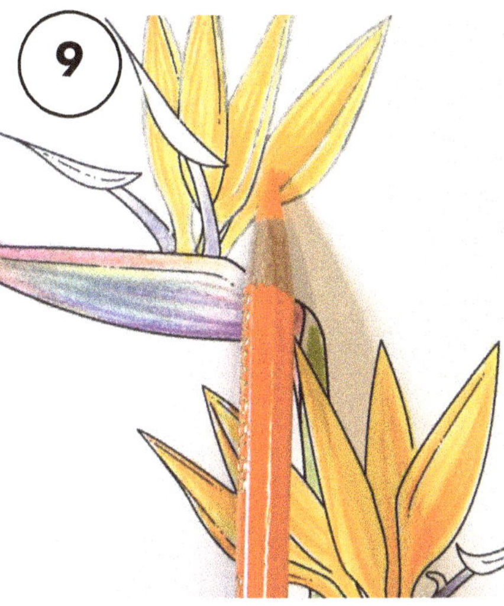

9

Now I use a sharp 918 Orange held vertically to draw in the grooves in the petals. Starting from the bottom up, lessening the pressure towards the tip.

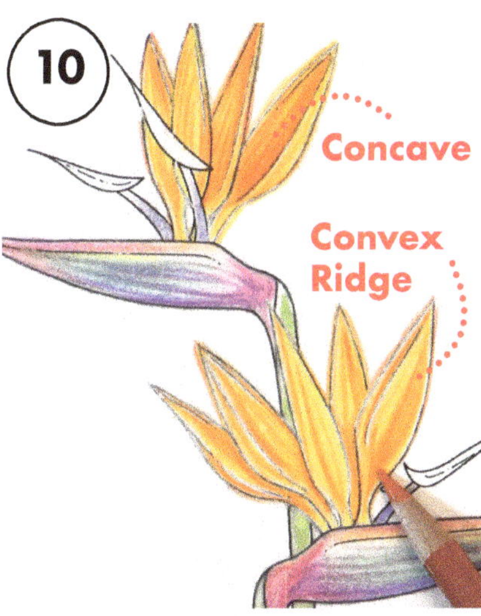

10

Then I add a few flicks of a sharp 922 Poppy Red to make a few lines and convex ridges stand out. I deepen the inside edges of the concave petals.

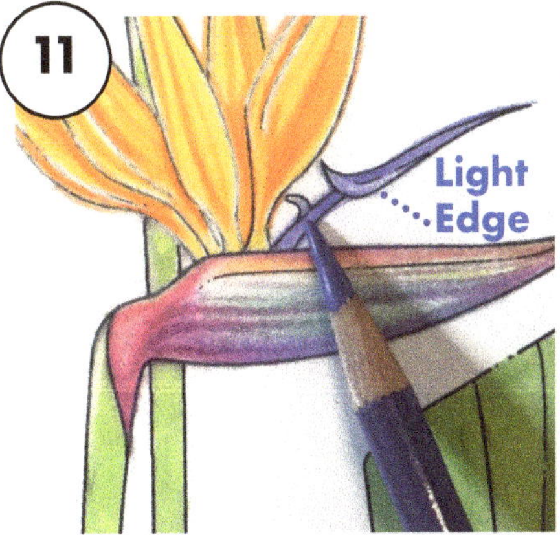

11

I use 1007 to complete the violet petal – deepening the bottom section and the top plane. The edge is a bit lighter.

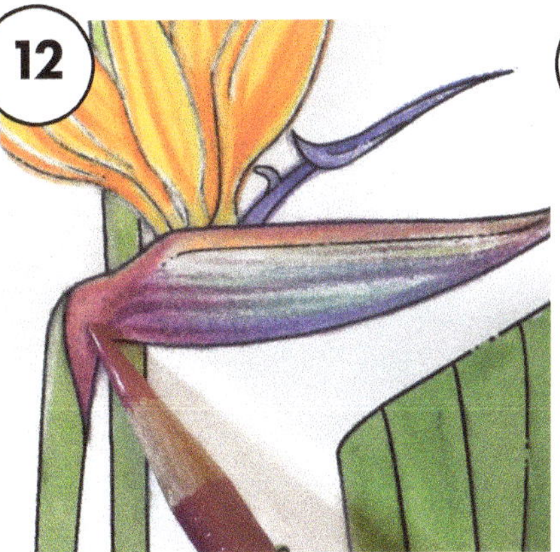

12

One more time with a sharp 994 to really etch in those details and create an eye-catching emphasis.

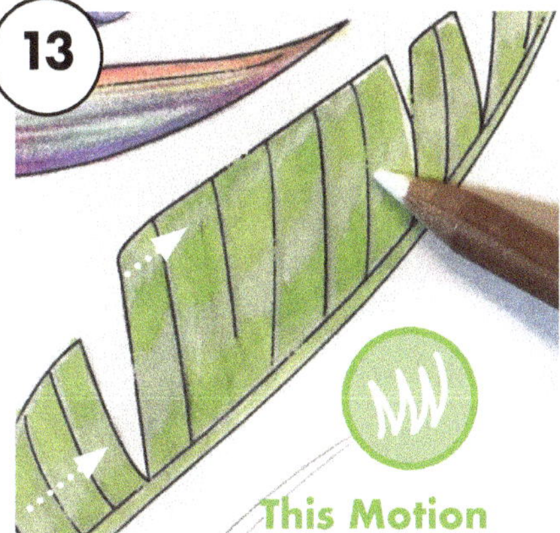

13

Now I use a White Luminance to create white bands spanning the length of the leaf, using up and down motions.

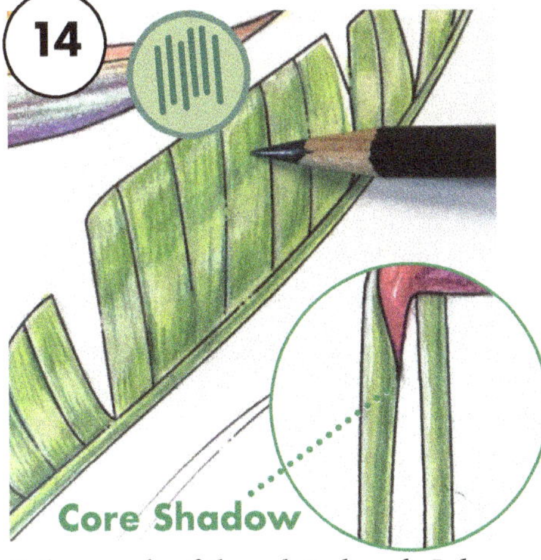

14

Below each of the white bands I do the same as in Step 13, only using straight lines with a sharp 907 Peacock Green pencil. I also add a long, vertical stroke – a core shadow – to all the cylindrical stems as seen in the inset.

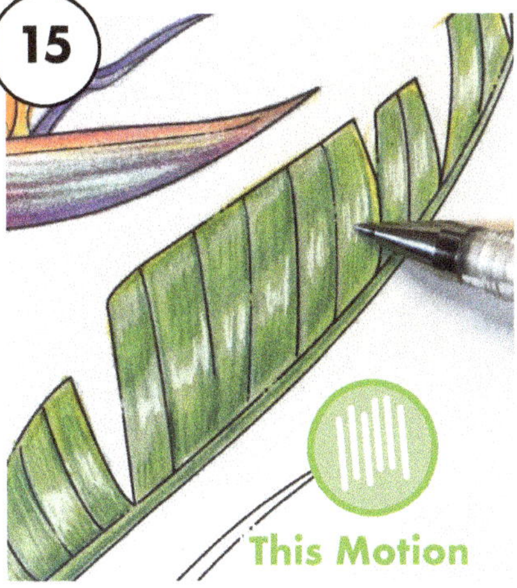

15

Finally I use the same motion with a white gel pen to make the leaf look shiny and textured. I add touches of white on the flower too. If the orange on the petals isn't bold enough, use a neon gel pen to pump up the intensity!

Did you know?

GEL PENS are a magical tool!
But if you are "erasing" black line art from ink-jet printed PDF pages, the black ink may smear into the white gel pen ink turning it gray! One way to prevent this from happening is by using a waxy white pencil over the lines BEFORE white gel pen. The black ink gets sealed in!

Another cool way to use gel pens: If the colored pencil colors in a drawing aren't looking bright enough, add a few bursts of NEON gel pen on top. It just adds that extra oomph! I've outlined my final petals in neon orange!

Lovely Luna + Smokey Night Effect

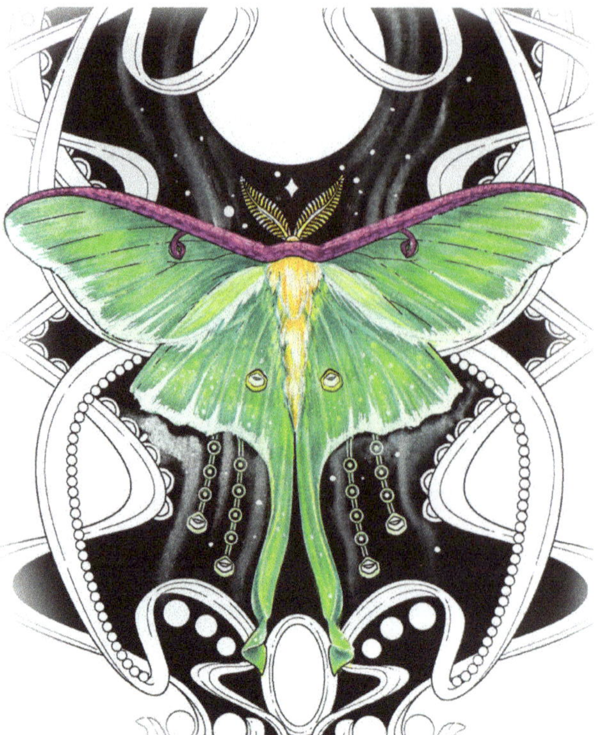

You will need:

- The Lovely Luna line art page
- Copic Marker YG45, Y15 (or TouchNew 46, 45) + Arrtx 85 (WN BrushMarkerV735 is not quite as red but will work)
- Prismacolor Premier pencils: 907, 913, 1002, 918, 931, 934, 1004
- White Uniball Signo Angelic gel pen + neon green, neon yellow and neon pink gel pen, such as Lolliz (or PC Pencils 920, 993)
- White Posca marker
- Optional: 100.5 TitaniumWhite PanPastel + cotton swabs or Sofft pointed tool

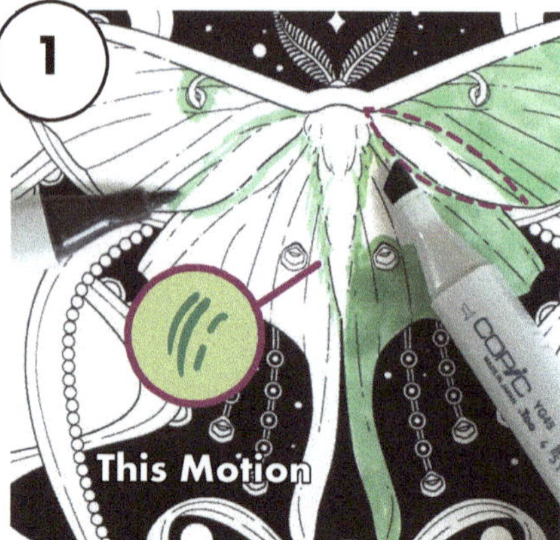

1 I begin by applying YG45 Cobalt Green, using the fine point end first to quickly go around the Moth's "eye spots" and body with short flicking motions. I then use the chisel to block in solid color, filling the wings except for the two "football" shapes where the translucent wings overlap. If you are using a brush marker you will only need to use that end.

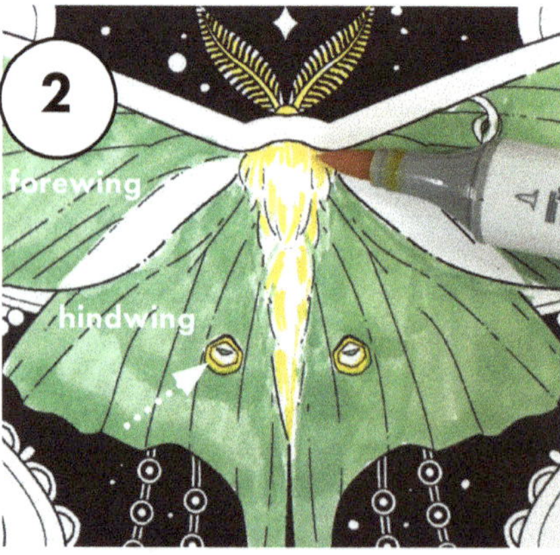

2 Next I use Y15 Cadmium Yellow in short, vertical flicking motions along the top edge of the furry body, plus a few on either side, as well as on the antennae and outside ring of the "eye spots."

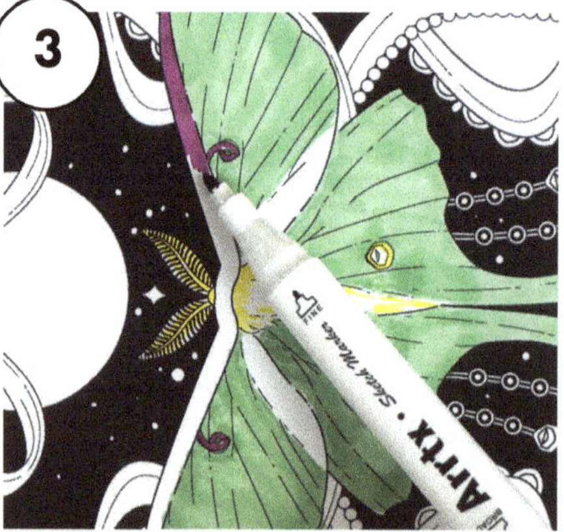

3 I rotate my page and use the fine point of my Arrtx 85 Vivid Purple marker to fill in the top edge of the forewing. I color toward myself for more control.

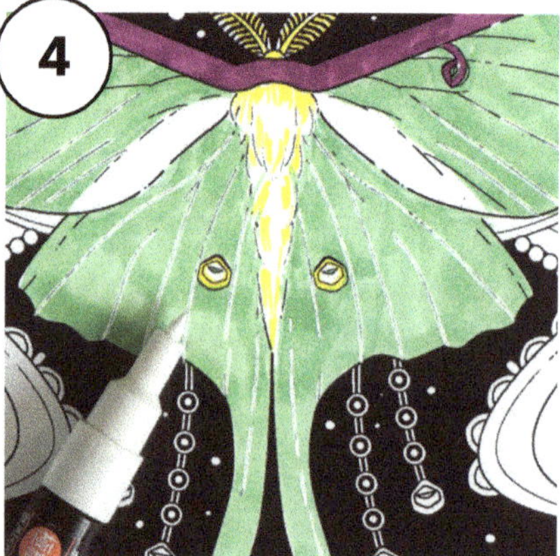

4 I shake my capped Posca, then *carefully* cover all of the black "veins" on the hindwing, and those closest to the bottom of the forwing, using two coats for opacity.

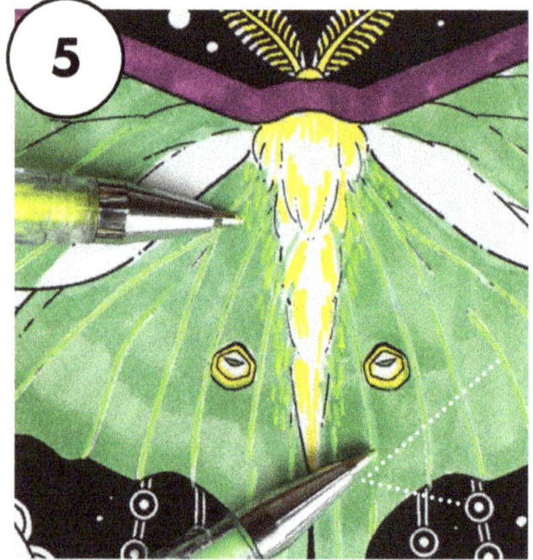

5 Now, I cover the veins and "dangles" with a neon green gel pen (or 920 Light Green pencil – the pen will be brighter). I use a fluo yellow gel pen to add body hairs on top of the green marker. An alterative would be to use Posca and cover it with a 1004 Light Chartreuse pencil.

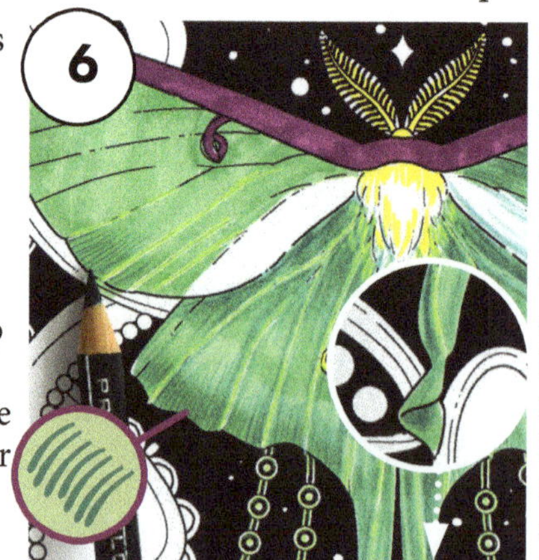

6 I use 907 Peacock Green on the outside top and bottom wing edges. To taper the strokes, I start from the outside moving inward toward the middle of the wing with less pressure. I add a few diagonal strokes in the "footballs" to suggest fur. I shade the creases of the tip of the tail. (See detail.)

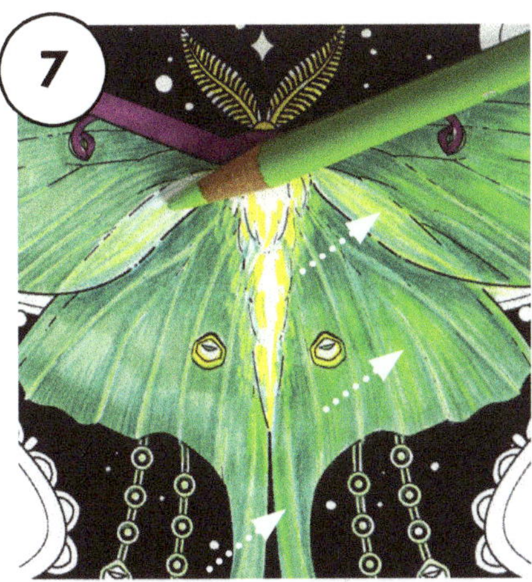

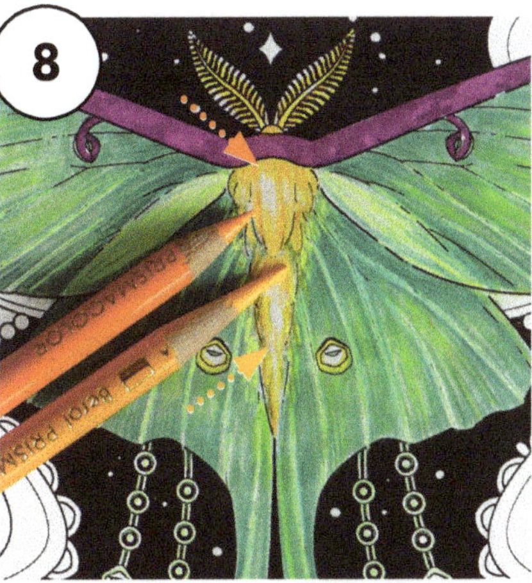

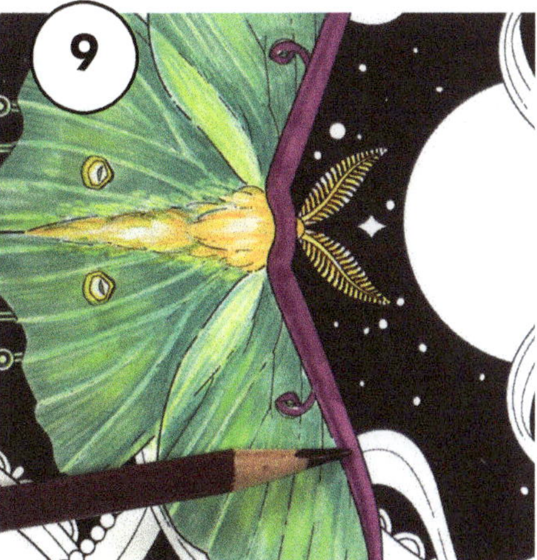

7 Now I use 913 Spring Green to fill in the overlapping "football" shapes, plus a layer mid-wing for both sets of wings to warm them up.

8 I then apply a layer of 1002 Yellowed Orange along the outside edges of the body. I add a few short vertical strokes of 918 Orange along the top edge and a few longer ones to break up the fur.

9 After rotating my page I use a single stroke of 931 Dioxazine Purple Hue to create a core shadow close to the edge of the purple shape, leaving a little room for the next step, reflected light.

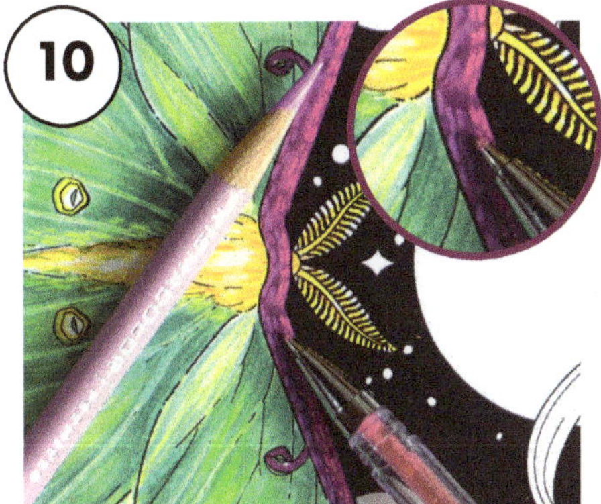

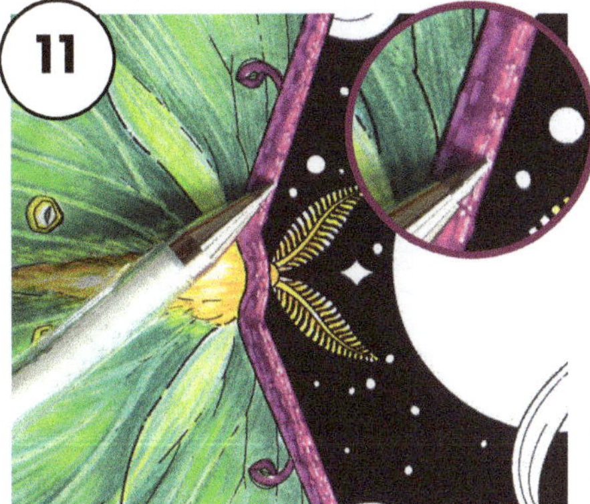

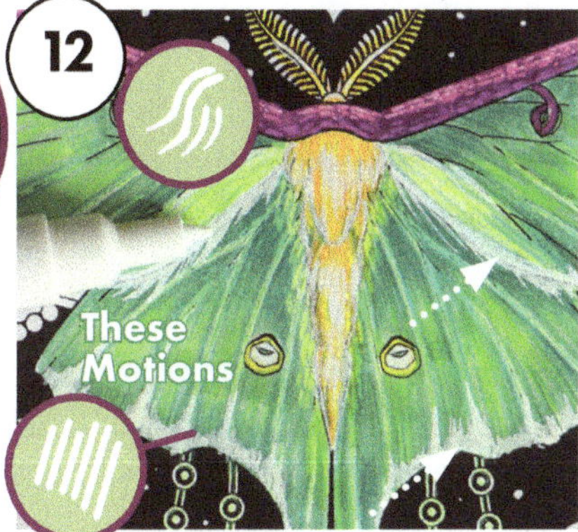

10 To create the furry texture I use a sharp 934 Lavender pencil to draw short tick marks running along the bottom edge – the cooler reflected light. I add pink gel pen ticks along the top edge. The closest alternative is a 993 Hot Pink pencil.

11 Now I add tiny, shorter vertical flicks and dots with a thin white gel pen close to the top edge of the purple shape. This is the brightest highlight on the moth, and it should make the shape now look 3-D.

12 Once again, Posca is used but now to create the fur along the edges on both sets of wings. I use longer curved motions on the edge of the forewing where it's really furry, and short straight motions on the hindwing.

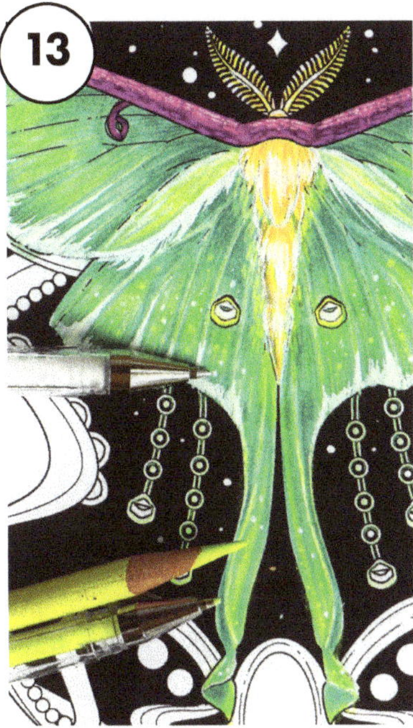

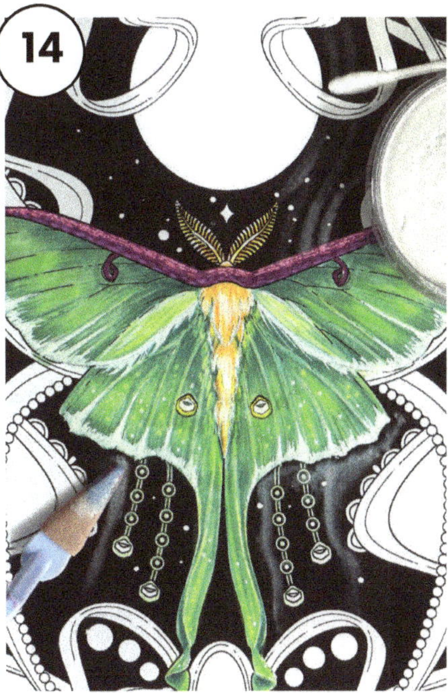

13 I add a layer of 1004 Yellow Chartreuse up and down the whole tail to warm it up and illuminate it! I add circular flecks of white gel pen and neon yellow gel pen in scattered areas of the moth's wings, and a stroke of white along the middle of the antennae.

14 Optional: I've created the smokey aura around the Luna using White PanPastel. With a small amount on my cotton swab or pointed Sofft tool, starting closest to the moth I drag it downward, gently bending the stroke to mimic the "dangles." I add a second layer to the top to make it bolder, and a few around the moon as well! To complete this page you might want to check out the Illuminated Moon tutorial and perhaps turn the decorative borders into metal – it's all in *The Secrets of Coloring 1*!

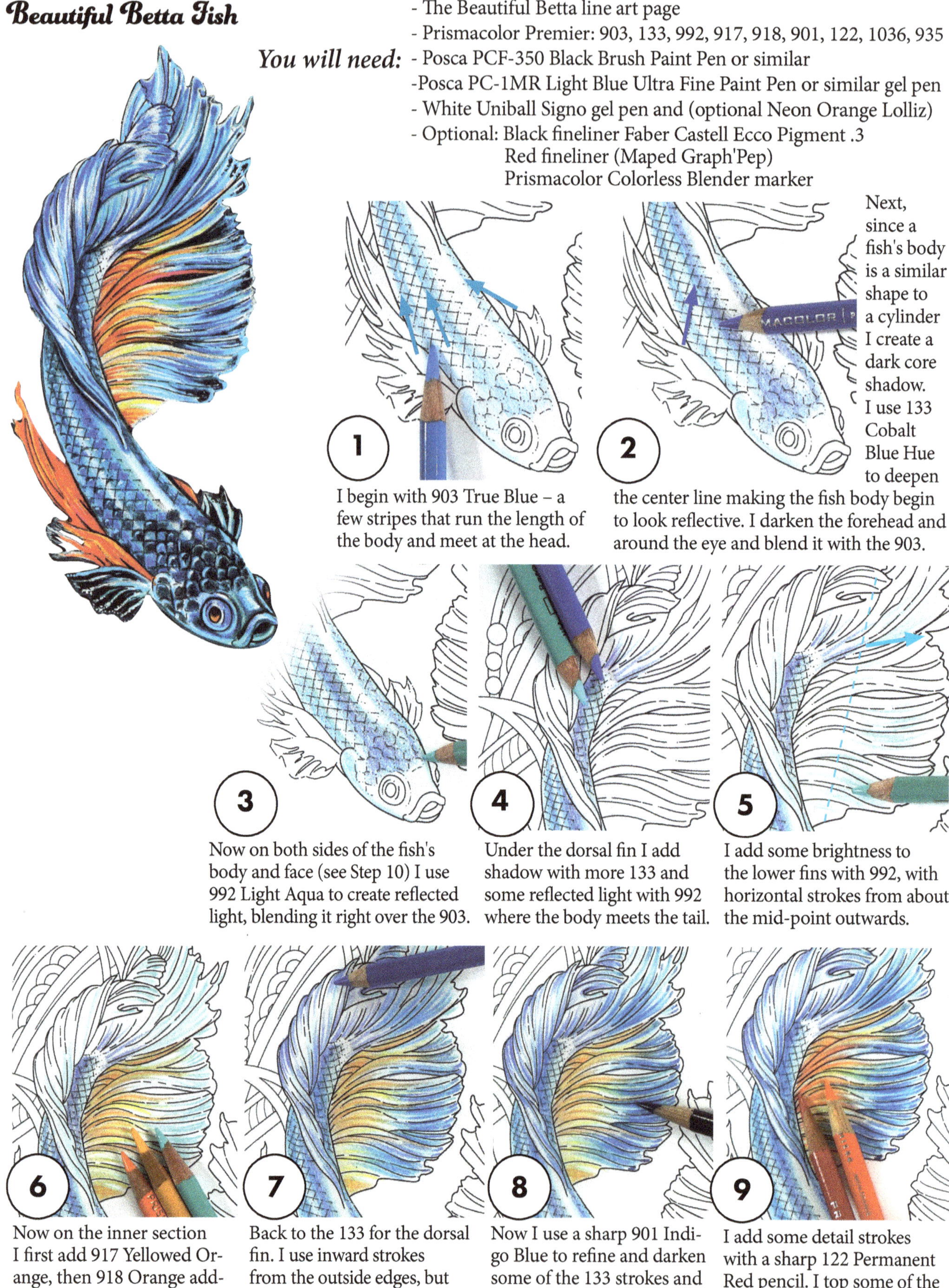

Beautiful Betta Fish

You will need:
- The Beautiful Betta line art page
- Prismacolor Premier: 903, 133, 992, 917, 918, 901, 122, 1036, 935
- Posca PCF-350 Black Brush Paint Pen or similar
- Posca PC-1MR Light Blue Ultra Fine Paint Pen or similar gel pen
- White Uniball Signo gel pen and (optional Neon Orange Lolliz)
- Optional: Black fineliner Faber Castell Ecco Pigment .3
  Red fineliner (Maped Graph'Pep)
  Prismacolor Colorless Blender marker

1 — I begin with 903 True Blue – a few stripes that run the length of the body and meet at the head.

2 — Next, since a fish's body is a similar shape to a cylinder I create a dark core shadow. I use 133 Cobalt Blue Hue to deepen the center line making the fish body begin to look reflective. I darken the forehead and around the eye and blend it with the 903.

3 — Now on both sides of the fish's body and face (see Step 10) I use 992 Light Aqua to create reflected light, blending it right over the 903.

4 — Under the dorsal fin I add shadow with more 133 and some reflected light with 992 where the body meets the tail.

5 — I add some brightness to the lower fins with 992, with horizontal strokes from about the mid-point outwards.

6 — Now on the inner section I first add 917 Yellowed Orange, then 918 Orange adding a few horizontal flicks on top. I add a few 992 accents on the tail and dorsal fin.

7 — Back to the 133 for the dorsal fin. I use inward strokes from the outside edges, but leave the middle white. I also add 133 in between the 992 strokes on the tail.

8 — Now I use a sharp 901 Indigo Blue to refine and darken some of the 133 strokes and to add dimension.

9 — I add some detail strokes with a sharp 122 Permanent Red pencil. I top some of the strokes in between with 1036 Neon Orange for brightness!

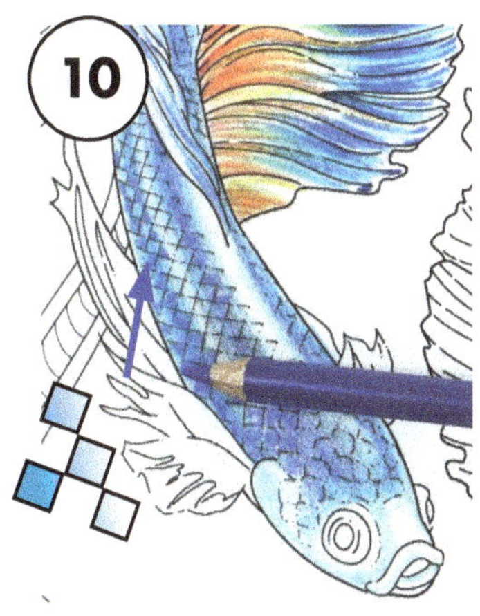

10

I am using 133 to fill in some diamonds (scales) that connect by their corners from the gill towards the tail, leaving the in-between ones alone.

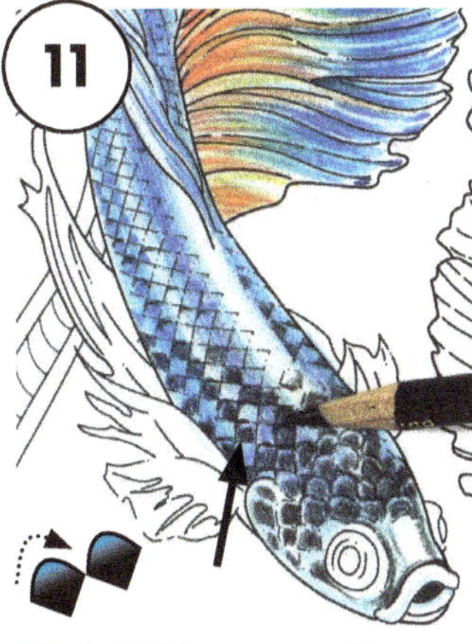

11

Black 935 is now used to darken in some of the scales from the fish's face backward. I curve the tops of some to make them more realistic.

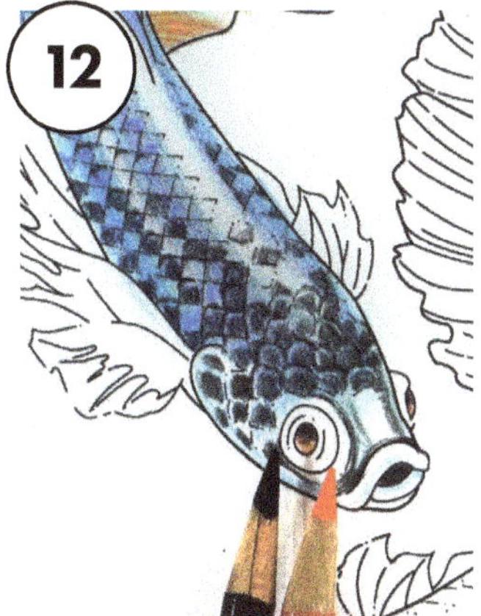

12

The lower half of each eye is filled with 1036 and the upper with 935. If this isn't bright enough in the end, add a dot of neon gel pen.

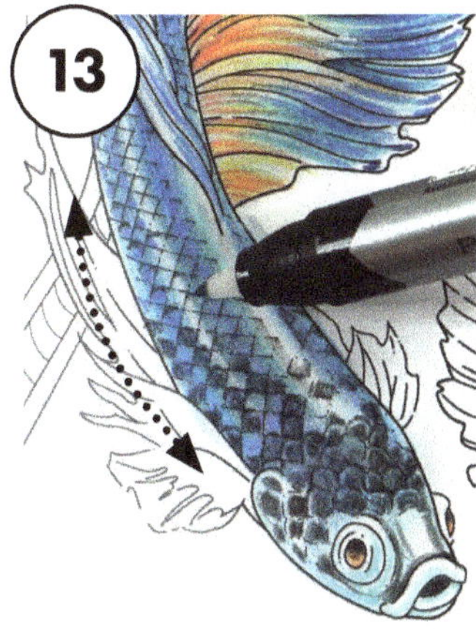

13

You may wish to use a blender marker to increase the vibrance and smooth the scales just a touch.

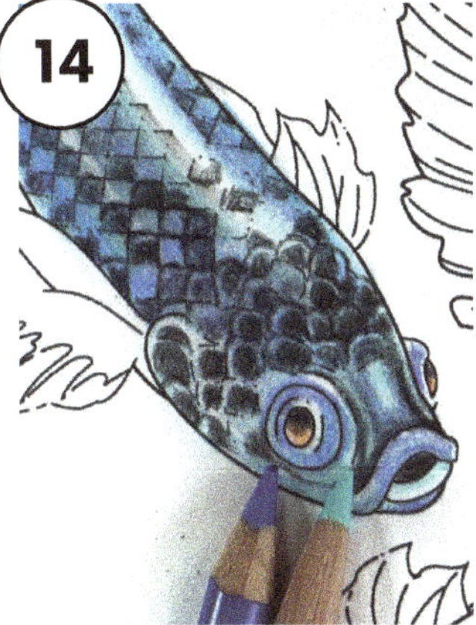

14

133 is used again, but this time inside the outer ring of the eye and lip. 992 is used on the area surrounding the eye, and remaining areas of the face.

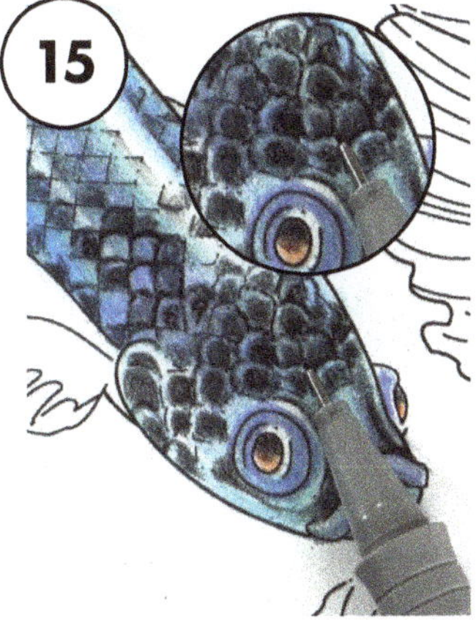

15

I want the forehead scales to stand out even more, so on top of the outlines in between the scales I "stipple" dots with a thin black fineliner.

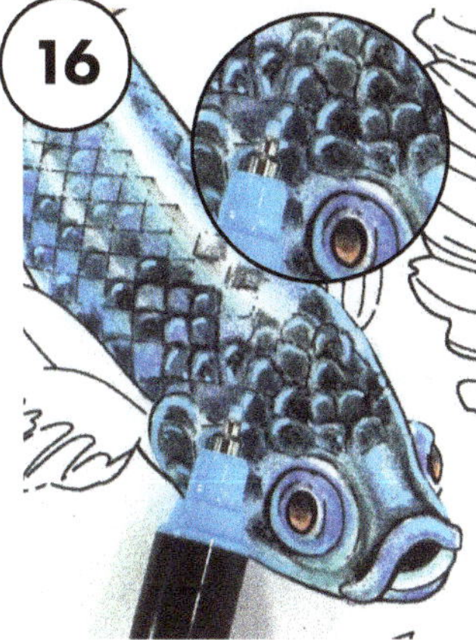

16

Now I am adding bold highlights, with a Light Blue Posca, to the top of each dark scale. I add some tiny ones to the scales moving towards the tail.

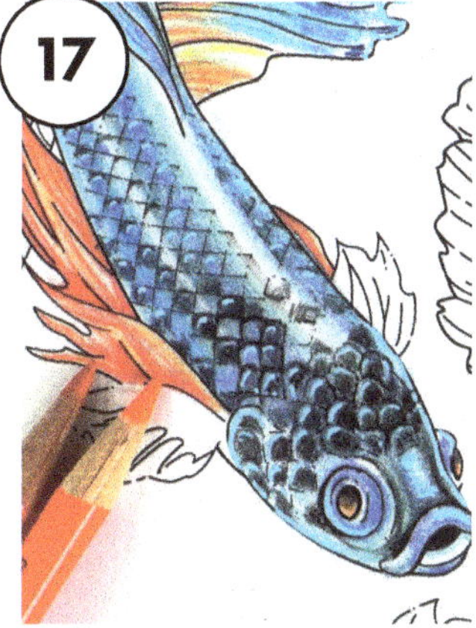

17

I use a combination of 1036 and 122 on the long front fins. The red goes in the creases and the orange goes in the areas that pop out.

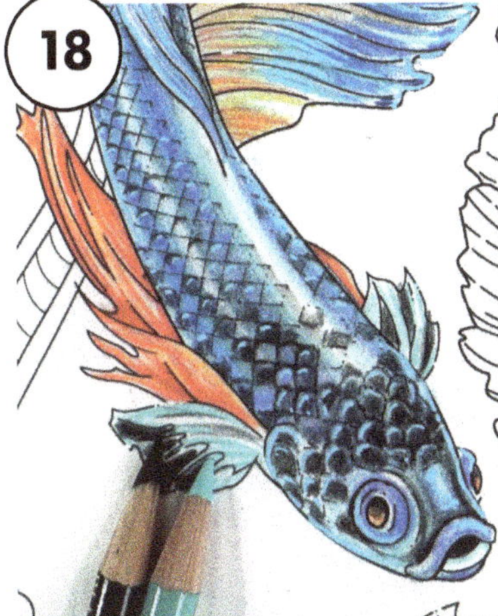

18

992 and 935 are used to fill in the two shorter fins. Blue in the inner shapes and black surrounding. After the background I'll add a touch of the PC-1MR and a few white gel pen "stipples" on the fins and face.

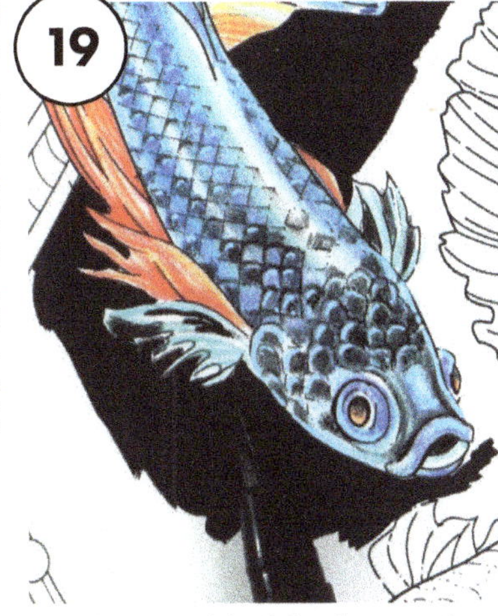

19

I've chosen a black background. I cover up the background with a brush marker using a Black Posca. I can draw right up to the fish and around the fins easily.

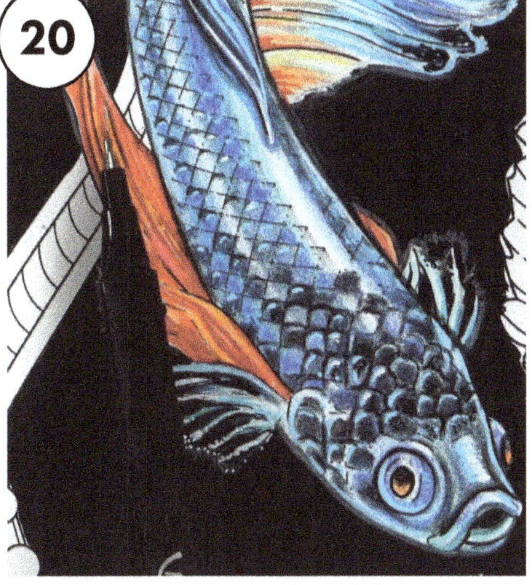

20

The last option is to use a red fineliner to make some of the details in the fin pop. I use it very sparingly in the creases. Tidy everything up and voîla!

Dazzling Dragonfly

You will need:
- The Dazzling Dragonfly and Lush Lotus line art page on toned paper
- Copic Marker B23 Phthalo Blue (Similar: Arrtx 183 /TouchNew 183)
- Prismacolor Premier Pencils: 938, 934, 1038, 992, 1035, 1007, 1065, 1063, 103, 932, 133, 935, 1077
- White and neon green gel pens + Posca PC-1MR Light Blue or other neon blue gel pen

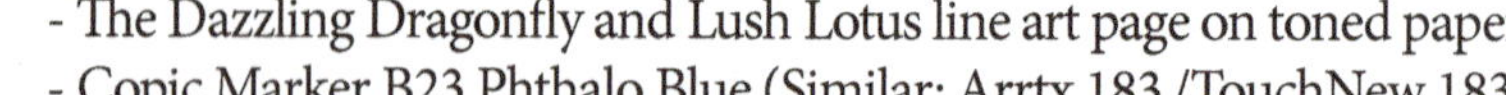

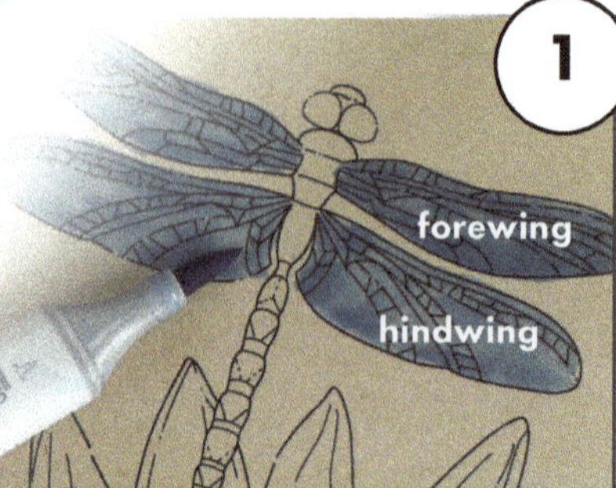

First I use a Copic B23 brush tip to quickly fill in the wings with a subtle blue color. **I will use the same colors *symmetrically* for both sets of wings on each step until Step 14.

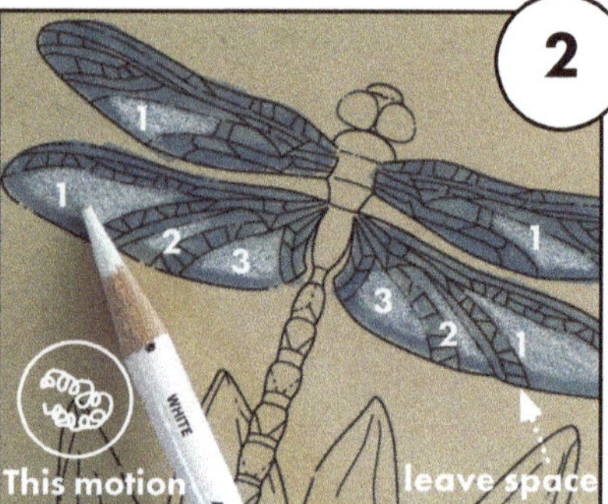

Next I use small circles to coat three sections (#1, #2, #3) of each hindwing and one section (#1) on each of the forewings with 938 White, leaving some space at the bottom of each wing.

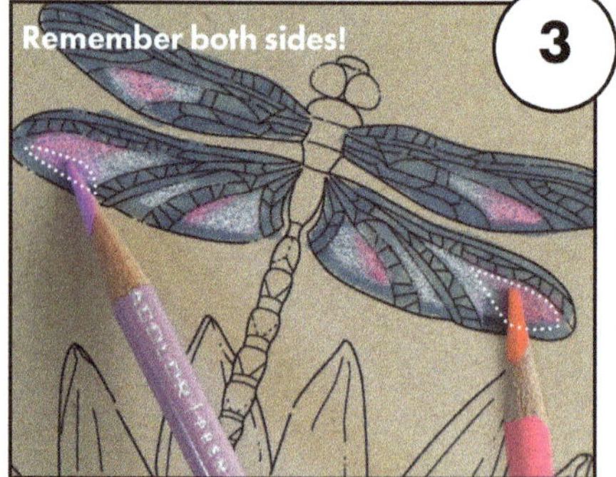

Then, on both sides, I add Neon Pink 1038 towards the outside half of both upper and lower #1 sections plus #3 sections. I add a little 934 Lavender to each #1 area towards the bottom – covering right over a little of the 1038. (See Step 4 photo for a better view!)

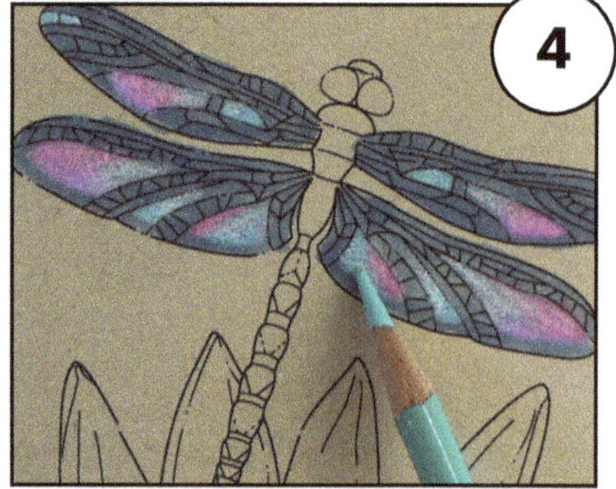

I use 992 Light Aqua in the remaining White areas of #3 sections and the bottoms of #2 areas that were White in Step 3. (I also add a touch to some small shapes.)

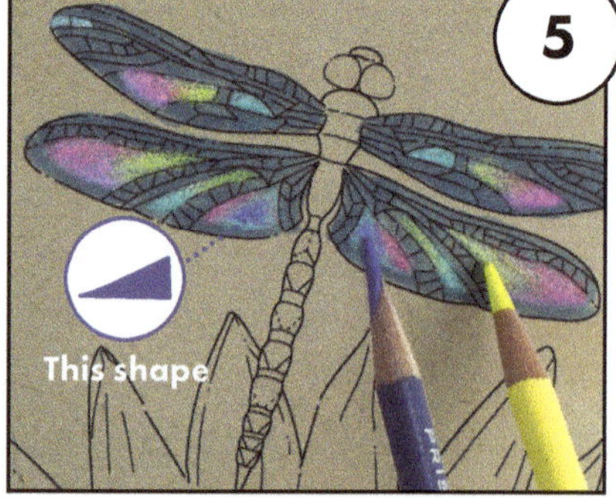

I use 1035 Neon Yellow to blend any of the remaining White parts of the numbered areas. I add a small triangle of 1007 Imperial Violet to each of the #3 shapes.

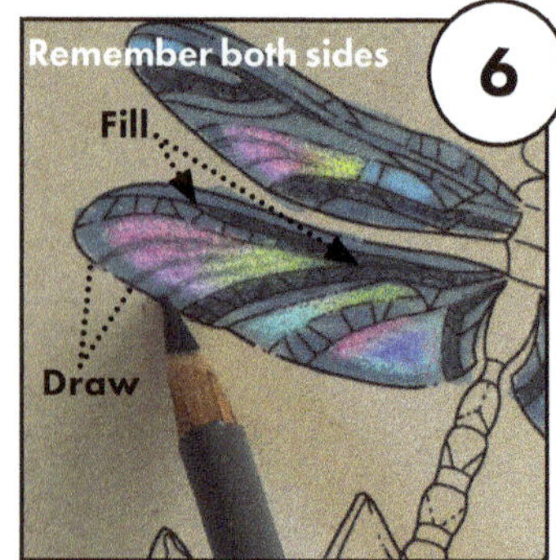

I begin the *texture* of the wings by drawing 1065 Cool Grey 70% lines in each of the colored sections to divide them into 2-4 strips. I also fill some of the narrow bands to add *contrast*.

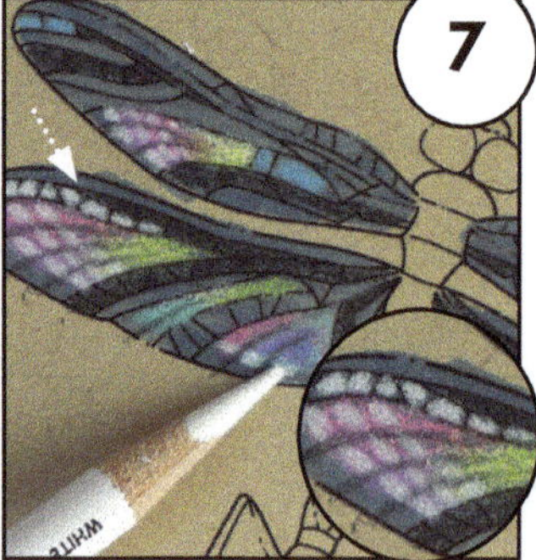

With a sharpened 938 pencil I make 3-4 stacked "dashes" in each strip, leaving a little space in between. I also fill in some of the little shapes above them solid White.

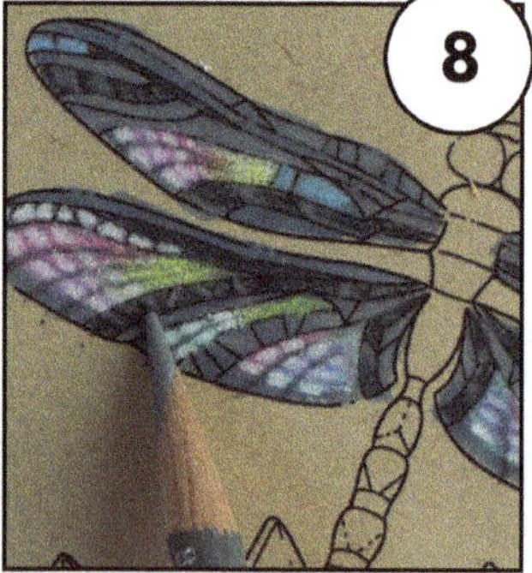

Now I add just a few random 1063 Cool Grey 50% lighter lines along the edges of some of the narrow band shapes that I have colored 1065, plus all of the yet uncolored spots.

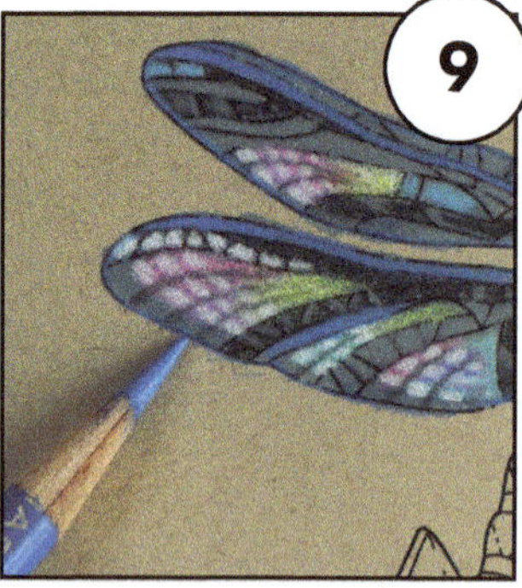

Then I use a sharp 103 Cerulean Blue to fill in the narrow solid strip that runs from one side of each wing to the other. I also outline the wings lightly.

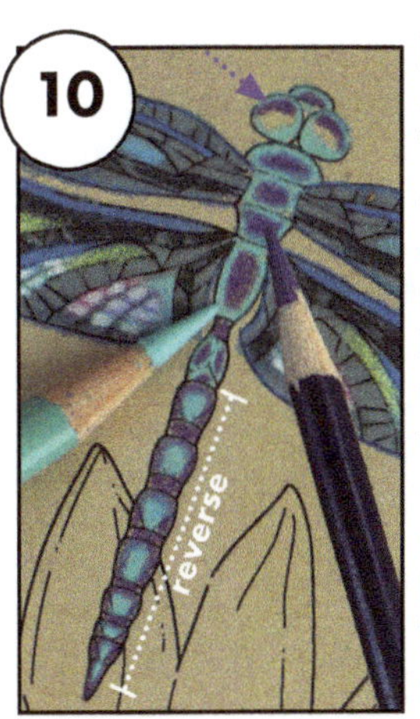

10 I add a curved stroke of 932 Violet to each eye and fill in the center of each section of the top half of the body. I then outline them with a sharp 992 so they glow! I do the reverse for the lower half of the body. I outline the eyes with 992.

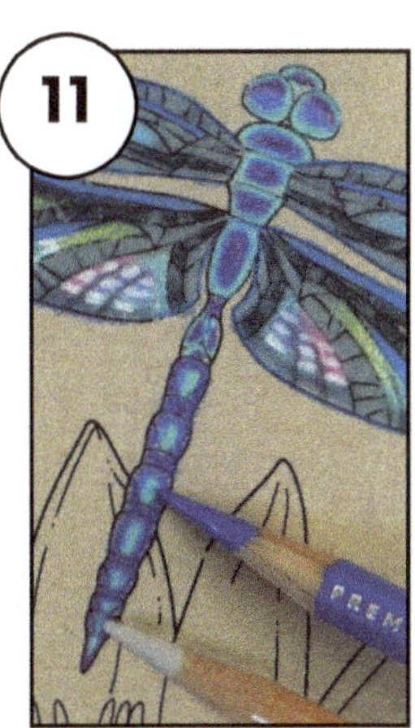

11 I add strokes of 133 Cobalt Blue Hue down both sides of the lower body, plus a touch to each upper segment and to fill in the eyes. I use a 1077 colorless blender to smooth each little area.

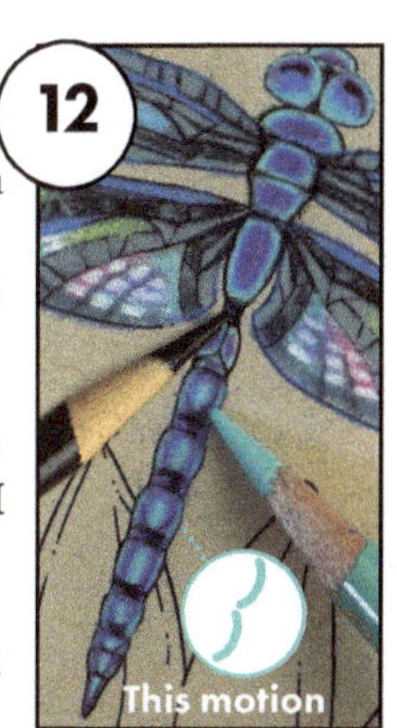

12 I use 935 Black to darken the top of each eye, between each segment and where the wings connect. With a sharp 992 I create short strokes around the outside of each segment as *reflected light*.

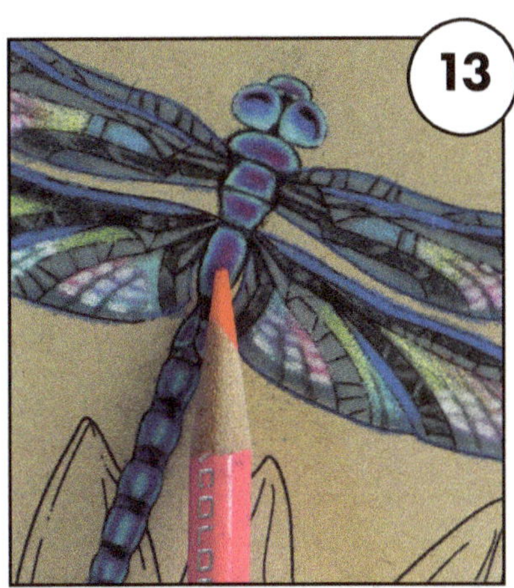

Once again I use 1038, but this time to add a little touch of iridescent glow to the upper body with a few Neon Pink marks on each segment!

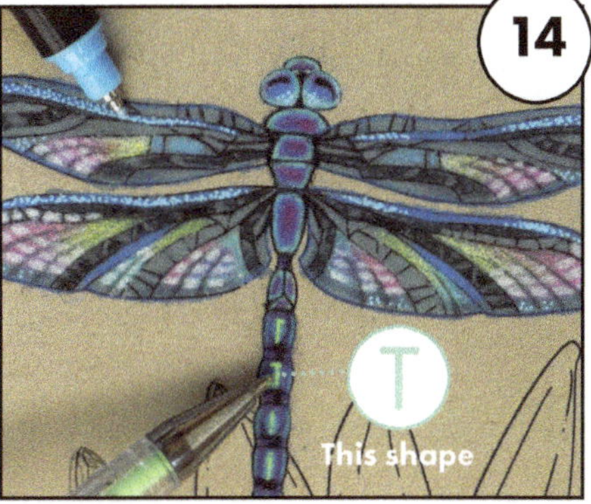

To make the dragonfly sparkle I add tiny stipples of Posca PC-1MR Light Blue over the long 103 sections. I have intentionally not done this part the same on both sides. I add a few random, scattered dots and then neon green gel pen skinny "T" shapes to the center of each lower segment!

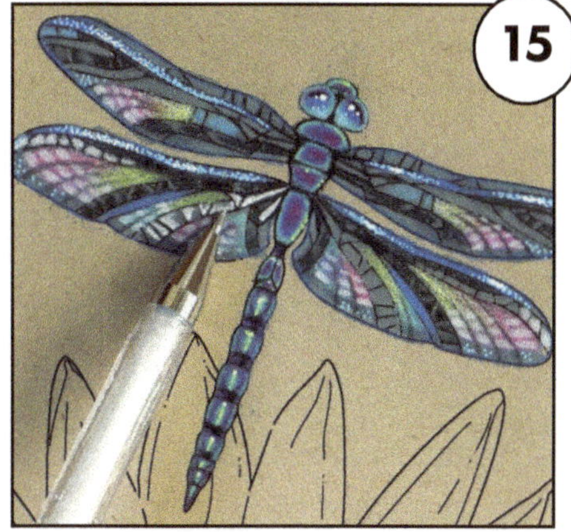

The final bit of shimmer is added with a white gel pen, more concentrated over a few of the light blue stipples than the others. I add a few random white shapes, dot the tops of the T's and give the eyes highlights. Doesn't the dragonfly shine?!

Lush Lotus

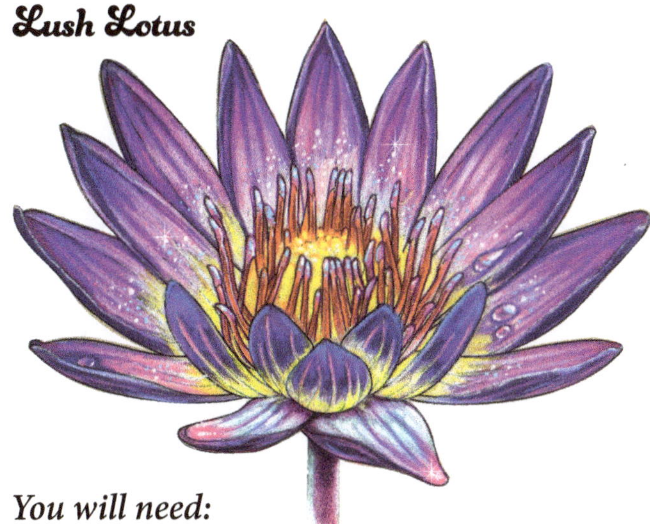

You will need:

- The Dazzling Dragonfly and Lush Lotus line art page printed on real toned paper (or use the practice page)
- I recommend a brush nib for this: Copic Sketch FV2 Fluorescent Dull Violet + V04 Lilac (or Prismacolor 127 + 168) If necessary, Arrtx 81 (similar) + 147 – these are chisel nibs
- Prismacolor Premier pencils: 938, 1102, 934, 1038, 1007, 932, 916, 931, 1036, 918, 1035, 132, 993, 910, 907, 920, 935
- Posca PC-1MR Light Blue, Yellow (or gel pens such as Lolliz)
- White Uniball Signo Angelic gel pen

Both dragonflies and lotus flowers exist in a variety of colors and shapes. You may wish to find some reference photos for inspiration and change your color palette to make them stand out against each other!

Tip: Use a darker color background around your dragonfly's wings to make them appear transparent! If a part of the wing overlaps an object in the background you can color in that part of the wing the same color as the object but a shade lighter. Be sure to blur the edges of the color! This will convey a sense of transparency.

The Petals & Stamens

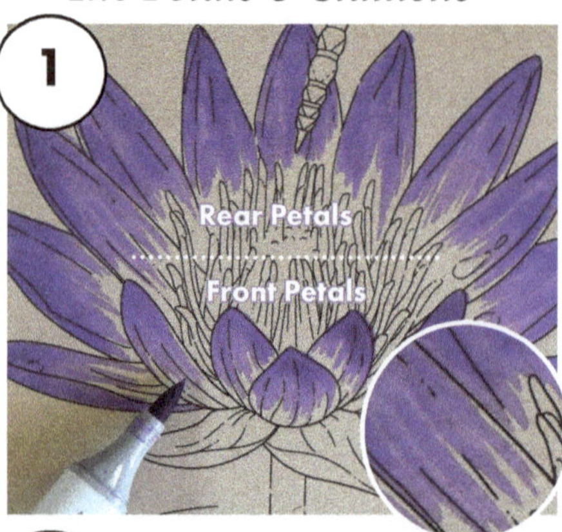

1 Please see inset photos for details of many steps! I begin with a Copic FV2 brush tip filling in all of the petals. I create lengthwise strokes, from the tip down, with ragged ends that stop just short of the "stamens" (middle) of the flower.

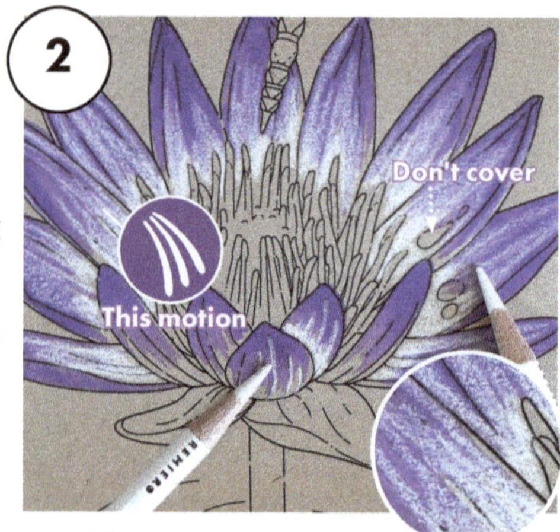

2 Next, with 938 White I create long lengthwise ridges directly over the FV2 for rear petals only, (leaving some dark areas) and from the ragged marker stroke ends down to the stamens. I trace the black lines on the front five petals.

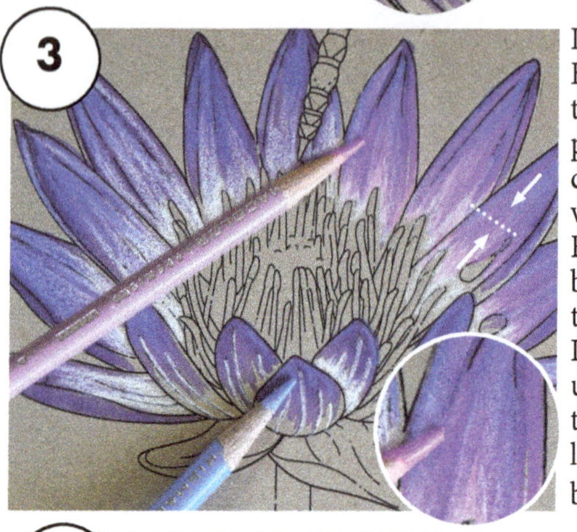

3 I then add 1102 Blue Lake, close to the top of each petal, moving downward with vertical strokes. From about the bottom of each of the rear petals only I use 934 Lavender upwards, until the two colors blend, leaving the very bottoms white.

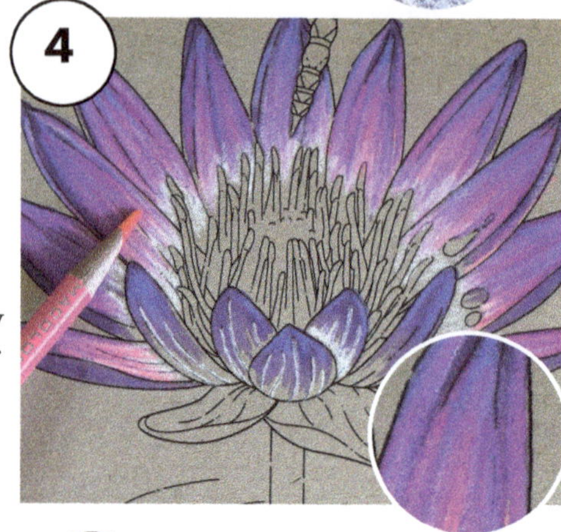

4 I use 1038 Neon Pink sparingly over some of the ridges – except on the front petals. Those I keep "cooler" because they are backlit! I use more 1038 on the petals that surround them.

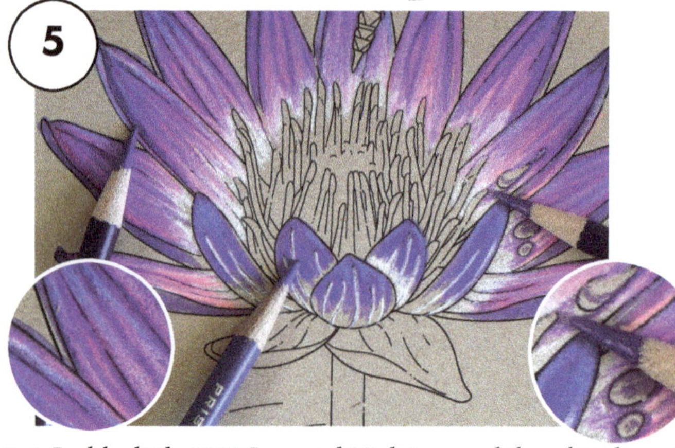

5

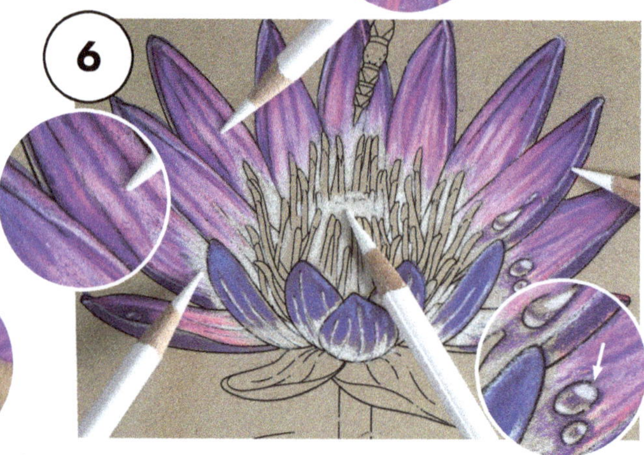

6

5-6: I add a little 1007 Imperial Violet around the white lines in the middle of the front petals. I use 932 Violet to add some darker vertical shadows on each petal to create more dimension around the ridges, plus a touch in the centers of the water droplets and around them as well. I then blend and lighten the middle of the ridges of each petal with 938, fill in the center of the flower, and add highlights on the petal edges as well as the inside right half of each water droplet.

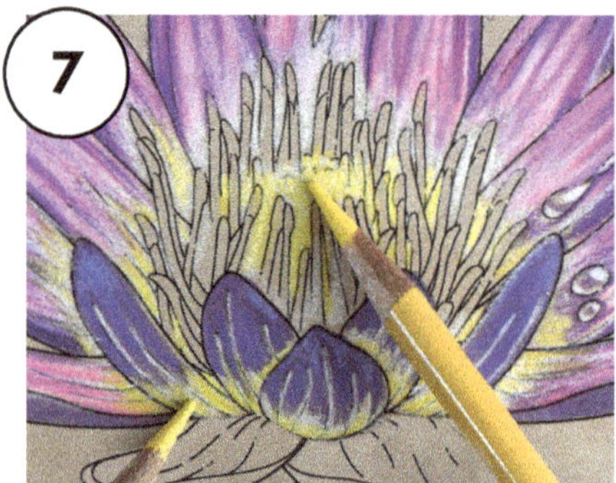

7 Here's the the start of the glow! I use 916 Canary Yellow at the base of each petal and in the center of the flower, being careful not to color the stamens.

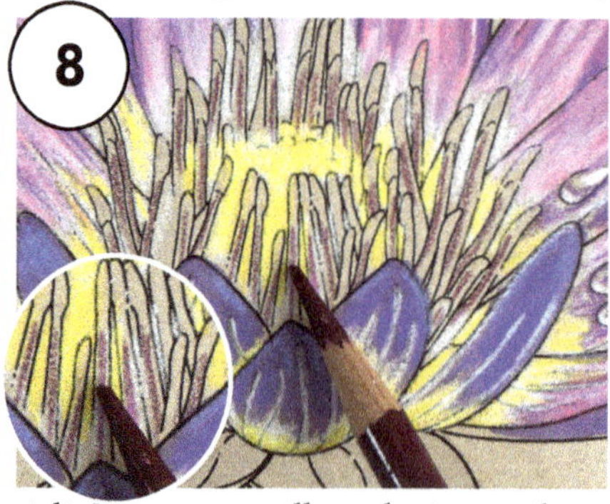

8 A little contrast will set the inner glow off...I use a sharp vertical stroke of 931 Dark Purple in the center of the stalk (main part) of each stamen.

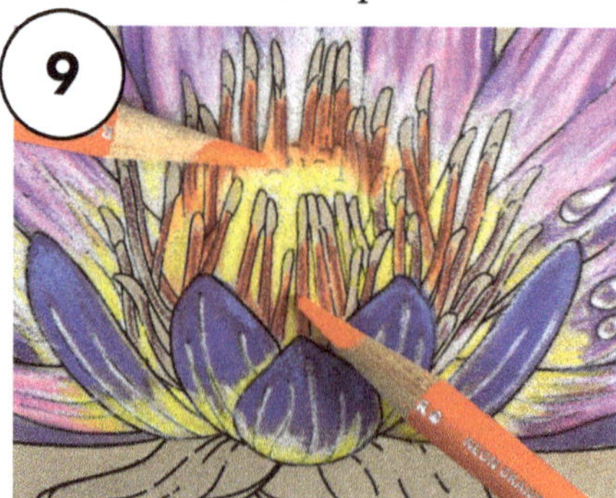

9 I use a few coats of 1036 Neon Orange to color on top of each stroke of 931. I also lightly blend the back "wall" of the stamens into the yellow center of the flower.

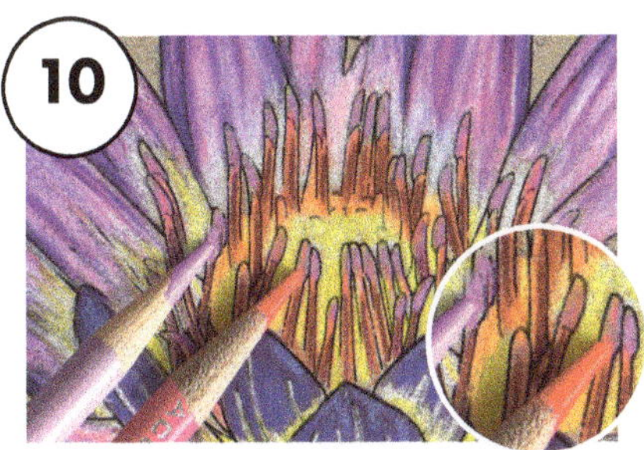

Now I tackle the tips of the stamens, or "anthers" by filling them mostly with 934. With a sharp 1038 I add a few tiny flecks. In the end you will barely see them.

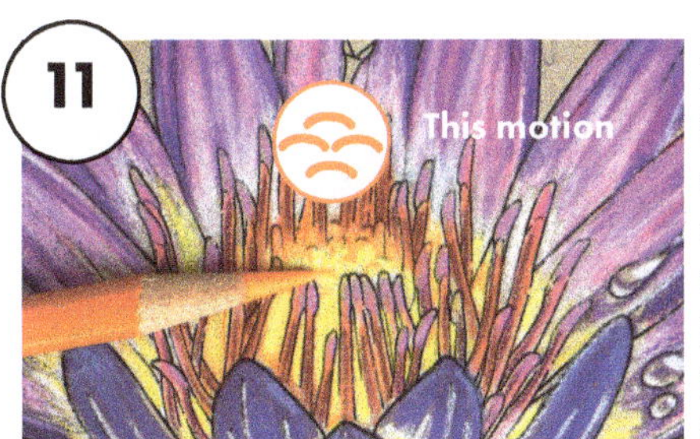

Now I use a sharp 918 Orange to add some short curved strokes that create the bumpy texture of the center of the flower.

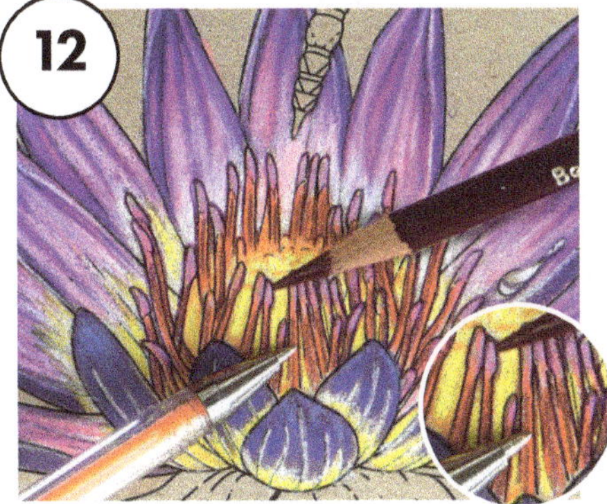

Next, with a razor-sharp 931 again, I outline the completed stamens to make them stand out a bit. I also add super skinny vertical strokes of neon orange gel pen on some of the stamen stalks.

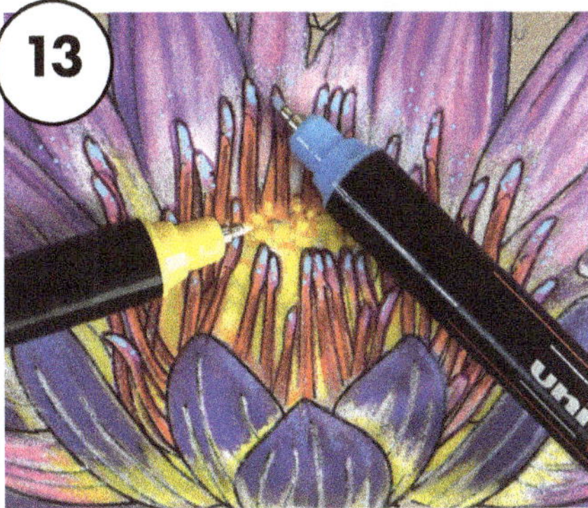

The magic really begins when I dot the tips of the anthers with a Light Blue Posca PC-1MR, as well as making little Yellow PC-1MR dots under the curved strokes in the center of the flower.

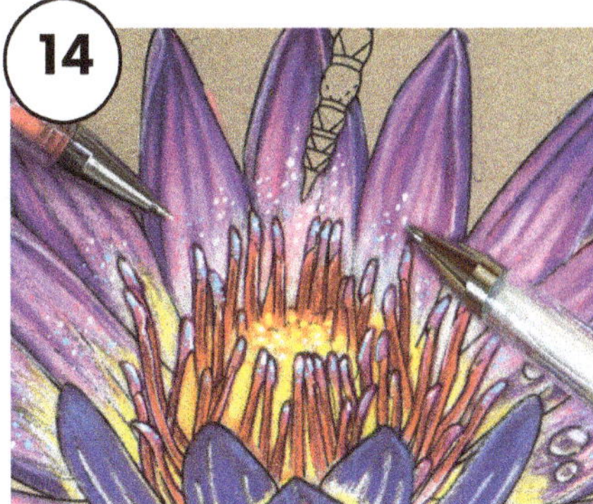

I add a few dots on the petals too with the Light Blue, as well as some neon pink gel pen. Finally, a few tiny dots of white gel pen act as highlights on the anthers, center, and petals making them glisten.

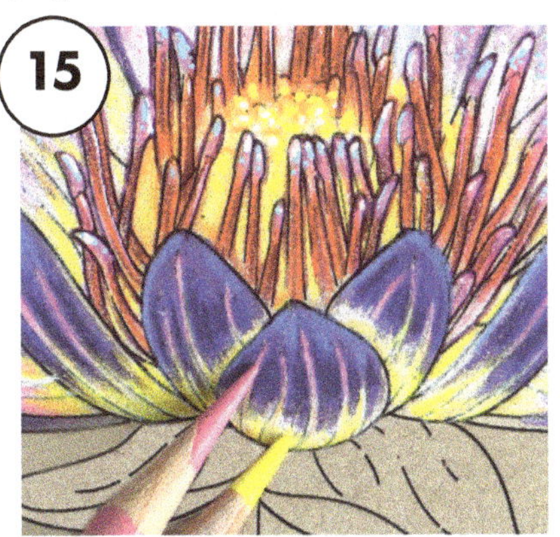

To add to the glowing effect, I brighten the yellow on the front petals with 1035 Neon Yellow. I add a layer of 993 Hot Pink over the 938 lines I traced earlier.

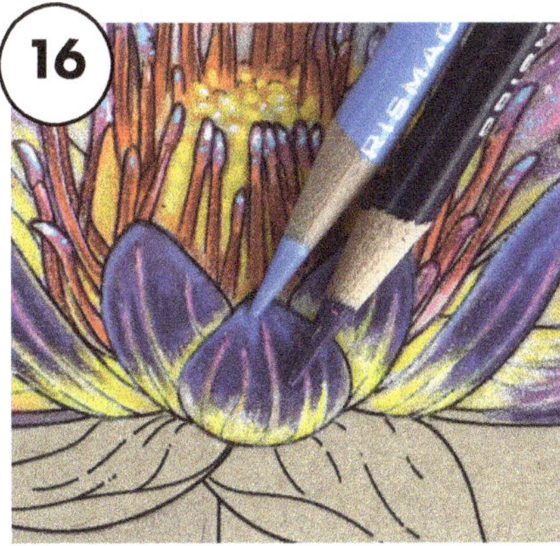

I need to balance the glow radiating from within the flower through these traced lines by cooling off and darkening the area around them. I add another layer of 1102 towards the top edges only and deepen across the centers of the petals with 132 Dioxizane Purple Hue to really set it off!

The Water Droplets

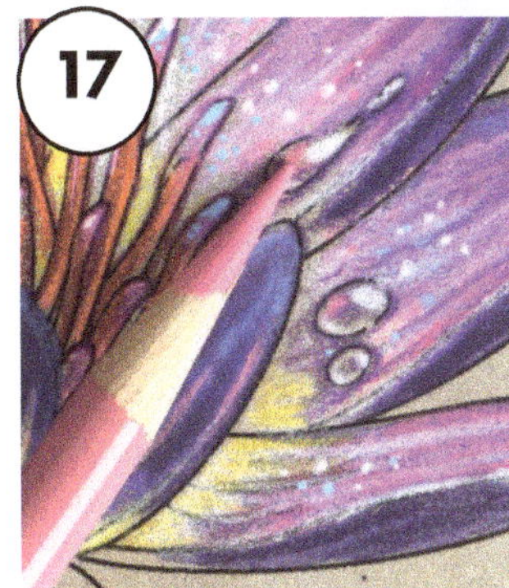

To complete the realistic water droplets I add a touch of 993 in the center of each shape, next to the Violet from Step 5-6.

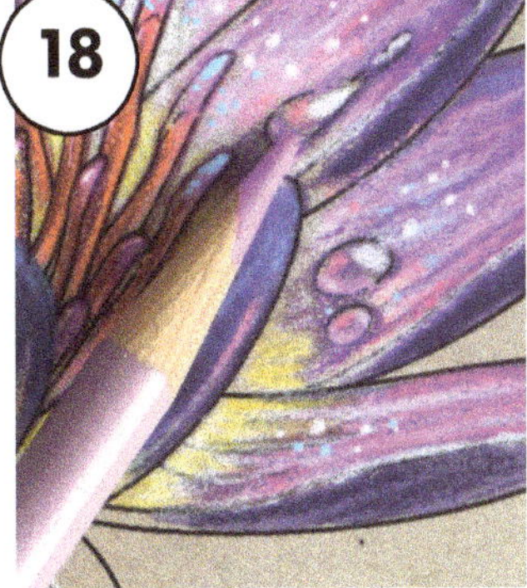

I use a little 934 towards the bottom of each drop to fill in the paper. The white area on the top droplet was a little too bright, so I tone it down a little as well.

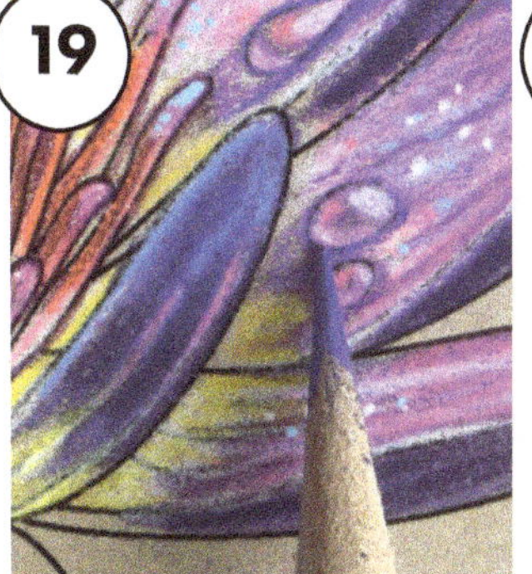

Now I create a thin outline of 1007 around each to make them more obvious. This small amount of *contrast* makes the lighter colors sing!

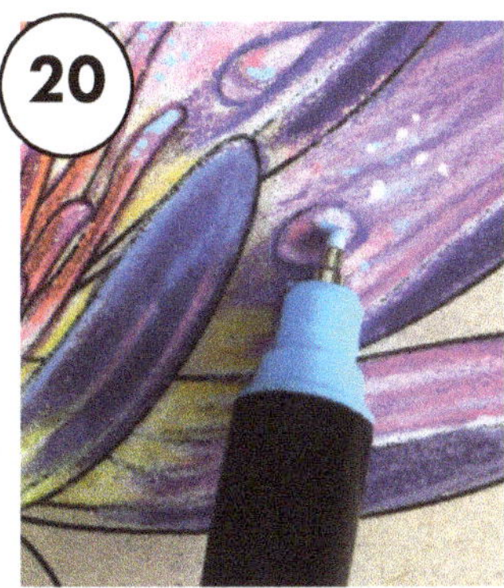

A couple flecks of Light Blue Posca really bring the water droplets to life! In the end you may want to also add a fleck or two of white just inside the 1007 border!

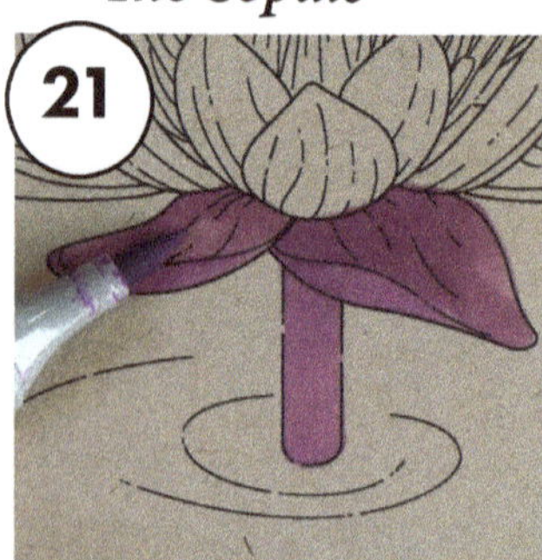

21 The Sepal is the leafy part of a flower where the petals come together. This one is a bit complex so we will do it separately from the rest of the flower. I use a Copic V04 brush nib to fill in the sepals and stem.

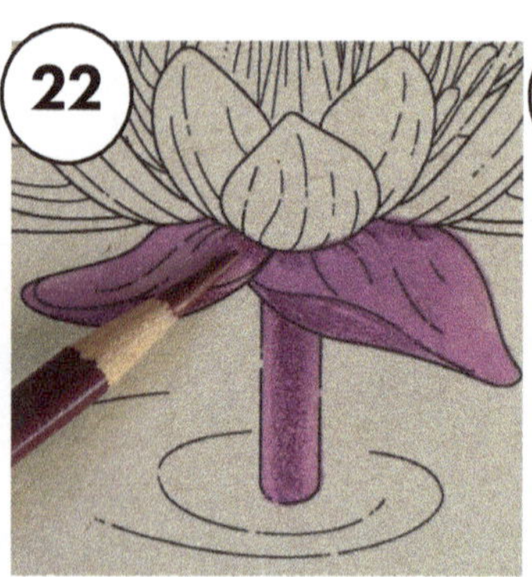

22 With 931 Dark Purple I add a cast shadow along the top of the sepals, a bit along the sides of them too, and a core shadow on the stem which will immediately help to create a sense of dimension.

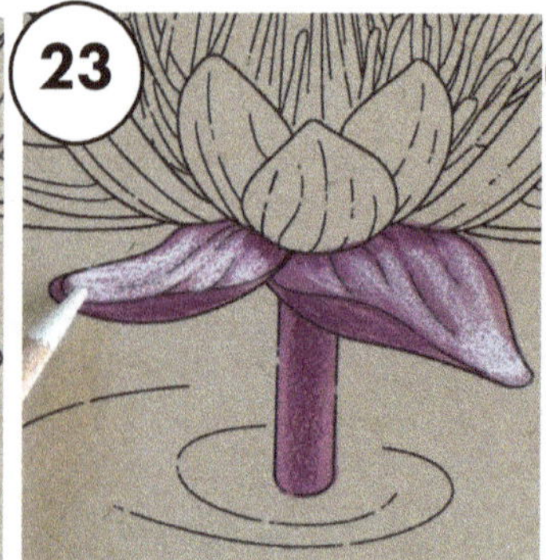

23 I add a coat of 938 White on the top plane of the sepals. I've left space around the line art details (where the curves indicate subtle texture). This helps to make it look pillowy.

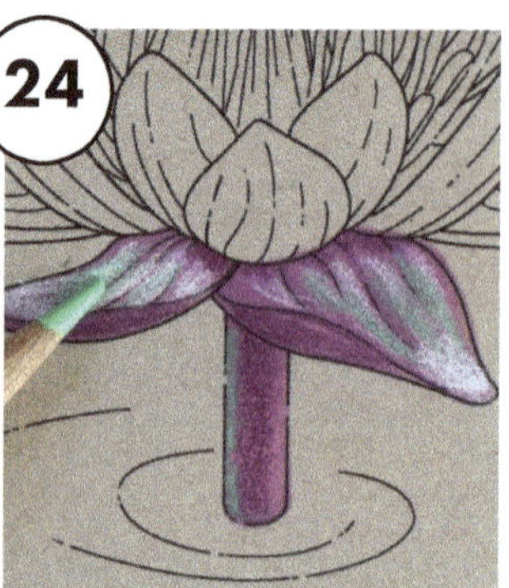

24 Now I use 910 True Green to add a little color in the middle of each sepal and along the left side of the stem to create the true variation these plants have.

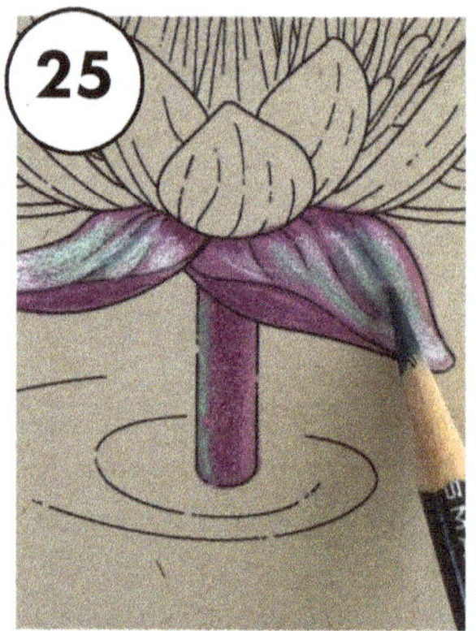

25 I use a touch of 907 Peacock Green along the indentations to give them more *form*.

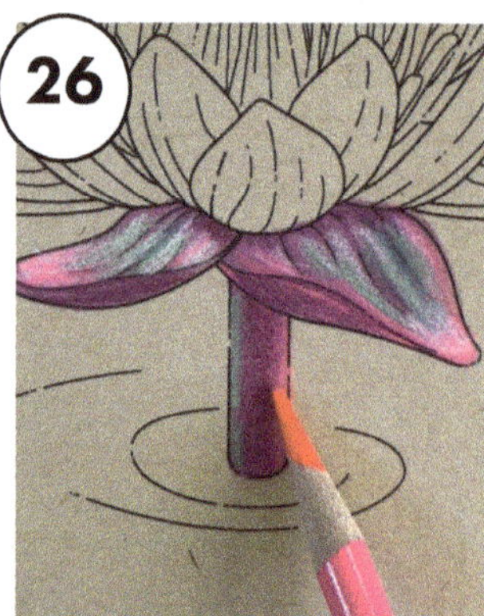

26 To make the tips and edges stand out I add some 1038 Neon Pink. I also brighten up the right side of the stem.

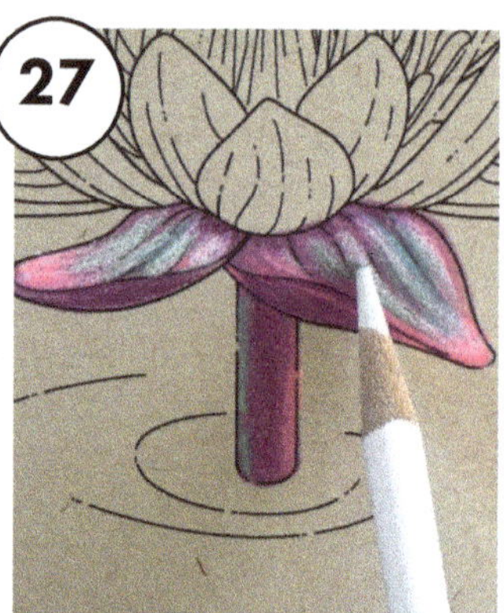

27 I blend these two colors a little using a light layer of 938 in between each indentation along the length of the sepal. Don't overdo it!

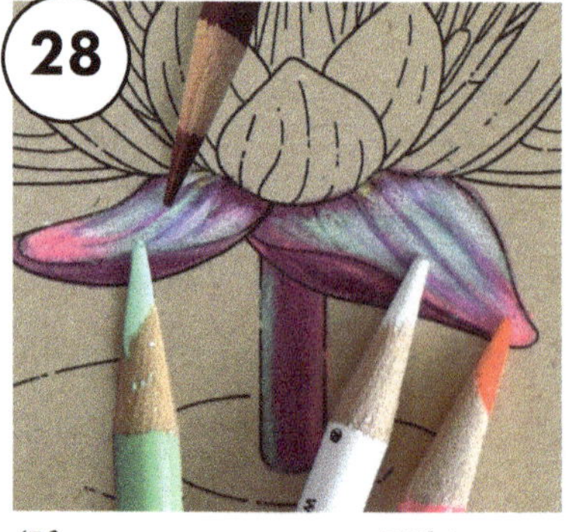

28 I go back in with the 931 Dark Purple to carve in the indentations, and I blend the lighter areas with 920 Light Green.

(If necessary use your White pencil again to add more contrast and your Neon Pink to brighten the tips more.)

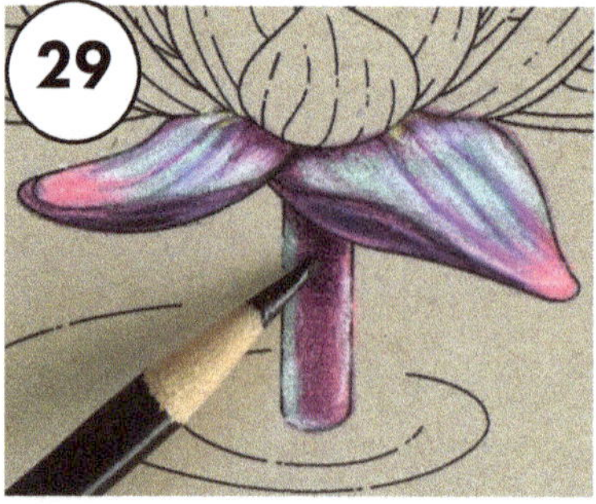

29 I deepen the sides of the sepals and part of the core shadow at the top of the stem with 935 Black.

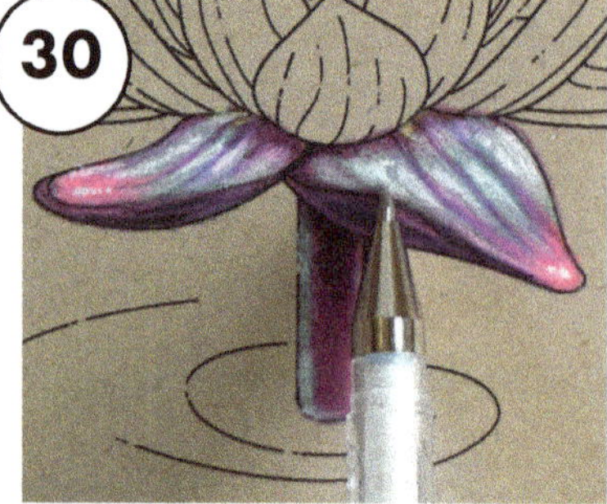

30 I add a few highlights with white gel pen to really set it off!

Chapter 11: Coloring Pages and More...

The final chapter of The Secrets of Coloring 2 consists of coloring pages that coordinate with all tutorials, color conversion charts, a copy permission agreement & links to resources in this book. The secret code for ModernColoring.com limited time bonus download pages, and purchaser-only videos can be found on the backside of a page near the end of the book. Don't forget to use it!

Practice Makes Perfect

The next couple of pages are for practice before delving into the final images! Try the irresistible sweets here before the final or just test different color palettes!*

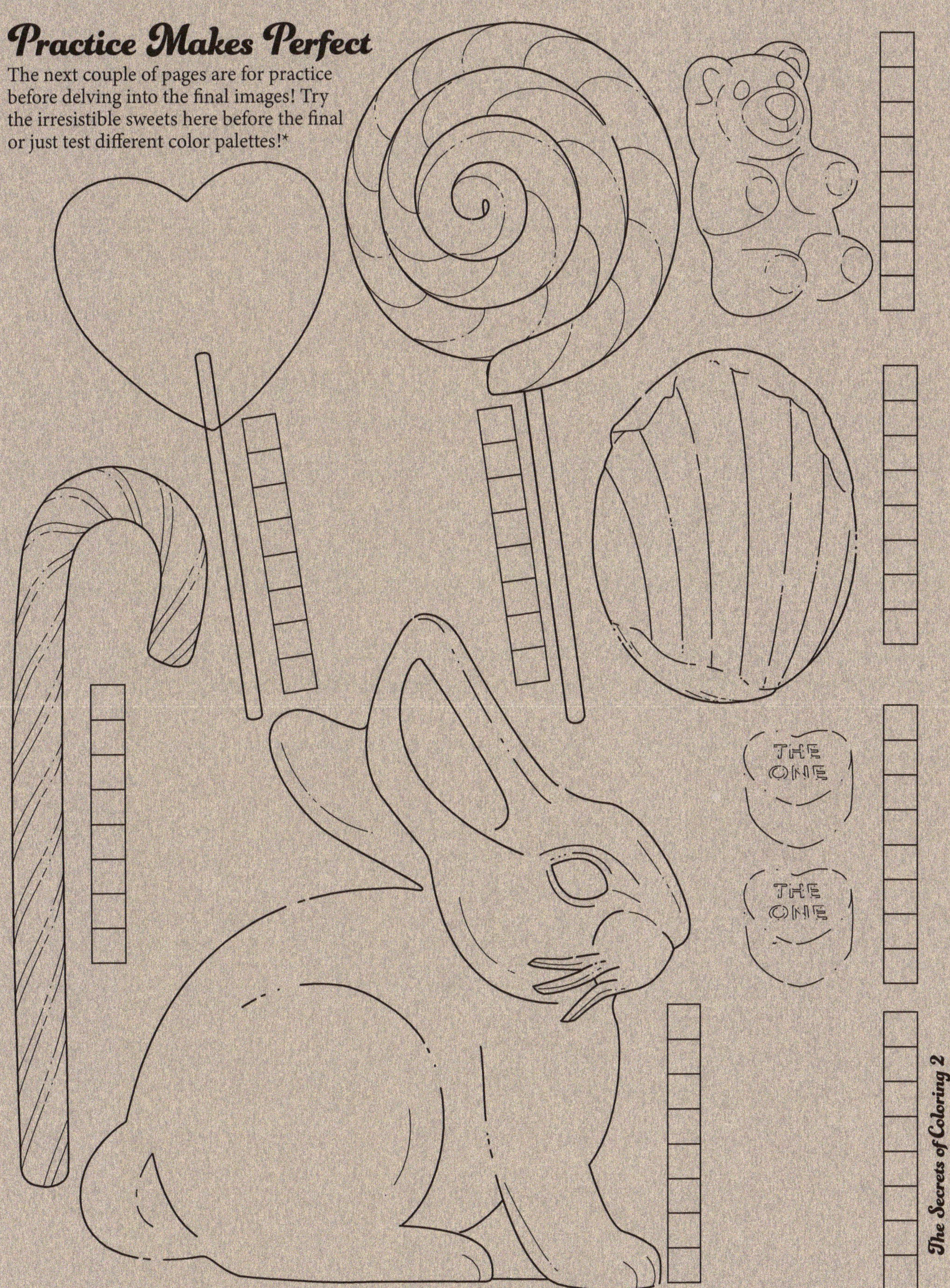

It is recommended to print pages such as these onto <u>real</u> toned paper for best results. *<u>For a limited time</u>, the bonus B&W line art PDF "Candy Shoppe" and "Crystal Queen" images are available with your secret code, free on ModernColoring.com. If you have no toned paper, a "Faux Toned" PDF printed onto card stock is the next best alternative. A PDF may be purchased at: Etsy.com/shop/ModernColoring. This image and several other pages in the book are printed on "Faux" backgrounds. However, the book's paper texture may vary and may not allow as many layers as real toned paper or card stock.

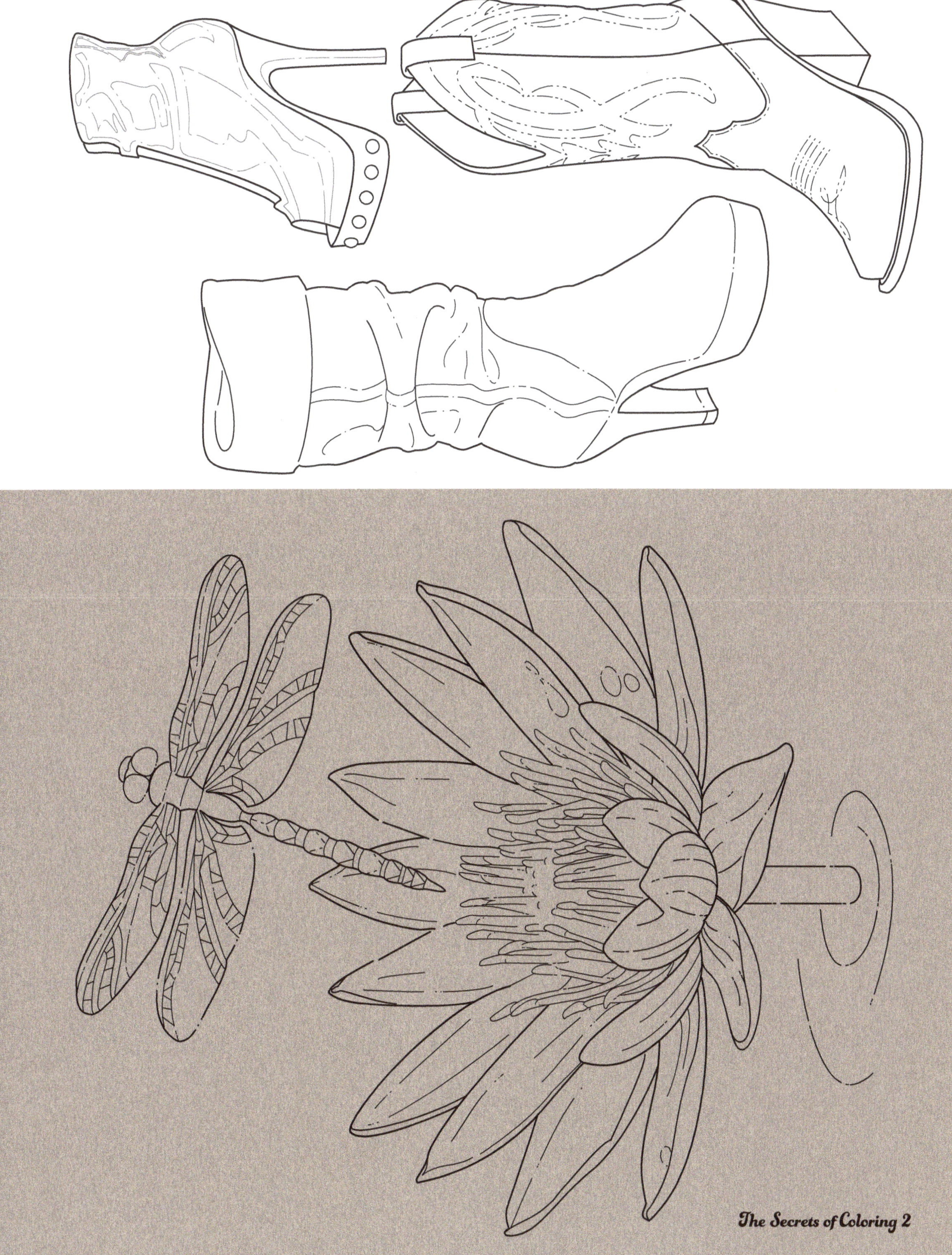
The Secrets of Coloring 2

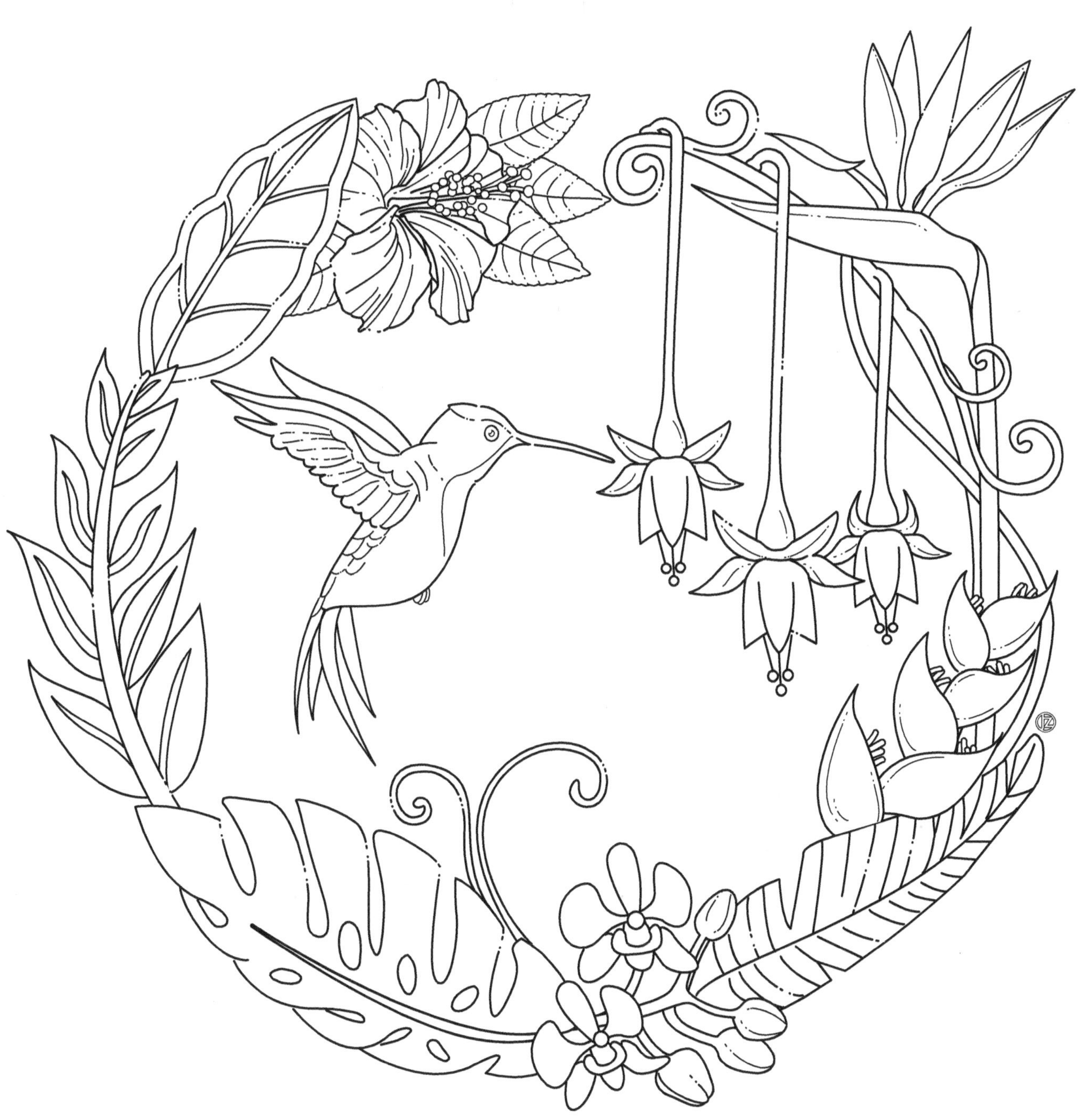

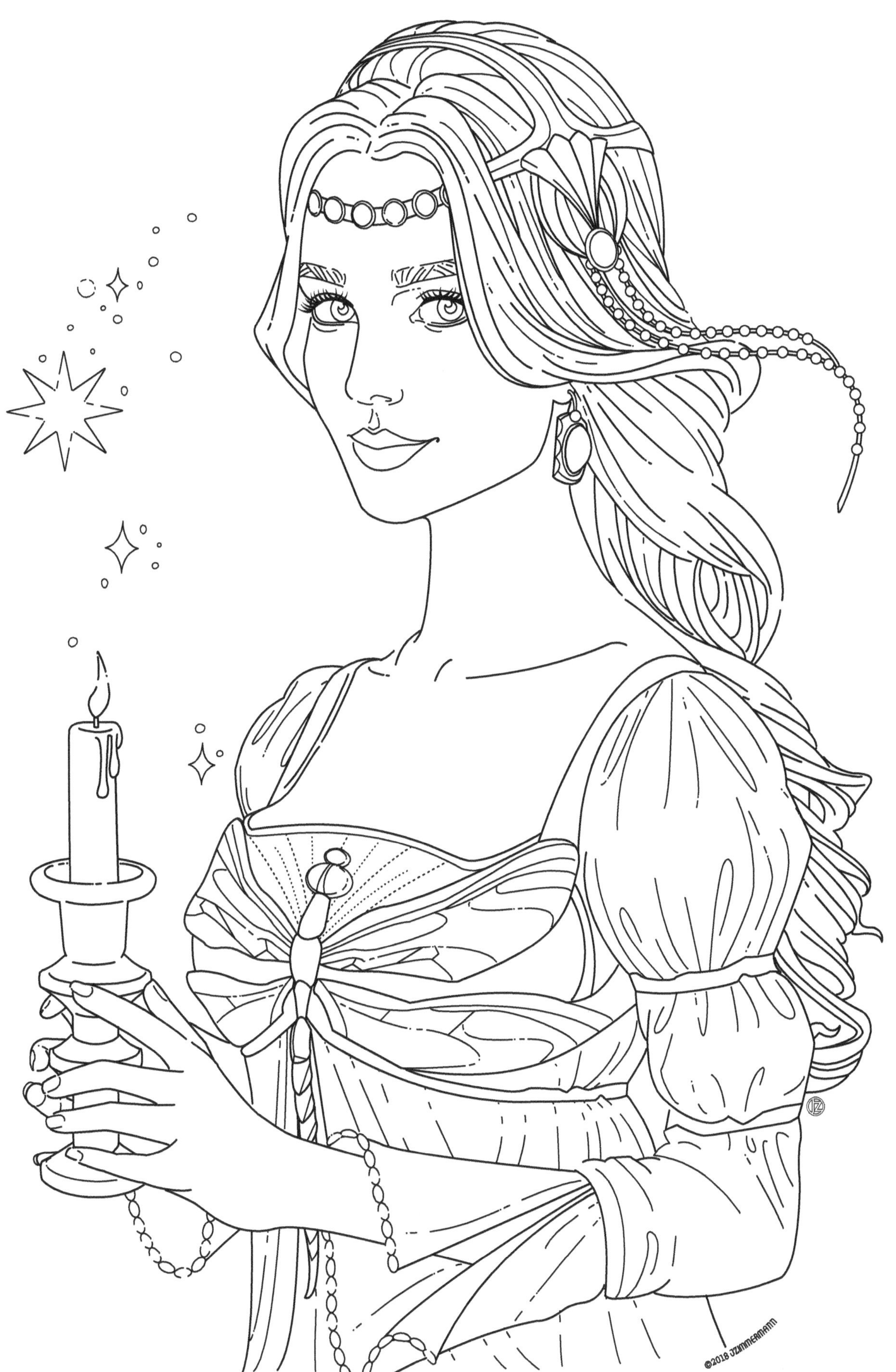

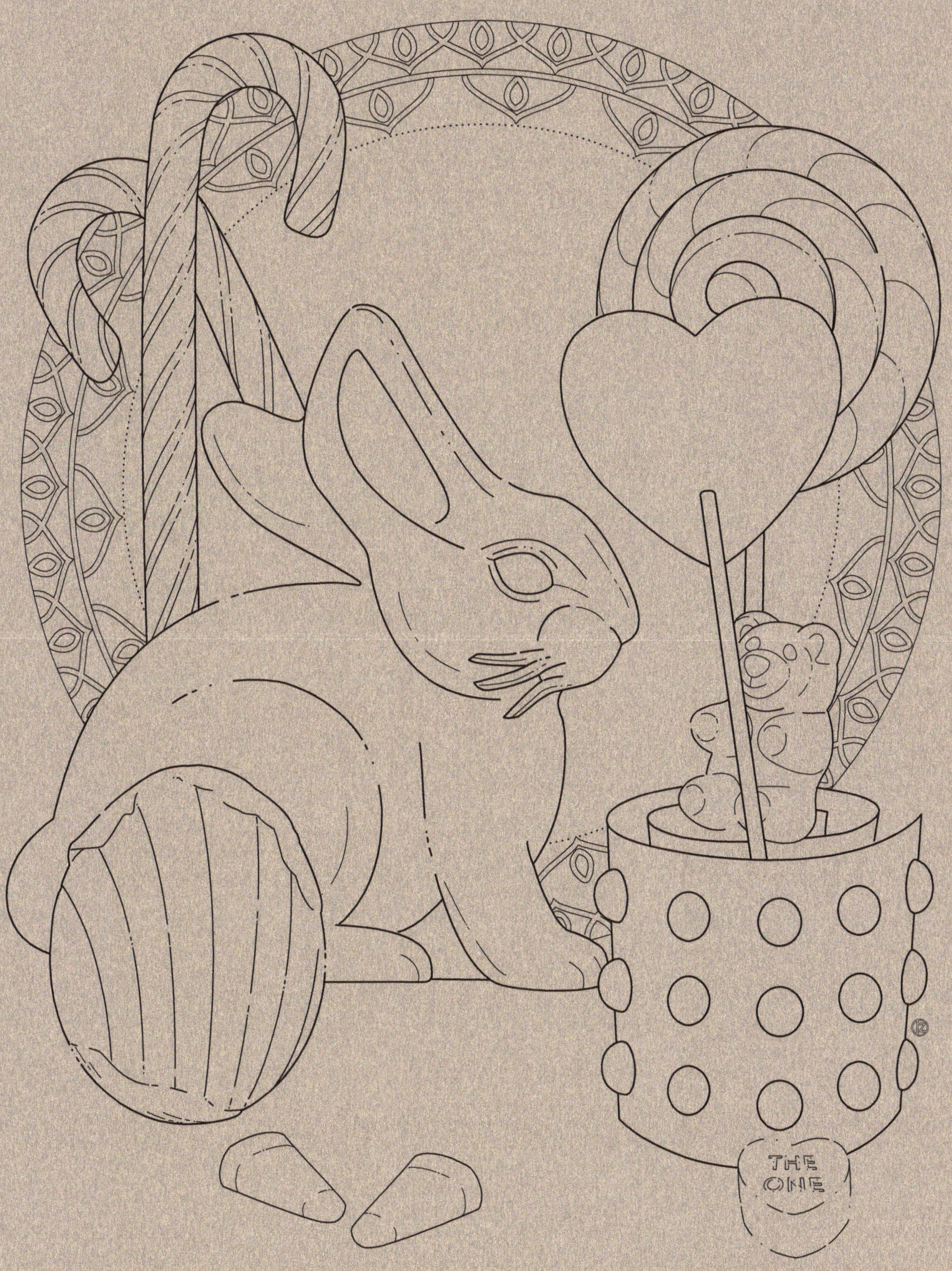

The Secrets of Coloring 2

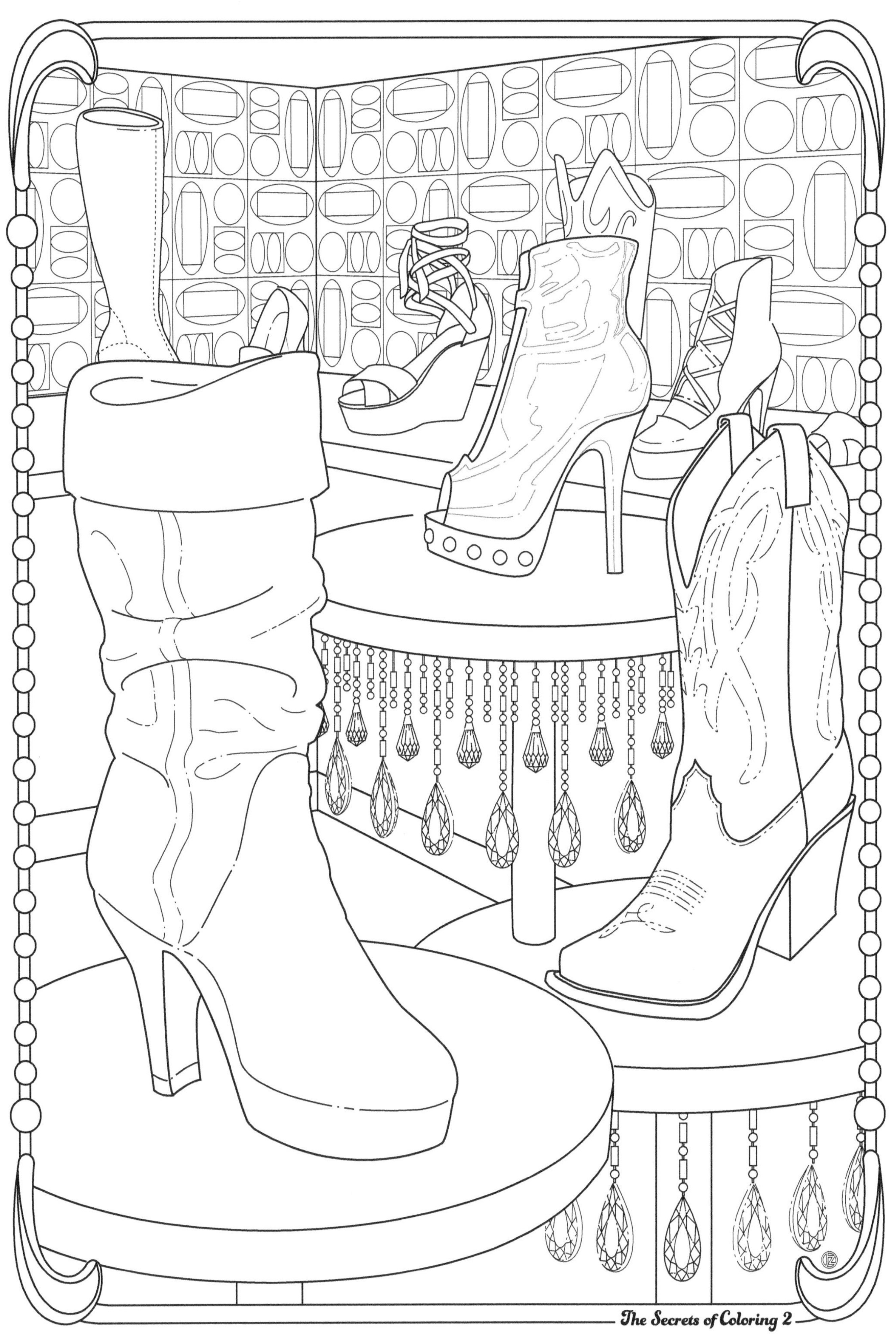
The Secrets of Coloring 2

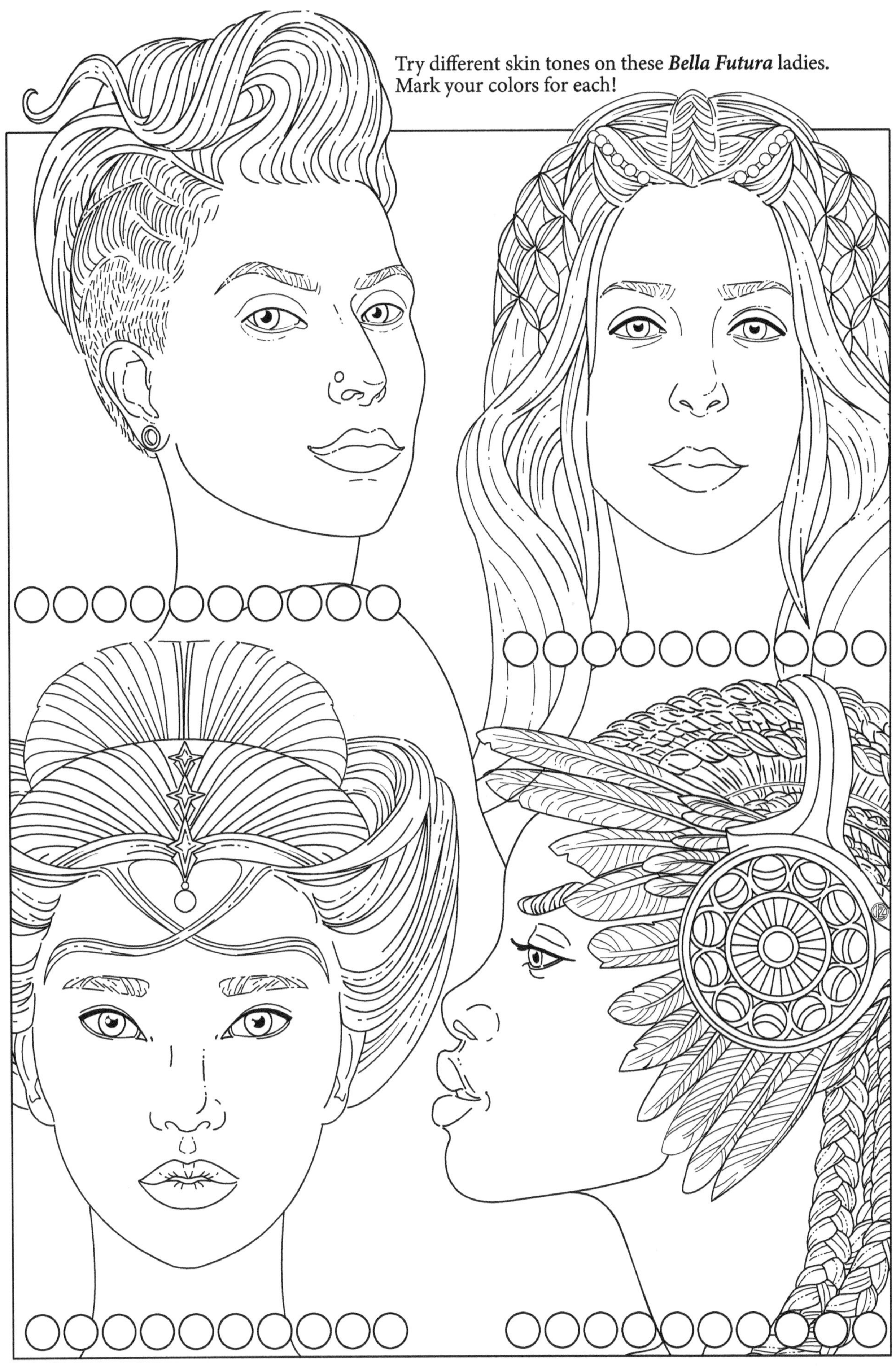

Try different skin tones on these *Bella Futura* ladies. Mark your colors for each!

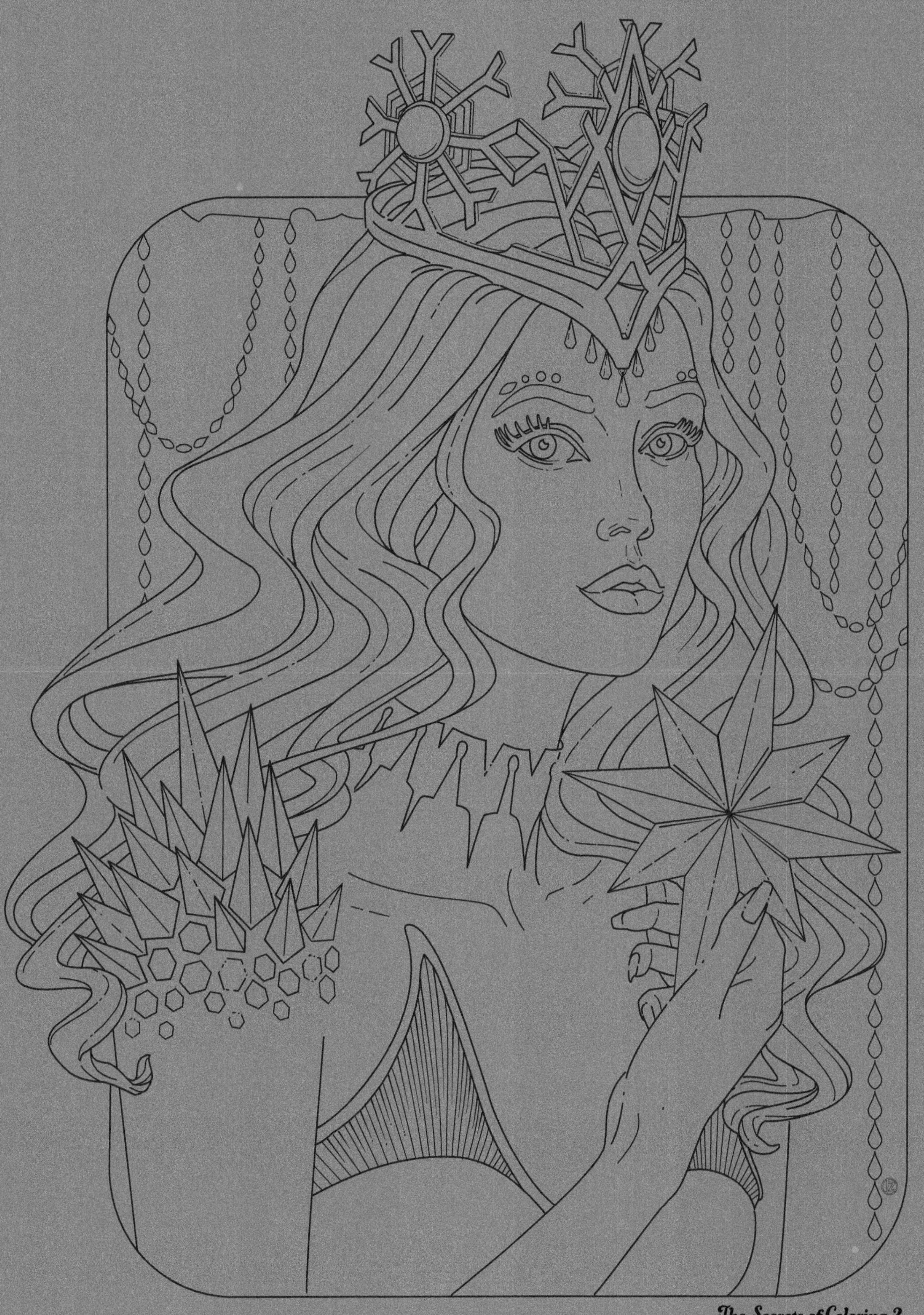

The Secrets of Coloring 2

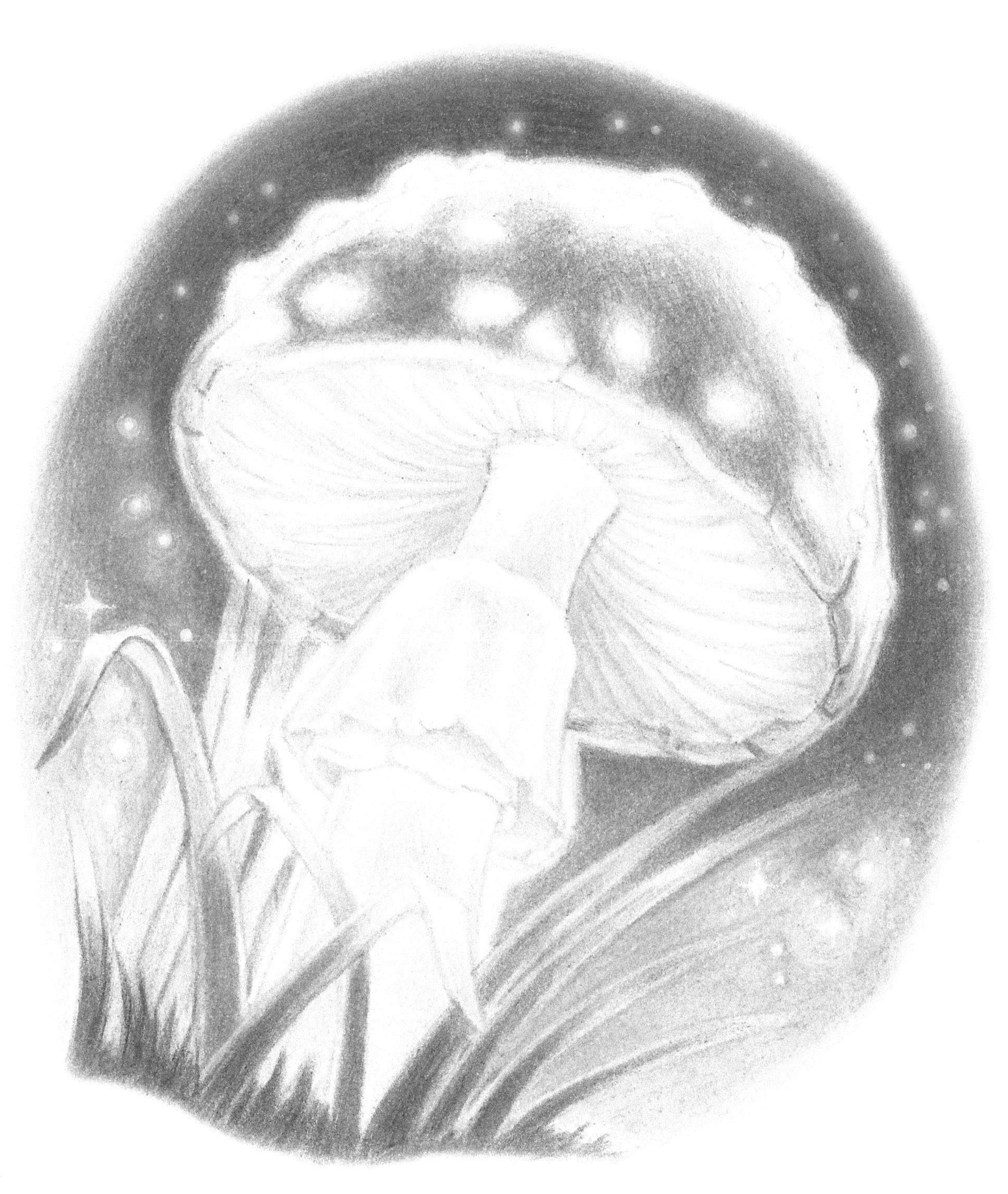

The Secrets of Coloring 2

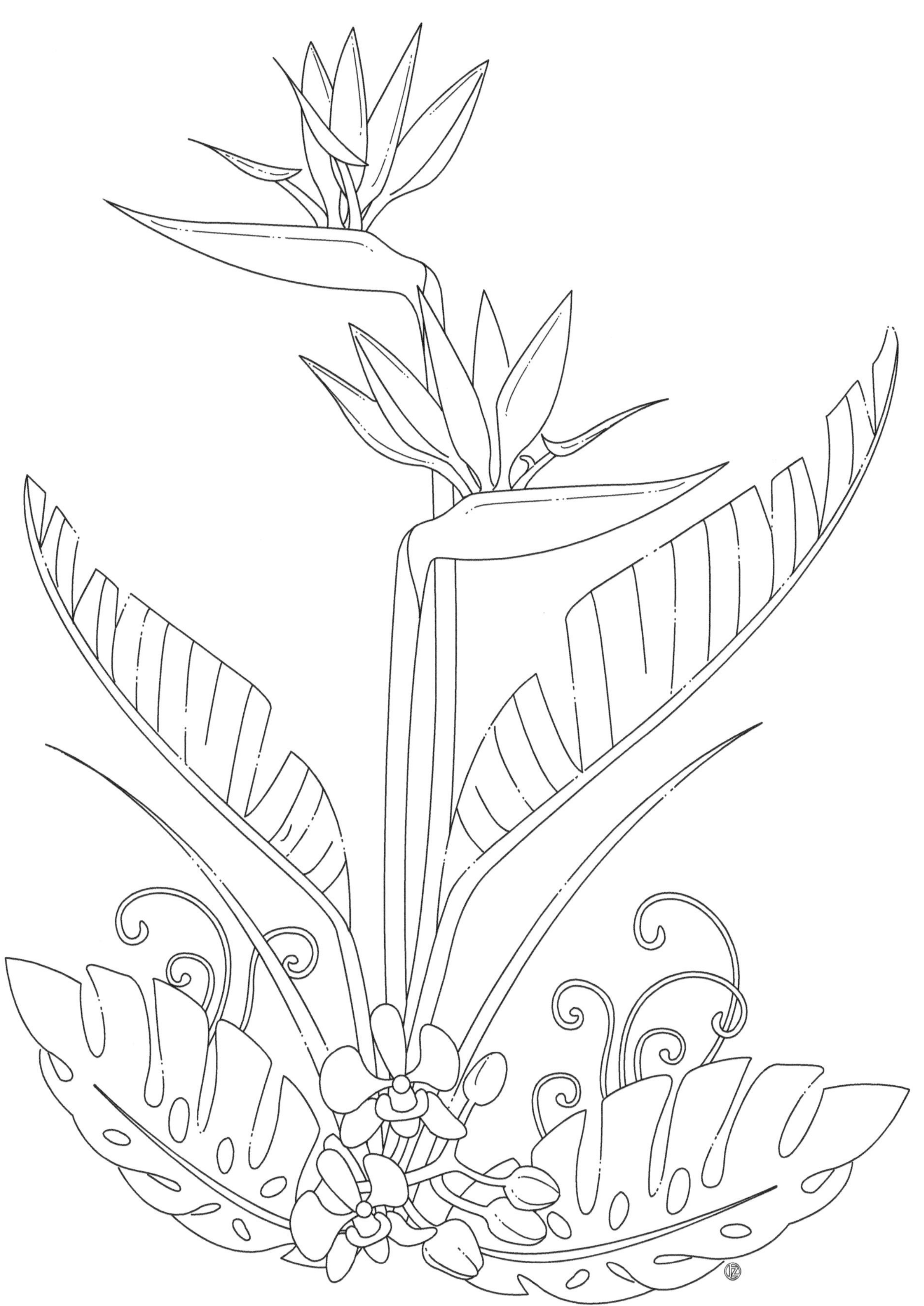

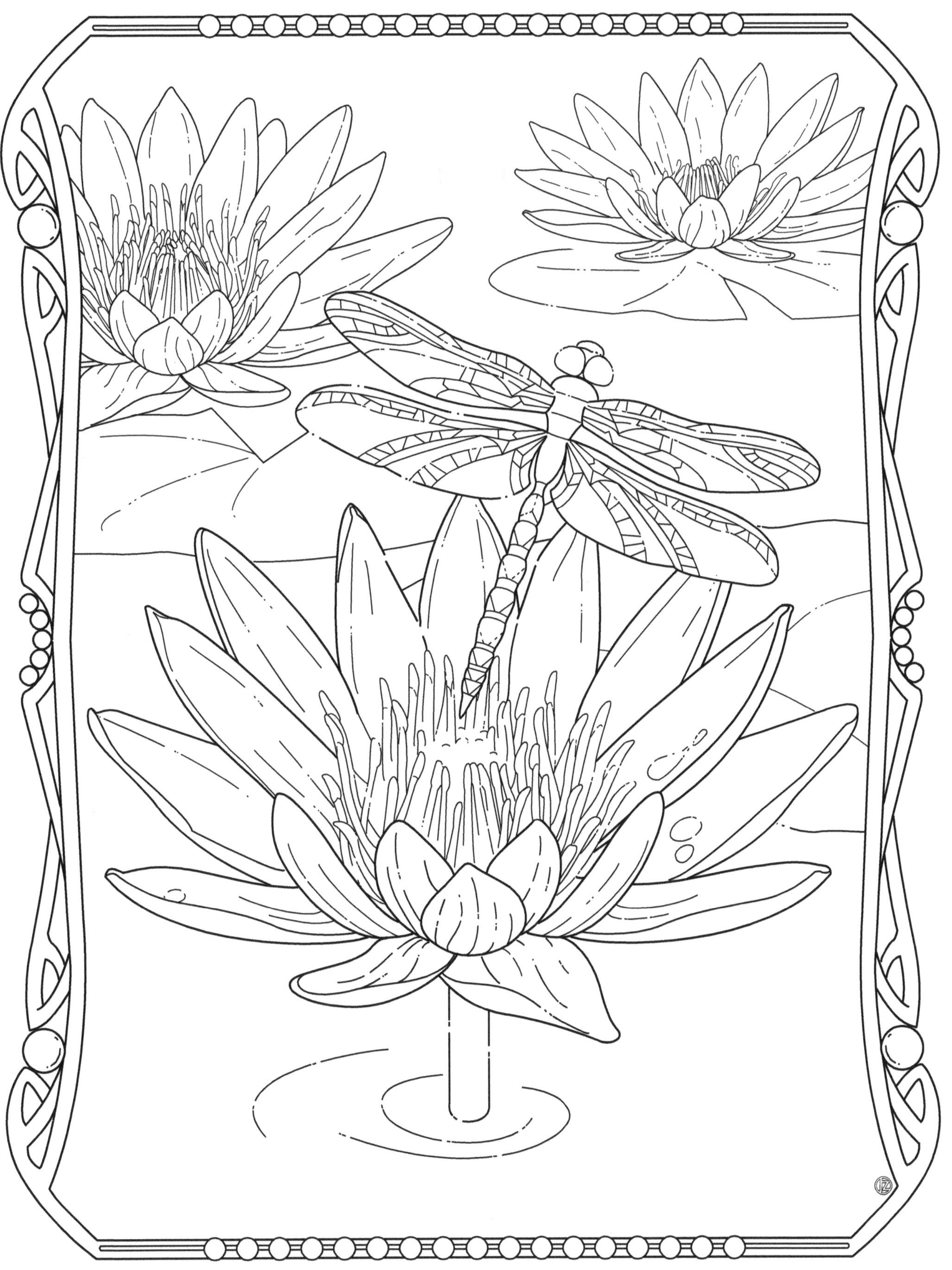

The Secrets of Coloring 2

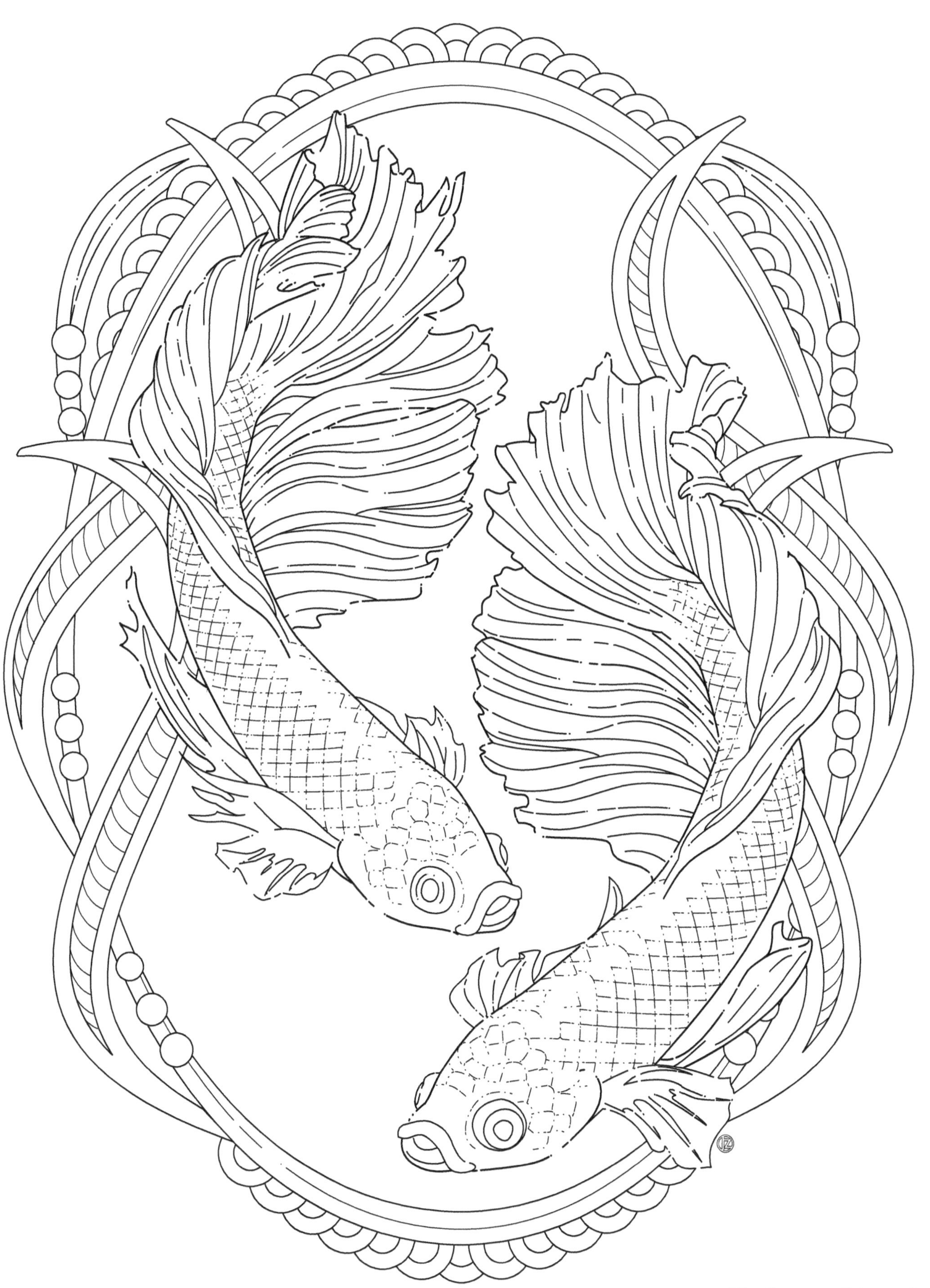

The Secrets of Coloring 2

*Use a blotter page under this page if you are going to
use marker on the previous page*

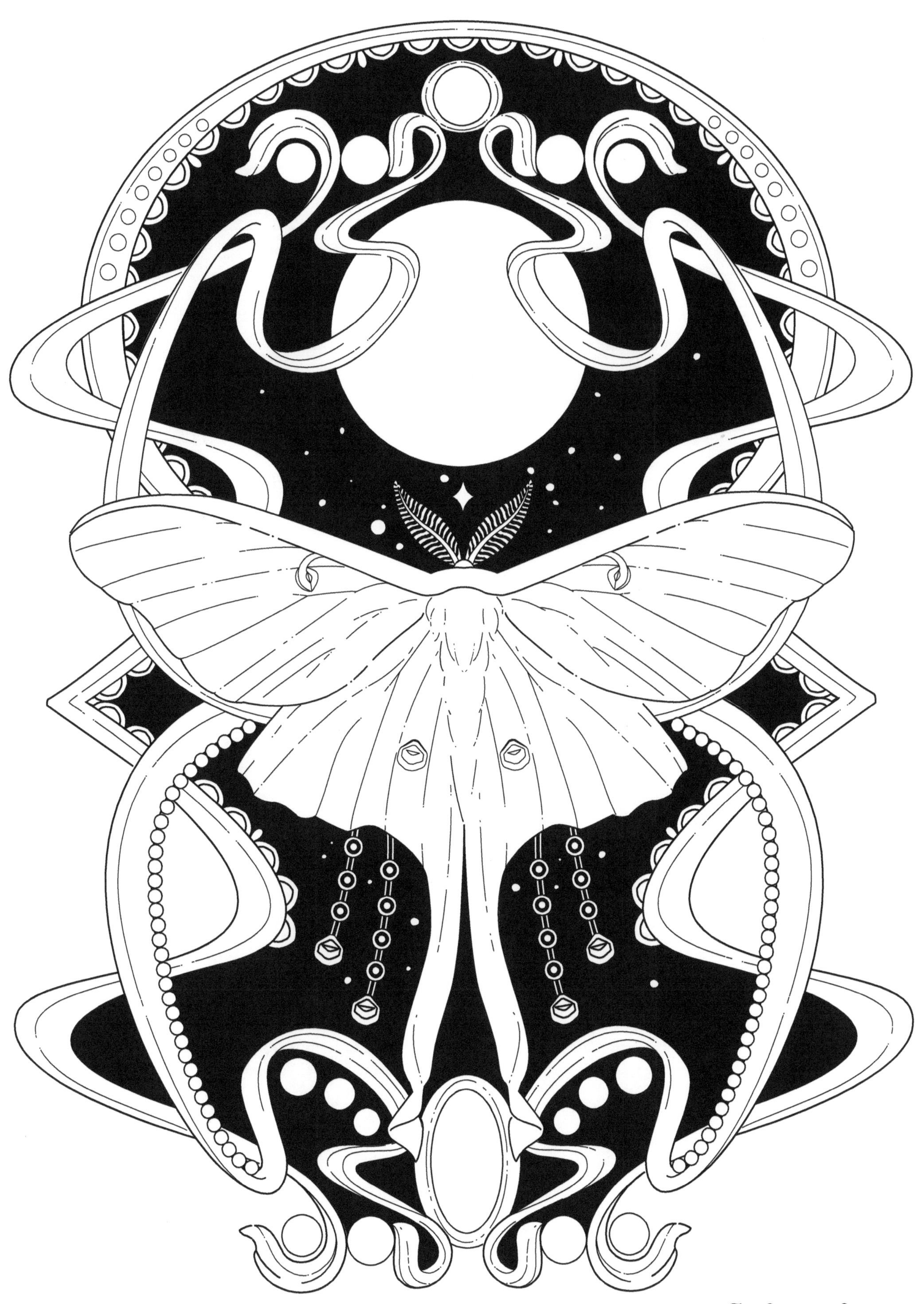

The Secrets of Coloring 2

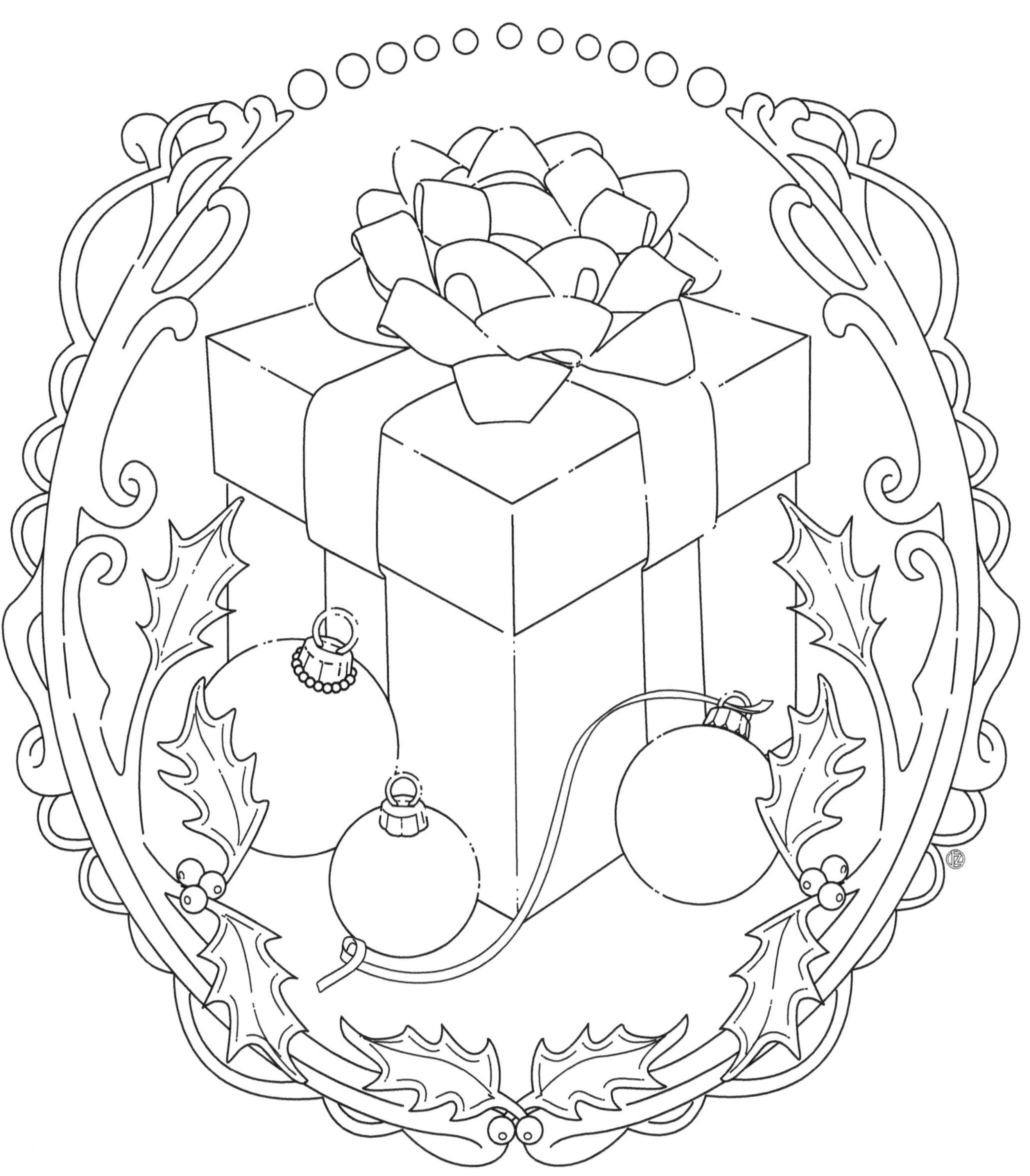

The Secrets of Coloring 2

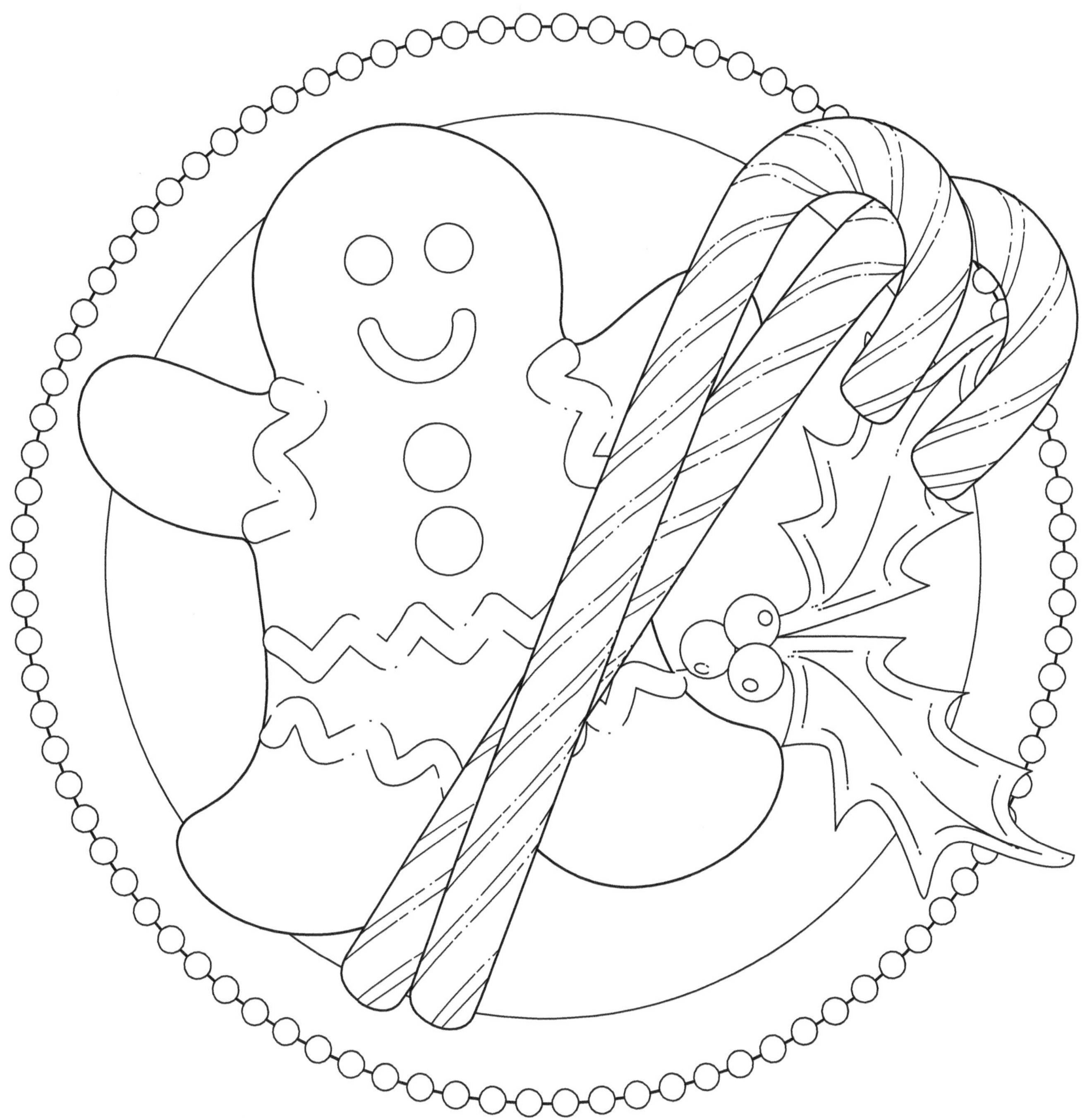

These coloring conversion charts are handy for those who don't have access to Prismacolor Premier pencils. As stated earlier, when using substitutes please understand that there's no guarantee you will achieve the same results that you see in the book. However, finding the closest colors to those I have used will most definitely make it more likely that you'll be on the right track. The next three pages contain conversions that I have made for the *closest* color match available, from five of the most popular brands listed in Chapter 3. Please remember – this is not an exact science – it is somewhat subjective and almost impossible to find a perfect equivalent. Some colors may be slightly darker, lighter, or the intensity may differ from the Prismacolor hues. As you may notice on the first page of conversions, many grey, neutral, metallic and fluorescent colors don't have a match from the popular alternative sets with fewer pencils. These more obscure colors are not usually top priority for the manufacturers of 72- pencil sets, but some sell them separately. More conversions will be created in the future if there are requests for them! You can "Like" my Facebook artist page and post your suggestions for conversions there: **www.faceboocom/moderncoloring**

Thank you for not sharing these charts online, as they are exclusive to the purchaser of this book.

modernCOLORING Color Conversion Charts: Prismacolor 150 vs. Popular Brands 72+

Prismacolor Premier

	1084	1083	1099	1050	1051	1052	1054	1056	1058	1059	1060	1061	1063	1065	1067	935	1068	1069	1070	1072	1074	1076	936	938	949	950	1028	1035	1036	1038
Black Widow	SD013					SD018	CB69		BW111							SD024				BW16				BW91						
Colleen				600									602			Blk				603				Wht						108
Schpirerr-Farben						690 077								700 054		720 033								010 034						
Castle				120		67							019	066		071							104	072						
Marco Raffine				564		566		568							720	570								501	572	571				

©2019 Jennifer Zimmermann/ModernColoring.com All rights reserved.

modernCOLORING Color Conversion Charts: Prismacolor 150 vs. Popular Brands 72+

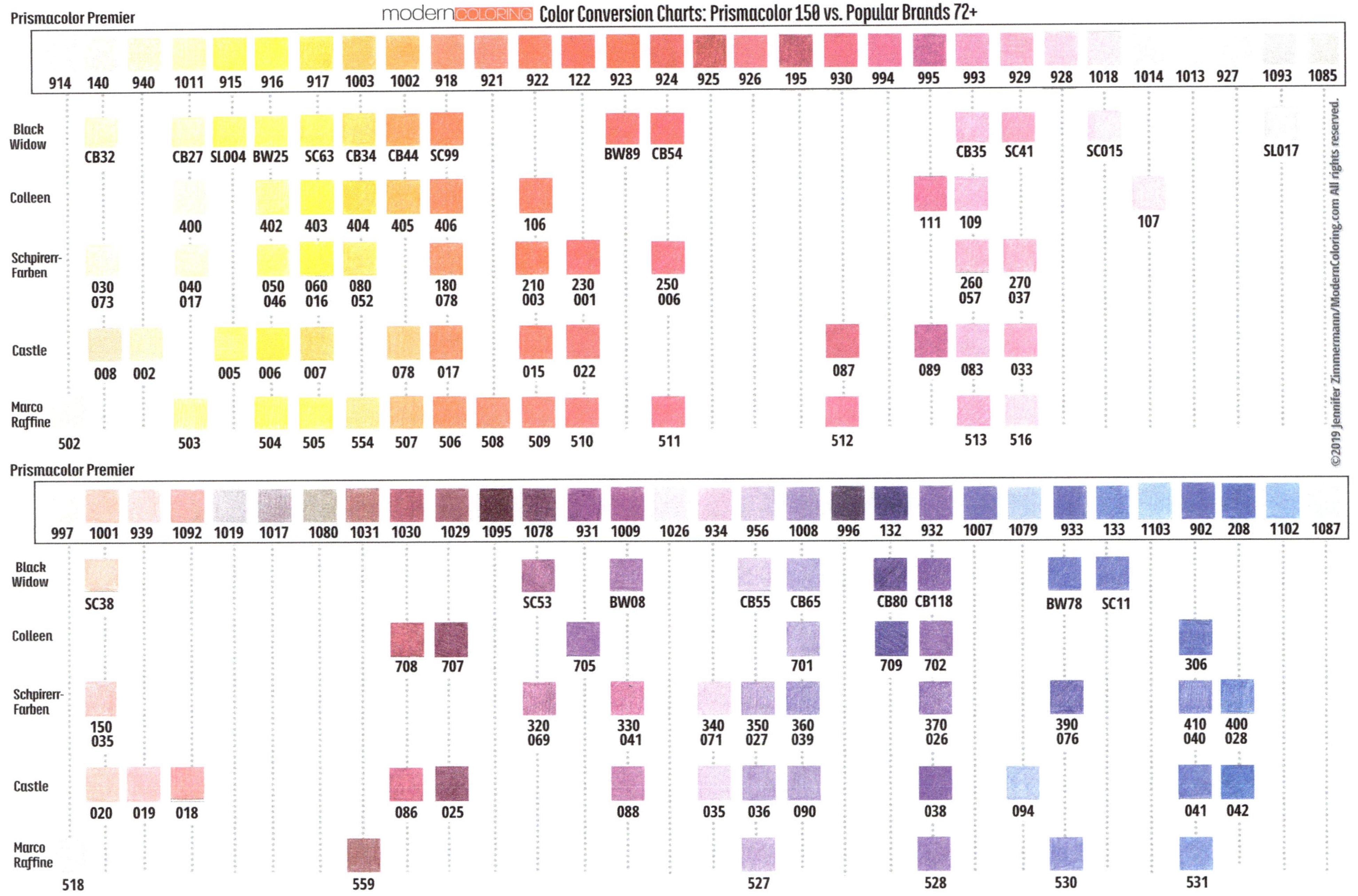

Prismacolor Premier	914	140	940	1011	915	916	917	1003	1002	918	921	922	122	923	924	925	926	195	930	994	995	993	929	928	1018	1014	1013	927	1093	1085
Black Widow		CB32		CB27	SL004	BW25	SC63	CB34	CB44	SC99				BW89	CB54							CB35	SC41		SC015				SL017	
Colleen				400		402	403	404	405	406		106										111	109			107				
Schpirerr-Farben			030 / 073	040 / 017		050 / 046	060 / 016	080 / 052		180 / 078			210 / 003	230 / 001	250 / 006							260 / 057	270 / 037							
Castle		008	002		005	006	007		078	017			015	022					087		089	083	033							
Marco Raffine	502			503		504	505	554	507	506	508	509	510		511				512			513	516							

Prismacolor Premier	997	1001	939	1092	1019	1017	1080	1031	1030	1029	1095	1078	931	1009	1026	934	956	1008	996	132	932	1007	1079	933	133	1103	902	208	1102	1087
Black Widow		SC38										SC53		BW08		CB55	CB65			CB80	CB118			BW78	SC11					
Colleen									708	707		705						701		709	702						306			
Schpirerr-Farben		150 / 035										320 / 069		330 / 041		340 / 071	350 / 027	360 / 039		370 / 026				390 / 076			410 / 040	400 / 028		
Castle		020	019	018					086	025				088		035	036	090			038		094				041	042		
Marco Raffine	518							559									527				528			530			531			

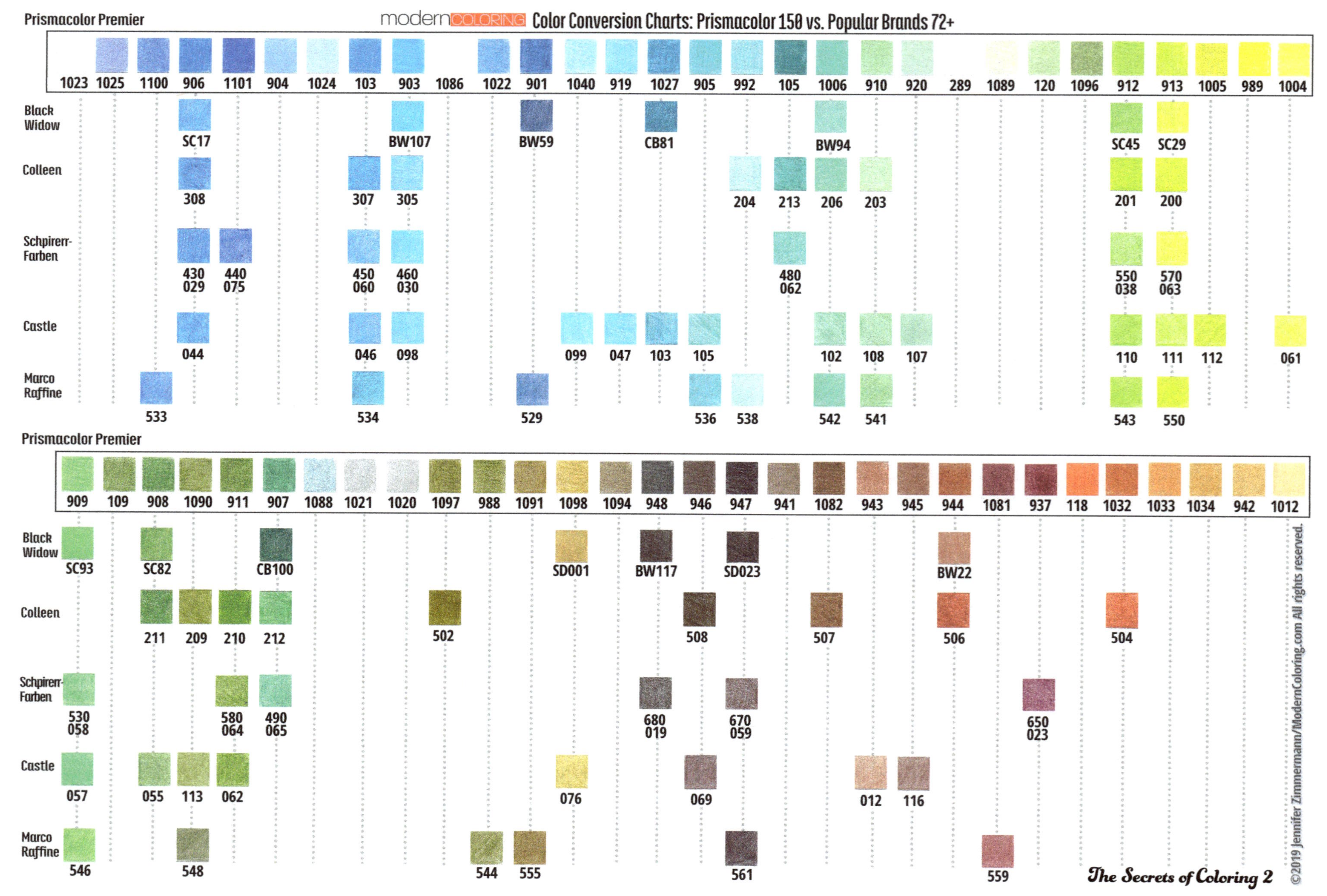

Prismacolor Premier
modern COLORING Color Conversion Charts: Prismacolor 150 vs. Popular Brands 72+
1023 1025 1100 906 1101 904 1024 103 903 1086 1022 901 1040 919 1027 905 992 105 1006 910 920 289 1089 120 1096 912 913 1005 989 1004
Black Widow: SC17 BW107 BW59 CB81 BW94 SC45 SC29
Colleen: 308 307 305 204 213 206 203 201 200
Schpirerr-Farben: 430 029 440 075 450 060 460 030 480 062 550 038 570 063
Castle: 044 046 098 099 047 103 105 102 108 107 110 111 112 061
Marco Raffine: 533 534 529 536 538 542 541 543 550
Prismacolor Premier
909 109 908 1090 911 907 1088 1021 1020 1097 988 1091 1098 1094 948 946 947 941 1082 943 945 944 1081 937 118 1032 1033 1034 942 1012
Black Widow: SC93 SC82 CB100 SD001 BW117 SD023 BW22
Colleen: 211 209 210 212 502 508 507 506 504
Schpirerr-Farben: 530 058 580 064 490 065 680 019 670 059 650 023
Castle: 057 055 113 062 076 069 012 116
Marco Raffine: 546 548 544 555 561 559
©2019 Jennifer Zimmermann/ModernColoring.com All rights reserved.
The Secrets of Coloring 2

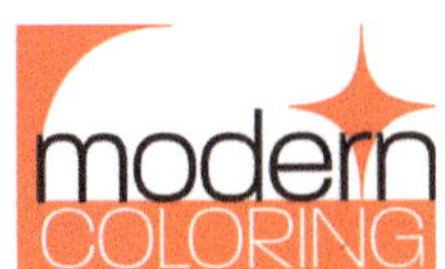

To Whom It May Concern,

Please allow the colorist ______________________________________,
to print the pages I've supplied strictly for personal use only.
Permission is granted to the colorist who has signed below, to copy
ten **(10)** pages from this book, *The Secrets of Coloring 2*, in a single
visit to your printing facility, for personal and individual use only.

**Mass production of this book is not allowed and business use is
strictly forbidden.**

Best,

Jennifer Zimmermann
Author/Artist
ModernColoring.com

· ·

Please defend the rights of artists and respect copyright law. Artists depend on the income
from the sales of their books and artwork to make a living. Misuse creates hardships for the
artists that produce the pages you love to color. Sharing of the colored pages in this book is
strictly forbidden, both by copying them for someone else and by posting uncolored on social
media. The only exception is made for reviewers, whom are kindly requested not to display
this book in its entirety, but only portions of pages. If you are posting a review and including
images of the uncolored line art pages, please lay a pencil across the image to help prevent
theft. If in doubt always contact the artist. It is requested that still photographs of color
conversion charts not be shared in reviews or on social media.

You, the colorist, are very welcome and encouraged to share and post your own finished
coloring pages from this book, and it is kindly requested that you list the book as the source if
you do. Thank you for your understanding, assistance and educating others in this matter.

I've read the above guidelines and agree to them.

Signed (the colorist):

______________________________________ Date: ________________

Resource Guide

Here you can find some of the materials and inspo throughout The Secrets of Coloring 2. You can find links to many of these products on my Amazon Influencer page: www.amazon.com/shop/modern_coloring

Arrtx - alcohol and watercolor markers .... amazon.com

Black Aneri - inspirational colorist account .... instagram.com/black_aneri/

Black Widow - colored pencils .... blackwidowpencils.com

Bio-Shield Citrus Thinner - non-toxic solvent (4 oz. $9.95) .... greenbuildingsupply.com/bioshield-citrus-thinner

Castle Art Supplies - colored pencils... castleartsupplies.com

Caran D'Ache - colored pencils, blenders .... store.carandache.com/us/en/

Colleen - colored pencils .... amazon.com

Coloured by Me - inspirational colorist account .... instagram.com/coloured_by_me

Copic - alcohol markers, blenders, AtYou Spica pens .... copic.jp/en/

Canson - Mi-Tientes, Colorline papers .... en.canson.com

Faber-Castell - colored pencils, Ecco Fineliners .... fabercastell.com

Georgia-Pacific - papers, card stock .... georgiapacificpaper.com

Hammermill - papers, card stock .... hammermill.com

Lilicence - inspirational colorist account .... instagram.com/lilicence

Lolliz - gel pens .... amazon.com

Maped - pencil sharpeners, water-based fineliners .... uk.maped.com/en_uk/

Micron - waterproof fineliners .... sakuraofamerica.com

Marco Raffine - colored pencils .... amazon.com

ModernColoring - Etsy - faux toned PDF, coloring pages, prints .... etsy.com/shop/ModernColoring

PanPastel - pan-based pastels .... panpastel.com

Posca - paint markers, pens... www.posca.com

Prismacolor - colored pencils, alcohol markers, blenders and erasers .... prismacolor.com

Q-Tips - Precision Tip cotton swabs .... qtips.com

Sakura - gel pens .... gellyroll.com

Schpirerr Farben - colored pencils .... schpirerrfarben.com

Sharpie - permanent markers .... sharpie.com

Sofft - pastel knives and covers .... sofftart.com/products.html

Strathmore - toned, Artagain papers .... strathmoreartist.com

Superglue - adhesive .... loctiteproducts.com

Tombow - blender, brush and Mono Zero eraser pens................................ tombowusa.com

TouchNew - alcohol markers .... amazon.com

Uni-ball Signo - Uniball gel pens .... uniball-na.com/

Winsor & Newton - BrushMarkers, watercolor paint .... winsornewton.com/na/

X-Acto - utility knives, blades .... xacto.com